D0153574

PROFESSIONAL ETHICS

SECOND EDITION

PROFESSIONAL ETHICS

SECOND EDITION

Michael D. Bayles

Florida State University

Wadsworth Publishing Company
Belmont, California
A Division of Wadsworth, Inc.

Philosophy Editor: *Kenneth King*
Editorial Assistant: *Cheri Peterson*
Print Buyer: *Randy Hurst*
Designer: *Adriane Bosworth*
Copy Editor: *Sylvia Stein*
Cover: *Al Burkhardt*

©1989, 1981 by Wadsworth, Inc. All rights reserved. No part of this book may be reproduced, stored in a retrieval system, or transcribed, in any form or by any means, electronic, mechanical, photocopying, recording, or otherwise, without the prior written permission of the publisher, Wadsworth Publishing Company, Belmont, California 94002, a division of Wadsworth, Inc.

Printed in the United States of America
1 2 3 4 5 6 7 8 9 10—93 92 91 90 89

Library of Congress Cataloging-in-Publication Data

Bayles, Michael D.
  Professional ethics / Michael D. Bayles.

    p. cm.
  Bibliography: p.
  Includes index.
  ISBN 0-534-09546-1
  1. Professional ethics. I. Title.
BJ1725.B29 1989   88-10208
174—dc19   CIP

To Marge, for making everything worthwhile

Contents

Preface

The ethics of professional conduct is being questioned as never before in history. Lawyers, physicians, engineers, accountants, and other professionals are being criticized for disregarding the rights of clients and the public interest. Perhaps society is reconsidering the role of professions and professionals. In any event, many difficult ethical challenges are being faced by both professionals and the public. Given the important roles professionals are playing in society during the last decade of the twentieth century, everyone is concerned with professional ethics.

The preceding paragraph is as true now as it was when I wrote it in the first edition of this book. Today's newspaper carries a report that unnecessary procedures by physicians are costing Medicare over $1 billion a year. The issues of professional ethics may change over time, but they do not disappear.

Much has been written on professional ethics since the first edition. My working bibliography for this revision, after significant winnowing, contained over 240 citations, almost all published since the book first appeared. As a result, the bibliography in this edition is much larger than in the first. Nonetheless, most of the literature still focuses a single profession and is written from the professional's point of view.

Thus, the original two primary aims of this book are still relevant. The first is to develop principles that apply to most or all professions. A major change in this edition is the inclusion of predominately employee or scholarly professions, although the predominately self-employed or consulting ones remain. Some of the problems confronted by self-employed and employee professionals differ, but many are the same, and the same principles apply. Employee professionals confront issues of their obligations to employers, and I have added a chapter to address these problems.

A second major aim of this book is to examine professions from the viewpoint of the average citizen in society. This book adopts the perspective of clients and other members of society. The overriding consideration is to determine the ethical norms citizens have good reason to accept. Citizens are presumably devoted to the values of freedom, protection from injury, equality of opportunity, privacy, and minimal well-being. This approach to the issues, then, renders the discussion relevant to those who are not planning to become members of professions as well as to those who are.

A wide conception of ethical issues is adopted. It includes issues of fees, advertising, and social organization to provide services, as illustrated by national health insurance, as well as professional discipline. Although some people deny that these are strictly ethical topics, they involve significant value choices confronting professionals and society. Elements of political, social, and legal philosophy are thus pertinent.

The first two chapters are primarily introductory and provide a background for those that follow. The first chapter discusses the scope of professional ethics, what can be expected from its study, and possible causes for the present concern with professional ethics. It then defines professions and notes significant characteristics of professions in the United States. Chapter 2 addresses the difficult subject of justification of professional norms and their relation to other ethical norms. The chapter then distinguishes between types of norms.

Chapters 3 through 7 analyze the substantive obligations of professions and professionals. Chapter 3 primarily concerns access to professional services. The first section discusses economic norms, such as those relating to unauthorized practice, fees, and advertising, which have often hindered access to services. The next section focuses on social organization, as illustrated by group services, national insurance, and national service, to provide medical and legal services. The chapter concludes with a discussion of the ethics of accepting clients who have unethical purposes. Chapter 4 considers the ethical obligations that arise from accepting a client. The first section considers the ethical nature of the professional–client relationship, and the second section deals with professionals' obligations to clients that result from viewing the relationship as fiduciary. A new short concluding section considers the obligations of clients to professionals.

Chapter 5 discusses the obligations of professionals to people who are not their clients and how these obligations are to be balanced against conflicting obligations to clients. Chapter 6 analyzes the obligations between employee professionals and employers. The first two sections analyze professionals' obligations to employers and argue that theoretically these obligations do not conflict with those that professionals have to clients and third parties. The next long section addresses authority relationships, deference to superordinates, whistle-blowing, unionization, and strikes. The final section briefly considers employer obligations to professional employees. Chapter 7 considers obligations professionals have to their profession. The first section considers obligations to help the profession through research and reform. The second deals with maintaining respect for the profession and identification with powerful clients.

The last chapter discusses methods of ensuring that professionals conform to ethical norms. The first section of the chapter reviews methods for controlling professional conduct, such as admission to professions and discipline. The next section considers self-regulation and alternatives to it. The last section discusses professionals' motives for unethical conduct and various methods for motivating them to ethical conduct.

This book is intended for use in a wide variety of courses. I have tried to present enough information about professions and to avoid technical philosophical vocabulary so that it can be used in lower division undergraduate courses. At the same time, I have tried to provide sufficient depth and detail so it can be used in upper division courses and in courses on the ethics of particular professions. For the latter use, teacher and students in classroom discussion should be able to supplement the examples with others from their particular profession.

Throughout the book, I have offered my own opinions about the obligations of professionals. Readers are encouraged to question and challenge my assumptions and arguments. One problem with traditional education in professional ethics has been that accepted norms, especially those enshrined in professional codes of ethics, have not been questioned. Only by challenging assumptions and reflecting on them can one come to understand the reasons for ethical norms and conduct.

The first edition of this book benefited greatly from comments by Michael Pritchard, Kenneth Kipnis, Wade Robison, and the publisher's anonymous reviewers. Michael Rumball, as my research assistant, was also very helpful. It was efficiently typed by Ann C. Marx, Pat Harris, Fran McFall, Lois Weston, Angela Robitaille, and others. Various forms of support were given by the University of Kentucky Research Foundation, the University of Western Ontario Foundation, Inc., and the Westminster Institute for Ethics and Human Values.

In preparing this edition, I was significantly aided by comments from the following reviewers: Nancie Fimbel, San Jose State University; Dana R. Flint, Lincoln University; Terry M. Lewis, Linfield College; and William Ruddick, New York University. Garrett Maass, my research assistant in spring 1987, did much library work. "Self-Regulation" in Chapter 8 is excerpted in revised form from "Professional Power and Self-Regulation," *Business & Professional Ethics Journal* 5, no. 2 (1986): 25–43, copyright © 1987 Michael D. Bayles.

1 Problems of Professions

In their daily practice, professionals confront a wide variety of ethical and value problems. Consider the following cases and the types of problems they present.

Clients may ask for help that requires conduct professionals consider ethically wrong. For example, a physician practicing in a remote Alaskan community is approached about an abortion by a seventeen-year-old woman who is three months pregnant. The physician is ethically opposed to abortion except to save a woman's life. This woman's health is not good, but she is likely to survive the pregnancy. She is unmarried and lives at home with her family. Her employment prospects are poor, and her father cannot easily support another child. After much discussion, she finally admits that her father is responsible for the pregnancy. If the physician does not perform the abortion, the young woman will probably not be able to afford the expense of traveling to another community to have one. Does the physician have an obligation to perform the abortion despite personal moral opposition?

Professionals also confront problems about the appropriate scope of their services. An architectural firm is temporarily short of clients and will have to let several employees go if it does not obtain more work. The local government is looking for a consulting engineering firm to design a sanitary sewer extension project. Although the architectural firm has not previously designed sewer systems, and such work is not usually considered appropriate for such firms, it believes it can do the job. Should it approach the government to try to secure a contract to design the sewer extension?

There are also problems about the types of fees professionals charge and arrangements for collecting them. A vice president in charge of production at a large corporation wants to build a new plant. To present his idea to the board of directors, he needs a rough design. He asks a friend who is a consulting engineer to make one. If the board approves the plant, the vice president assures his friend that he will get the design contract as well as payment for the rough design. Should the board not approve the new plant, then unfortunately the engineer will not be paid. Can the engineer ethically agree to make the rough design? Would it be fair to other engineers to obtain business by such a contingent fee agreement? Is it ethical for the vice president to make such an agreement?

Conflicts of interest raise still other questions. A member of an accounting firm serves without pay on the board of directors of a local nonprofit organization. If the director is not involved, may his firm ethically audit the books of the organization?

Other kinds of problems involve conflicts of interest between clients. For example, a large law firm has two clients being handled by separate legal teams. Their cases are in different courts within the state. The case for client A requires arguing for a particular point of law, but the case for client B involves arguing against the same point of law. Can the firm ethically represent both clients?

Obligations to inform clients also create problems. A dentist has a patient who constantly smokes a pipe. Clenching the pipe between his teeth has caused some teeth to shift, slightly affecting the alignment of his bite. The smoke badly stains his teeth and has caused some minor precancerous sores of the type that rarely become malignant. The patient is concerned about the sores. To try to get the patient to stop smoking, can the dentist ethically tell him that the sores are "precancerous lesions" without further qualifications?

Professionals also have problems about their obligations to others. A family physician sees one spouse and diagnoses a venereal disease. The patient requests that the other spouse not be told of the disease because it might destroy the marriage, which the patient still wishes to preserve. Should the physician advise the other spouse to be tested for venereal disease?

Another example is a criminal defense attorney whose client tells her he has concocted an alibi and wishes to take the stand to present it. What should the lawyer do? Should she place her client on the stand to perjure himself? Should she withdraw from the case? If so, will the client then simply not tell the next lawyer that his alibi is false? Should she simply put the client on the stand, let him tell his story without direction, and then not argue that evidence? If so, will not the jury conclude that the client is lying?

Other problems arise from professionals' positions as employees. One common difficulty is the extent to which a professional may engage in independent work. Should an agency social worker take on clients independent of the agency, say, if a client does not meet the guidelines for agency assistance?

Another difficulty is that employer guidelines can conflict with professionals' conceptions of the services necessary to solve a client's problem. A legal aid lawyer might think that to handle adequately a divorce client's problems a lawsuit for injuries suffered in an accident is also necessary, but agency policy might forbid performing such work. Or a physician working for a county health organization might be confronted with a seriously ill child. The physician's professional obligations are to treat those in need, but the child might not meet residency requirements for services— perhaps he comes from a county to which the agency does not provide services. Should the physician treat the child anyway?

Perhaps the most common problem of an employed professional is employer directives that the professional thinks technically or ethically wrong. An editor might rewrite a journalist's story, placing the matter in an entirely different light. Engineers might be told to use a less expensive design that they think is less safe. When should a professional follow such directives? When is one justified in refusing to follow them?

Other problems revolve around the ethics of research. For example, a university computer science professor is contacted by a government security agency. The agency would like her to develop a system for accessing computers when the codes are not known. Can the computer scientist ethically undertake this task?

Problems about informing on the ethics of colleagues also arise. A nontenured university faculty member learns that the department chairman frequently visits female graduate assistants at home and suggests that they sleep with him. Does the faculty member have an obligation to report the chairman's actions to the dean or another university authority? Another example is a junior member of an accounting firm who learns that one of the senior partners spends two to three weeks each year at a lodge owned by a corporate audit client. Does the junior accountant have an obligation to report this activity to the appropriate disciplinary committee?

THE PROBLEMS

These cases, some of them among the most debated in professional ethics, illustrate the types of ethical problems professionals face and also provide some idea of the scope of professional ethics as a field of study. Some people restrict professional ethics to ethical dilemmas faced by particular professionals, so that matters of fees, advertising, the specification of the separate spheres of practice of professions, and social schemes to make professional services widely available are not, in their view, properly a part of professional ethics. The preceding cases indicate the broader scope of professional ethics adopted here.

Broadly construed, professional ethics encompasses all issues involving ethics and values in the roles of the professions and the conduct of professionals in society. Four broad areas of concern can be distinguished. First, the goal of making professional services equally available to all raises questions about the legitimacy of advertising, the cost of services, and the appropriateness of restricting certain services to particular professions. The question of the desirability of insurance or legal services corporations are also part of this concern. The second area of concern is the relationship between clients and professionals, in which problems such as taking advantage of client dependence, withholding information, and disregarding confidentiality of information can arise. The third area of concern is the effects on others of professional conduct in behalf of clients. These others may be either a specific individual, as in the example of a physician telling a patient's spouse of the risk of a venereal disease, or society more generally, as in a lawyer's client committing perjury (which is a crime against society's interest in the legal process). Fourth a professional's status as an employee raises many concerns. Obligations to employers and their effects on obligations to clients and others are crucial. Also important is the extent to which superiors should override the judgments of subordinates. Thus, professional ethics is not simply an application of narrow ethical theory. It involves aspects of political, social, and legal philosophy as well.

The study of professional ethics will not automatically make one an ethical professional or enable one to always know what is right or wrong. Although intellectual study cannot develop a motivation to ethical conduct, most people most of the time want to do what is ethically correct. Sometimes, however, they fail to see the ethical questions surrounding a course of action. The study of professional ethics will hopefully sensitize one to the ethical dimensions of professional practice and help one think clearly about ethical problems. In addition, conflicting considerations often make many ethical choices difficult. The study of professional ethics can enable one to develop some general principles to use in difficult or unusual cases. Finally, consideration of the social or political aspect of professional ethics will enable one to understand better the role and importance of professions in contemporary society.

Historical Perspective

Why has professional ethics become such a popular and important topic in recent years? The reasons for its popularity may not be the same as those for its importance, but they are closely related. The popularity of professional ethics largely stems from dramatic, widely publicized cases. Watergate stands out as the most spectacular of recent examples of unethical professional conduct, largely by lawyers. Watergate also brought with it exposures of corporate fraud and bribery that accountants and investment advising firms failed to detect or covered up. Recent instances of trading on inside information rocked the stock market. Physicians have been exposed and criticized for unnecessarily prescribing brand name drugs in exchange for benefits from the pharmaceutical industry and accused of defrauding the government in Medicare and Medicaid programs by billing for services that were not performed.

Historically, the professions have controlled admission to their ranks, regulated the conduct of their members, and defined their role in society. The lay public regarded professionals with respect and entrusted their lives and fortunes to their judgments. Although antipathy and suspicion have occasionally been directed toward individual professions, such as the attacks on lawyers in Charles Dickens's novels, by and large people concurred in professionals' self-judgment that all the decisions in and about their respective fields should be exclusively theirs. Now, however, criticism has become widespread and is directed at almost all professions.

Contemporary discontent with professional conduct may be deeper than professionals believe and may be based on more than the occasional ethical aberrations of a tiny minority of professionals, as the professions themselves are apt to see it. An eminent sociologist has written that "the professional complex, though obviously still incomplete in its development, has already become the most important single component in the structure of modern societies."[1] In the twentieth century, the number of professions and their members has grown dramatically. Although their origins date back several centuries, accounting, psychiatry, and many branches of engineering are largely twentieth-century professions. In 1900, there were 1,234,000 professional and technical workers in the United States, constituting 4¼ percent of the working population.[2] By 1984, the number of professional workers alone had vaulted to 12,835,000, constituting 12¼ percent of the working population.[3] The increase is even greater than these rough figures indicate. The figures for 1984 omit technical workers and writers and entertainers (but add accountants).

As society has become more complex and dependent on technology, the professions have become increasingly central to its functioning. For years, violations of professional ethical codes were frequent and unpunished, yet did not spark the kind of criticism that is currently widespread.[4] At the least, the recent criticism reflects the development of consumerism. Concern about withholding information from clients, unnecessary surgery, advertising, fees, and the unavailability of professional services all reflect a new emphasis on consumer rights.

Modern society has become centralized on the basis of complex technology and an increasingly complex legal system. As a result, many more decisions significantly affecting our lives are made by professionals. Control has shifted from the average individual or a political representative to professionals. Given the traditional self-regulation of the professions, democratic control, individual freedom, and other social values (discussed further in the next section) may be threatened.[5] The rise of modern industry during the late nineteenth and early twentieth centuries was accompanied by a political and social struggle to preserve and promote the well-being of the larger society. State and federal legislatures developed laws—such as worker's compensation—to restrict or meliorate the detrimental effects of large corporations on employees and the public. This effort culminated in the New Deal legislation of the 1930s. With the rise of the professions, a somewhat similar struggle may be occurring to redefine the professions' role in society so as to preserve and promote freedom, equal opportunity, and other values.

From this perspective, the study of professional ethics must be more than the application of traditional principles of professional ethics to new problems. It must be an analysis of the proper roles of professions in society. One cannot simply accept the prescription by professionals of their own roles. As one lawyer notes, "The public contempt for lawyers stems rather from their adherence to an unethical code of ethics, paradoxical though that may seem."[6] Although the responsibilities and situations of individual professionals vary, common elements stem from their role as professionals.

Professions have evolved differently in various societies. In France, their development has been closely tied to the growth of the government bureaucracy. Although there has been a greater similarity of professional development in Anglo-American societies, many differences remain. In England, trial lawyers or barristers are a separate group from lawyers (solicitors) who prepare cases for trial and handle office matters. Some differences stem from alternative modes of organizing society, and others from different underlying social values. Professional ethics can be properly analyzed only against a set of social values and a conception of the general role of professions in society.

Social Values

If the professions are to serve society, their roles must be examined from the viewpoint of average members of society. Therefore, this book analyzes professional ethics from the perspective of the average citizen, who is a consumer of professional services and is affected by professionals working for others. Even professionals are such consumers with respect to other professions. Citizens need good reasons to accept the ethical norms that regulate professional practices.

Much disagreement exists about how ethical norms and social values are justified. Little more can be done here than to state the method used and to indicate some social values that are largely assumed. Norms must be justifiable to a reasonable or rational person living in the society in which the norms operate.[7] A reasonable person is not mentally ill and has sufficient intelligence to understand the norms and their implications. Such a person uses logical reasoning (including scientific method) and all available information in acquiring desires and values, deciding what to do, and accepting norms. The person considers arguments for and against norms, accepting those that are sound and rejecting those that are not. Information is relevant to accepting a norm if it indicates that the norm's use has or lacks some normative characteristic, such as fairness, or that the probable use would be good or bad.

Reasonable people might have different desires. Some might like tapioca and others not. However, certain basic desires are presumably reasonable and widely shared. These desires are for bodily and mental integrity (including life), at least the wealth of personal property, reputation, and security in these. More controversially, it is assumed that people are self-interested with limited benevolence. That is, although they have some concern for others, they do not care for all others as much as for themselves.

Given these desires, a reasonable person has good reason to accept certain social values. The chief values relevant to professional ethics are freedom, protection from injury, equality of opportunity, privacy, and minimal well-being. Space does not permit a full discussion of these values and the arguments for them.[8]

Freedom and Self-Determination. People should be free from limits imposed by others to act as they desire to the extent that such freedom is compatible with other values. If one is free, then one's decisions determine what one will do and to that extent what will happen to one. Freedom is valuable both for its consequences and for its own sake. One often knows better than others what will most promote one's interests. So one's decisions will have better consequences than those of others. Freedom in society is likely to result in others' developing new ideas, methods, and goods leading to social improvement. Moreover, freedom or self-determination is often desired for its own sake, even if one might make mistakes others would avoid if they decided for one. It represents that one is respected as an agent capable of directing one's life.

Protection from Injury. People should be protected from injury—loss of life, bodily or psychological integrity, or wealth—by force, theft, or fraud. The basis of this value is obvious. If one desires life, bodily and mental integrity, and wealth, then one desires to retain them. One wants to be protected from others depriving one of them. Without protection from injury caused by others, social life is not possible.

Equality of Opportunity. People should have the same chances to reap the benefits of society. Discrimination on the basis of sex, race, religion, or ethnic origin, for example, deprives people of an equal opportunity. So far as human beings control social conditions, only ability and effort should be relevant to social success. Self-interested people want as much opportunity as possible for themselves. They have no reason to accept a value that would give them fewer opportunities than others. But if no one has good reason to accept fewer opportunities than others, the only solution acceptable to all is equal opportunities. Note that the concern is with opportunities, not outcomes. People of limited benevolence have a motive to assure others an equal chance, even though they desire their own success more than that of others.

Privacy.   People should have privacy, that is, control over the information others have about them. Privacy takes several forms—solitude, intimacy, and private or personal affairs. A reasonable person has good reason to accept privacy as a social value. Lack of it can adversely affect one's wealth and reputation (business deals can be lost if others know of plans in advance). Privacy is an essential element of personal relationships. For example, there might be matters about one's bodily function that one would disclose to a physician but not a journalist. Psychological benefits stem from occasional solitude to reflect and collect one's thoughts.

Minimal Well-Being.   People should have the goods and services needed to fulfill wants necessary for a minimal standard of living. A minimal standard of living refers to the conditions for normally good health, personal necessities, and security in them. That each reasonable person values minimal well-being is little more than a restatement of the desires for bodily and mental integrity, wealth, and security. Given the fundamental importance of minimal well-being to each person, a reasonable person has good reason to support this social value. Anyone can suddenly confront a loss of minimal well-being via natural disasters such as hurricanes and social disasters such as stock market collapses. Moreover, persons of limited benevolence would desire that others have minimal well-being, even if they desire more for themselves.

The role of professions in society should ultimately be tested against these values. To the extent professions preserve or promote them, they are properly constituted. Freedom and self-determination can be lost if professionals make decisions for one without one's consent. Protection from injury is relevant to the honesty of professionals and their protection of others from clients. Equality of opportunity is especially relevant to access to professional services and membership in professions. Privacy is especially relevant to confidentiality of professional–client relations, business and trade secrets, and discipline of professionals. Minimal well-being is relevant to the availability of professional services and research and reform to provide it for all. Professionals can affect many other values of clients or others in addition to these social values and be held to additional ethical standards in their dealings with clients and others.

THE PROFESSIONS

No generally accepted definition of the term *profession* exists, yet a working concept is needed for our study of professional ethics. Because our purpose is to consider common ethical problems raised by and within professions, a good definition will delineate characteristics of occupations with similar ethical problems. (These characteristics may prove to be related to some of those problems in important ways.) One need not characterize professions by a set of necessary and sufficient features possessed by all professions and only by professions.[9] The variety of professions is simply too great for that approach. Rather, some features can be taken as central or necessary for an occupation to be a profession, and others as simply common to many professions and as raising similar ethical concerns.

Three central features have been singled out by almost all authors who have characterized professions. First, a rather extensive training is required to practice a profession. Lawyers now generally attend law school for three years, and in the past they underwent years of clerkship with an established lawyer. Many, if not most, professionals have advanced academic degrees, and one author has plausibly contended that at least a college baccalaureate is necessary to be a professional.[10]

Second, the training involves a significant intellectual component.[11] The training of bricklayers, barbers, and craftspeople primarily involves physical skills. Accountants, teachers, engineers, lawyers, physicians, and nurses are trained in intellectual tasks and skills. Although physical skill may be involved in, for example, surgery or dentistry, the intellectual aspect is still predominant. The intellectual component is characteristic of those professionals who primarily advise others about matters the average person does not know about or understand. Thus, providing advice or service rather than things is a characteristic feature of the professions.

Third, the trained ability provides an important service in society. Physicians, lawyers, teachers, accountants, engineers, and architects provide services vital to the organized functioning of society—which chess experts do not. The rapid increase in the numbers of professions and professionals in the twentieth century is due to this feature. To function, technologically complex modern societies require a greater application of specialized knowledge than did the simpler societies of the past. The production and distribution of energy requires activity by many engineers. The operation of financial markets requires accountants, lawyers, and business and investment consultants. In short, professions provide important services that require extensive intellectual training.

Another common and perhaps central feature is credentialing. A process of certification or licensing often exists. Lawyers are admitted to the bar, and physicians receive a license to practice medicine. However, licensing is not sufficient to make an occupation a profession. One must be licensed to drive a car, but a driver's license does not make one a professional driver. Many professionals need not be officially licensed. College teachers are not licensed or certified, and many accountants are not certified public accountants. However, in many of these occupations, credentials are needed to be employed. Thus, almost all college teachers have advanced degrees in their fields, and accounts are distinguished from bookkeepers by their college education. Credentialing refers back to the extensive training; such training is needed to obtain a position in the field.[12]

A common feature to professions is an organization of members.[13] All major professions have organizations that claim to represent them. These organizations are not always open to all members of a profession, and competing organizations sometimes exist. Some bar associations, at least in the past, did not admit all lawyers. The organizations work to advance the goals of the profession—health, justice, efficient and safe buildings, and so on—and to promote the economic well-being of their members. Indeed, one author has stated that "the ethical problem of the profession, then, is . . . to fulfill as completely as possible the primary service for which it stands while securing the legitimate economic interest of its members."[14] If this claim is even approximately correct, one must expect professional organizations to be deeply involved in securing the economic interests of their members. Nevertheless, such organizations do generally differ from trade unions, which are almost exclusively devoted to members' economic interests. One does not expect to find carpenters' or automobile workers' unions striking for well-designed and constructed buildings or automobiles, yet public school teachers do strike for smaller classes and other benefits for students, and physicians and nurses for improved conditions for patients.

Another common feature of the professional is autonomy in his or her work. Given the present concern with reconciling professions and social values, how far such autonomy should extend is an open question. The minimum lies perhaps in the tasks of the work itself.[15] For example, surgeons are free to use their judgment about the details of operating procedure and lawyers to use their judgment about how to draft a contract, provided they remain within the bounds of acceptable professional practice. If professionals did not exercise their judgment in these aspects, people would have little reason to hire them. However, many professionals now work in large bureaucratic organizations in which their autonomy is limited by superiors who direct their activity and overrule their judgments. Nurses are often thought to have an equivocal status as professionals simply because physicians can overrule their judgments about specific aspects of their work. In these cases, however, an element of autonomy remains because the professionals are expected to exercise a considerable degree of discretionary judgment within the work context. Thus, an element of autonomy is a common and partially defining feature of a profession, though it might not be a necessary feature and the extent of such autonomy is debatable.

One may bias an investigation of professional ethics by using normative features (those saying how matters *should* be) to define or characterize professions. One common bias is to characterize professionals as primarily devoted to providing service and only secondarily to making money.[16] Such claims may be legitimate contentions about what should govern professions and motivate professionals, but they do not define the professions. If lawyers are, in the words of one of the earliest American writers on legal ethics, George Sharswood, "a hord of pettifogging, barratrous, custom-seeking, money-making" persons, they nonetheless constitute a profession.[17] An extreme example of the use of normative features to define professions is the following "consideration" presented by Maynard Pirsig: "The responsibility for effectuating the rendition of these services to all that need them and in such a manner that the public interest will best be served is left to the profession itself."[18] In this one condition, Pirsig manages to assume three different normative principles. First, services should be provided to all who need them. Second, the services should be provided so as best to promote the public interest. Third, the profession itself should be the sole judge of the method of achieving the first two principles. Even if these normative principles are correct, they should not be erected into the defining features of a profession.

Use of these criteria exclude some occupations that claim professional status. For example, realtors must be licensed, perhaps they perform an important service, but they do not meet the criterion of extensive training. Similarly, most administrators do not qualify. An extensive training in business administration is not a required credential for a position. Indeed, many administrators come from other professions such as law, engineering, and accounting. Two exceptions here are public school and perhaps hospital administration.

Similarly, other occupations have an equivocal status as professions. Some fields such as journalism are still quite open to people with training in other areas. For example, the syndicated columnist George Will has a Ph.D. in political science. Moreover, although college and university teachers must have advanced degrees, their training is not in teaching. One graduate dean turned down a request from a history department to grant graduate students credit for a course on teaching history! He did not think such a course appropriate, even though most history Ph.D.s go into teaching.

It is useful to distinguish between an occupation being a profession and it undergoing professionalization. The latter involves developing standards of performance and some training in them. For example, the professionalization of law enforcement officers means training personnel in techniques and methods and evaluating their performance against standards. This contrasts with the previous system, still common in sheriffs and some of their deputies, of being well liked and elected. The professionalization of law enforcement need not imply that it constitutes a profession. College level training is not yet required, although it is becoming increasingly common.

Two cross-cutting distinctions that are important for some ethical issues can be made among professionals. The first is between those who are self-employed and those who are employees. Many if not most physicians and lawyers are self-employed. Teachers and most engineers, journalists, and social workers are employees in large organizations. Self-employed professionals confront many ethical problems related to acquiring clients that employed professionals do not usually face. However, employee professionals confront ethical issues in their relations to their employers that self-employed ones do not.

The second distinction is between professionals who have individual human beings as clients and those who have large groups of persons as clients. Most health care professions have individual clients—patients. Lawyers also have individual clients, but they need not be human beings. Often their clients are corporations, and obligations to corporate clients might be different from those to specific human beings. Other professionals serve groups of people as clients. For example, the clients of journalists—the persons they serve—are their audience. The clients of some industry engineers are the end users of products they design. Academic and industry researchers, especially those in basic research, do not have anyone who might plausibly be considered a client. Teachers and group therapists fall somewhere in between the two categories. Their primary focus is on the class or group, but they also have ethical obligations to individual members.

Significant differences exist between members of the same profession. They can differ with respect to employment status and clients. Some physicians are self-employed with individual clients, and others are salaried researchers with no clients. Professionals also differ in many other respects. The differences in income, status, and type of practice between a partner in a Wall Street law firm and a small-town solo practitioner are tremendous. The large law firm usually has retainers from corporate clients, whereas the solo practitioner handles one matter for one client. Large accounting firms also can be virtually certain of continuing to work for corporate clients, but small accountants have little such security. The disparity is so great in the legal and accounting professions that different ethical or enforcement procedures have been suggested for large and small firms.[19] The conditions they face, it has been claimed, require such different applications of the same general ethical principles as to make a single system inappropriate. The medical profession is not as stratified as the legal and accounting professions, but a great difference still exists between a well-known specialist in a large urban center and a general practitioner in a rural community. The status of specialties has been evident in the career choices of medical students during the past decades. Medical research and surgery have been the most prestigious, and general or family practice the least. Although family practice is becoming more respected and the choice of more students (as a specialty!), this difference has not disappeared.

Three salient features of the role of professions in the United States at the end of the twentieth century lie at the heart of the problem of their position in society. First, they all provide an important service. Engineers and architects design the structures and facilities essential to modern life—buildings, power stations, transportation systems, and so on. Most of us depend on the medical and dental professions to protect our health and well-being. The legal profession provides services essential for legal justice and equality before the law. Accountants, as auditors, testify to the financial integrity of institutions and keep track of the wealth in society. Teachers and journalists provide the knowledge and information so important in an information age. The services of professionals are important for individuals to realize values they seek in their personal lives—health, wealth, legal justice, comfort, safety, and knowledge.

Second, the professions have a significant or monopolistic control over the provision of services and entry into them. In some professions, especially health care, one must be legally licensed to practice. Laws make it a criminal offense to practice medicine or law without a license. Physicians and lawyers determine who will be licensed. Attempting to do without these professionals or to be one's own professional can realistically have only minimal success. If one decides to be one's own physician, one cannot obtain access to the most useful medicines and technology; most drugs can be obtained legally only with a prescription from a licensed physician and from another professional, a pharmacist. The United States limits the access to medications more strictly than other countries such as Mexico and even Canada. Although one may legally represent oneself, the legal profession has waged continuous war against allowing people access to help in handling their own legal problems, such as divorce and probate of wills.

Although the law does not prohibit practice by nonprofessionals in many professions, the professions still often retain significant control over who can practice. In some, one must be certified to use a particular name, say, architect or certified social worker. Employed engineers do not even have to be certified. But realistically, to obtain a job, one must have graduated from an accredited engineering school. Such accreditation is often determined by private professional organizations.

The monopolistic aspect of professional practices has frequently brought professions into conflict with each other and with other occupational groups over the provisions of services. Architects and engineers have long debated their respective spheres of practice, as have lawyers and accountants. The legal profession has also been anxious to define the respective spheres of practice of realtors and insurance and title companies. The medical profession now confronts questions concerning the services provided by nurse practitioners and physician's assistants.

The legal monopoly of professional services, when it exists, has an important implication for professional ethics. Professionals do not have a right to practice; it is a privilege conferred by the state. One must carefully distinguish between a right and a privilege in this context. *A right* is a sound claim that one be permitted (or assisted) to act in some manner without interference. *A privilege* is a permission to perform certain acts provided specified conditions are fulfilled. With a privilege, the burden is on the person obtaining it to demonstrate that he or she has the necessary qualifications. For example, one must pass tests for the privilege of driving a car. In the case of a right, the burden is on anyone who fails to respect it, for example, by prohibiting the publication of one's opinions. Individual professionals have only a privilege to practice; in addition, the profession as a whole is privileged activity created by the state to further social values.

A third feature of the professional's role is that although some professions have secured legally protected monopolies, few of them have been subject to much public control. Monopolies such as public utilities that provide essential services have usually been subject to strict public control as to the conditions and types of services provided. In contrast, the professions have claimed and been accorded a large degree of self-regulation. They have claimed that because of the intellectual training and judgment required for their practice, nonprofessionals are unable to evaluate their conduct properly. Thus, in addition to control over membership and the disciplining of members, the professions also often control the conditions of practice (including, until recently, setting fees and regulating advertising).

The combined effects of these three features—serving basic social values, monopoly, and self-regulation—are central to the issue of the role of professions in a modern society. Monopoly and self-regulation, if exercised improperly, can be detrimental to society and the quality of human life. As the number of professions and professionals increases and their decisions become more essential for the operation of a technologically complex society, the conduct and ethical principles of the professions as well as the enforcement of standards become a matter of increasing importance to everyone. If the principles of professional conduct are designed to favor professionals more than their clients and others, then social values are threatened. Monopolies are created for the benefit of society, and if they do not serve society well, then they are not justified.

Some problems with professional principles may arise from a failure of professions to revise accepted ethical principles adequately to reflect the changing condition of society and professional roles. Two sociologists suggest that the professions are beginning to adopt characteristics of modern industry, specifically a more bureaucratic structure of practice.[20] They specify six differences between traditional professional practice and the modified form they see evolving.

1. Practice as an isolated individual is changing to team practice.

2. The use of knowledge from a single discipline is being replaced by use of knowledge from diverse disciplines.

3.   Compensation is changing from fee-for-service to salary.

4.   The limits on altruism involved in solo professionals' entrepreneurial private practices (the concern with attracting clients and making a living) are decreasing.

5.   The opportunity for colleague evaluation is increasing.

6.   The privacy of the professional–client relationship is decreasing.

Examination of these six changes indicates that the last three depend on the first three. Colleague evaluation and privacy in the professional–client relationship depend largely on whether a professional practices as an individual or as part of a team. The entrepreneurial limit on altruism depends on the fee-for-service system. With a fixed salary, a professional can literally afford to be altruistic.

The factors of team approach, use of knowledge from diverse fields, and compensation by salary partially result from the increasing knowledge required for professional practice. The growth of engineering knowledge and the complexity of many structures now being built require the efforts of many different types of engineers. Electrical, structural, and other engineers must be involved in the design and construction of skyscrapers, large bridges, and so on. The growth of medical knowledge has forced specialization because physicians cannot keep fully informed about all aspects of medicine. No one specialist can provide total patient care, so the team approach involving various physicians, therapists, social workers, and nurses is now often used for hospitalized patients. Although compensation by salary is not as widespread among physicians as among accountants and lawyers, as group practice develops, more physicians will become salaried. Similar developments have occurred in the legal profession. Although the profession is just beginning to officially recognize specialization, it has existed in practice for a number of years. The development of large corporate law firms during the late nineteenth and early twentieth centuries encouraged specialization and salaried employment. In addition, the enormous proliferation of laws, especially with the advent of governmental regulatory activity in the 1930s, has made it difficult for any one lawyer to keep abreast of the entire legal field.

These claims about the changing nature of professional practice are not that clear. They seem most applicable to the health professions. The percentage of lawyers in solo practice has also declined, in 1980 constituting about 33 percent of all lawyers.[21] Yet during the 1970s, the percentage of self-employed professionals increased.[22] Some of the traditional employed professions, such as social work, have experienced tremendous growth as well as a significant increase in self-employed practitioners.[23] Nevertheless, most professionals, such as teachers, nurses, and engineers, have always been employees.

SUMMARY

Professional ethics seeks to determine what the role of professions and the conduct of professionals should be. As a discipline, it includes aspects of social, political, and legal philosophy as well as individual ethics. The study of professional ethics will not automatically make one more ethical, but it should develop sensitivity to ethical problems and clearer thinking, provide some general guiding principles, and help one better understand the role and importance of professions in contemporary society. Professional ethics has gained popularity due to recent dramatic cases of unethical conduct or difficult issues, but deeper reasons may underlie this new popularity. The contemporary concern with professional ethics reflects consumerism and the need for society to reconsider the role and conduct of professionals. This study adopts the point of view of the average citizen interested in preserving the social values of freedom, protection from injury, equality of opportunity, privacy, and minimal well-being.

The professions are characterized by three or four central features—extensive training, a significant intellectual component to practice, the provision of an important service, and perhaps credentialing. They also have two common features—the organization of members and autonomy in work. It is important to distinguish between employed and self-employed professionals and between those who have individual people as clients and those who have groups as clients or no clients. Members of a profession are not homogeneous but range from those working in large organizations to solo practitioners, from world famous surgeons to small-town physicians.

Three salient features characterize the role of professions—provision of services related to basic values, control or monopolization of the provision of services and membership in them, and self-regulation. These features lie at the heart of the relation between the professions and social values. The structure of professional practice might be changing from that of a single practitioner paid on a fee-for-service basis to one of team practice using knowledge from diverse disciplines and paid by salary. The changes differ among the professions, and most professionals have been and are employees.

NOTES*

1. Parsons, "Professions," p. 545.

2. From U.S. Bureau of the Census, *Historical Statistics of the United States, Colonial Times to 1970,* bicentennial ed., part 1 (Washington, D.C.: GPO, 1975), p. 140.

3. U.S. Department of Commerce, Bureau of the Census, *Statistical Abstract of the United States, 1986,* 106th ed. (Washington, D.C.: GPO, 1985), p. 400.

4. See Chapter 8, "Self-Regulation."

5. Branson, "Secularization of American Medicine," notes the conflict between traditional medical practices and the values of freedom and equality.

6. Lieberman, *Crisis at the Bar,* pp. 15–16.

7. See Brandt, *Theory of the Good and the Right,* pp. 10–16; Bayles, *Principles of Legislation,* pp. 51–54.

8. For a general development of these political values and principles, see Bayles, *Principles of Legislation.*

9. Wilbert E. Moore recognizes this point and offers a scale of professionalism; see *The Professions,* pp. 4–5. The definition technique used here could be modified to a scale system by assigning points to the possession of those characteristics that are

---

*See the bibliography at the back of the book for complete references.

often found in professions. Both the scale system and that used here agree that an occupation may be a profession yet lack some features found in most professions.

10. Ibid., p. 11.

11. Professionals "profess to know better than others the nature of certain matters, and to know better than their clients what ails them or their affairs. This is the essence of the professional idea and the professional claim" (Everett C. Hughes, "Professions," in *Professions in America*, ed. Lynn, p. 2).

12. See Freidson, *Professional Powers*, pp. 59–60, requiring that to be a profession working depend on credentials based on higher education.

13. See Moore, *The Professions*, pp. 9–10; Pound, "What Is a Profession?" p. 204.

14. R. M. MacIver, "The Social Significance of Professional Ethics," in *Cases and Materials on Professional Responsibility*, ed. Pirsig, p. 48.

15. See Freidson, *Profession of Medicine*, pp. xvii, 42, 70, 82.

16. Wade, "Public Responsibilities of the Learned Professions," in *Cases and Materials on Professional Responsibility*, ed. Pirsig, p. 38; MacIver, "Social Significance," (see n. 14 above), p. 48 Moore's use of this feature as one item on a scale is less objectionable because the service orientation is not a necessary feature; see *The Professions*, pp. 13–16.

17. Sharswood, *Essay on Professional Ethics*, pp. 147–148.

18. Pirsig, *Cases and Materials on Professional Responsibility*, p. 43.

19. Philip Shuchman, "Ethics and Legal Ethics: The Propriety of the Canons as a Group Moral Code," in *1977 National Conference on Teaching Professional Responsibility*, ed. Goldberg, p. 271; see also Abraham J. Briloff, "*Quis Custodeit Ipsos Custodes?* Accountants and the Public Good," *National Forum 58* (Summer 1978): 29.

20. Gloria V. Engel and Richard H. Hall, "The Growing Industrialization of the Professions," in *Professions and Their Prospects*, ed. Freidson, p. 85.

21. Curran, *Lawyer Statistical Report*, p. 13.

22. Freidson, *Professional Powers*, p. 121.

23. From 1975 to 1985, the number of clinical social workers increased about 140 percent; Frederic G. Reamer, "Social Work: Calling or Career?" in Special Supplement, *Hastings Center Report* 17 (February 1987). A 1975 survey found that only 2.4 percent of social workers indicated private practice as their primary employment, but a 1981 survey found 21.5 percent; Kelley and Alexander, "Part-Time Private Practice," p. 254. Even allowing for a significant bias in the second survey, this is a remarkable change.

STUDY QUESTIONS AND PROBLEMS

1.   Which of the following questions concern professional ethics? Why or why not?

    a.   Should a corporation pay a government lawyer an honorarium for a lecture?

    b.   Should carpenters be paid the same hourly wage as bricklayers?

    c.   Should a physician smoke marijuana?

    d.   Should an accountant report suspected illegal activity by a firm she is auditing to the Securities and Exchange Commission?

    e.   Should an engineer report to the police that his neighbor is driving a car with one headlight and both taillights out?

    f.   Should poorly paid and understaffed social workers in a probation office go on strike?

2.   Study the newspaper for a week and collect all the articles that concern professions. What ethical issues are raised? Are the stories favorable or unfavorable?

3.   Why have the professions grown so rapidly during the twentieth century? Name five professions that are new in the twentieth century.

4.   Are the social values mentioned in the text justifiable? Why or why not? Are some of them more important than others? If so, which ones? Why? Are there others that should be added? If so, what are they and why?

5.   Which of the following categories of occupations are professions? Why are they or are they not professions?

    a.   physicians

    b.   horticulturalists

    c.   law clerks

    d.   journalists

    e.   radiologic technicians

    f.   military officers

    g.   TV repair people

    h.   major league baseball players

    i.   editors of book publishing firms

    j.   practical nurses or nursing assistants

6.   What ethical difference does it make, if any, whether an occupation is profession? Why?

7.   What differences between professionals' mode of employment might be relevant to professional ethics?

8.   Do licensed barbers constitute a monopoly? How do they differ, if at all, from lawyers?

9.   Choose a profession and list as many differences as possible between the way it is practiced now and the way it was practiced sixty years ago. Are these differences also found in other professions?

2 The Structure of Professional Ethics

Professional ethics can be viewed as a system of norms. The term *norm* has several uses. In social science, it is commonly used descriptively to refer to criteria of behavior accepted within a group or to the statistical average of a characteristic. "Norm" can also be used evaluatively to specify how things should or ought to be. Our concern is with what the behavior of professionals should be rather than with what it is and with the criteria that should be used to evaluate professional conduct and professions rather than with those that are used. Consequently, *norm* is used as the most general term for criteria for evaluating professions, professionals, and their conduct.

Professional ethics does not concern all the norms that apply to professionals, only those that pertain to them in their professional conduct and activities. Thus, although a justifiable norm may specify that parents have a responsibility for the well-being of their children, this is not a norm of professional ethics. Even if professionals are also parents, caring for the well-being of their children is not part of their professional activities.

Some norms apply to all people; others apply to people in particular roles. The parental responsibility to provide for children applies to people in the role of parent. It does not apply to people who do not have children. These can be called role-related norms. Other, universal norms apply to people irrespective of their roles. Examples of universal norms are the requirements to keep promises and not to murder. These also apply to people in roles; parents are not to murder their children!

Consequently, both universal norms and professional role-related norms apply to professionals in their professional activities and are included in professional ethics. There are three crucial questions about the norms of professional ethics: (1) How are they justified? (2) What is the relationship between role-related and universal norms? (3) What kinds of norms are there? This chapter examines these three questions.

JUSTIFICATION

Ethical Relativism

The central feature of ethical relativism is that norms always refer to a particular reference group.[1] "X is wrong" if and only if "P disapproves of X," where P is the reference group. According to the ethical relativist, different norms can be correct in different societies or for different groups. The ethical relativist does not maintain merely that people have different beliefs (cultural or descriptive relativism), but that these different beliefs can all be correct.

Ethical relativism is subject to two major criticisms. First, it makes meaningful ethical disagreement impossible. If a Korean engineer says that bribing officials is permissible, and a U.S. engineer says it is not, they do not really disagree. The Korean is saying that most people in Korea believe it is permissible, and the American is saying that most people in the United States believe it is not. Both can be correct, and there is no disagreement. Second, the group cannot give a reason for its belief. If the claim "X is wrong" is correct because most people in the society think it is, then the only reason a member of the majority can give is that most people think so. Here, thinking makes it so. For these reasons, ethical relativism is not accepted for this book.

A version of ethical relativism is sometimes suggested to justify professional ethics. One author claims that social workers' ethics is determined by the preferences of most social workers.[2] In other words, social workers' conduct is right if most social workers think it is. However, this is just a version of ethical relativism and subject to the same criticisms. It protects the accepted social worker ethics from criticism. Suppose a person claims that some aspect of accepted social workers' ethics is incorrect. But if most social workers think it is correct, then it is. The critic must be incorrect!

Levels of Justification

Suppose a college professor changes the announced basis for grading in a course, say, by dropping an examination or changing the weight assigned to exams. A student might well complain that this is wrong. The student might have done poorly on an early exam and been counting on a higher grade on the dropped test or have done well on a test that is now assigned less weight.

How might a student justify the claim that the professor's conduct is wrong? First, the student might appeal to some norms. There might be a college (institutional) rule requiring professors to announce the basis for grading on the first day of classes. The student might also appeal to universal norms, claiming that the professor has broken an implicit promise to grade on the announced basis and lied to or deceived the students in originally giving the grading basis.

The professor, being a philosopher, might not be convinced. The professor might contend that breaking promises and institutional rules is justifiable whenever it produces more good than harm. Because most students did well on the first exam (or the one now weighted more heavily), breaking the norms produces more good than bad and so is justifiable. In short, the professor claims that the norms are not justifiable or have exceptions.

The student must now defend the norms to which she appeals. This could be done by appealing to values. Changing the grading basis deprives students of an equal opportunity to get high grades. She had planned to emphasize work in the course at the end of term, but now she has less chance to improve her grade. Moreover, a reasonable person who would be subject to a norm about keeping promises would not agree to someone breaking a promise whenever that person thought more good would result from doing so.

This example illustrates two of the three levels of justification. At the first level, claims about the ethics of particular actions are justified by appeals to norms. At the second level, norms are justified by appeals to social values. At a third level, the social values themselves must be justified (Figure 2.1). Each of these levels of justification is complex and requires further elucidation. The use of different types of norms to justify acts is considered later in this chapter.

Figure 2.1   Levels of Justification

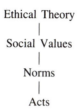

Ethical Theory

|

Social Values

|

Norms

|

Acts

Norms can be justified by their being acceptable to reasonable people expecting to live in a society in which they operate. Often this acceptability depends on the social values reasonable people have. Professional activities usually affect three or four distinct groups—the professionals, their clients, their employers, and the general public.[3] Professional activity should generally promote the wealth of professionals and their employers and the interests and values of clients related to the professional activity. It should not be detrimental to (should preserve or promote) the social values of clients and others in society. Different values and interests will be affected, depending on the context. For example, confidentiality promotes the value of clients' privacy, and making services available promotes equality of opportunity.

Norms are justified by balancing the effects of conduct conforming to them on the interests and values of the different groups. Sometimes a norm will promote one value or interest for at least one of these groups and preserve all values and interests for others. For example, a physician treating a bacterial infection in a client promotes the client's interest in health and preserves the values and interests of others. Sometimes this is not possible, and difficult choices must be made between favorable and unfavorable effects on different values or interests of various affected groups. Clients' interests and values sometimes coincide with, and sometimes conflict with, those of the broader community. A criminal lawyer's client has an interest in avoiding punishment that is contrary to society's interest in preventing crime and protecting its members from injury. Similarly, a patient with a highly communicable disease has an interest in being free in the community, which is contrary to society's welfare.

Professionals often mediate between individuals and society. Social workers serving as parole and probation officers mediate between social and individual concerns, trying to reconcile them. Sometimes the values of the general public do not all point in the same direction; for example, a housing project might promote the well-being of some persons but harm that of others who are forced to move. In such cases, norms must provide a proper balance between the effects on professionals, clients, employers, and the public. This balance is determined by considering what reasonable persons holding social values would desire in the respective roles.

If norms are justified by their acceptability to reasonable persons with social values, then the nature of those values is crucial. In a Nazi society, the norms for physicians might include identifying and killing those who, by Nazi standards, are unfit. A professional ethic completely incompatible with accepted social values will not endure; any viable professional ethic must be largely congruent with the accepted values of a society. However, as the Nazi example shows, the accepted social values might be unjustifiable. Consequently, the third level of justification involves justifying social values. The values of freedom, privacy, equality of opportunity, prevention of injury, and minimal well-being identified in Chapter 1 are here taken to be justifiable. Major differences from these values alter the norms that are justifiable. Although there are differences in interpreting these values, they are widely enough accepted in the United States and other Western countries to render viable a professional ethic based on them.

RELATIONSHIPS

At the beginning of this chapter, we noted the difference between universal norms applying to everyone and role-related norms applying only to people in a role. The nature of role-related norms needs to be further explicated; then we can consider the relationships between universal and role-related norms.

Norms have the following logical structure: person P, with characteristics C, in situation S may or should do A in manner M. A norm specifies who should or may do what, when, or how.

Social roles or positions are defined by such norms. These role-defining norms need not be ethical; they simply state the actions that people with certain characteristics may or must do. *Role-defining norms* specify the powers and tasks of a role or position. For example, the role or position of president of the United States is defined by the Constitution. It specifies certain characteristics that the president must have, for example, be a natural born citizen and at least thirty-five years old. It also specifies tasks and powers that the president has, such as commander-in-chief of the military and the power to grant pardons.

Similar norms define professional roles. Sometimes one can determine professional roles by examining statutes and other licensing regulations. They specify the qualifications for being an accountant or nurse, for example, and the kinds of activities these professionals are entitled to perform. Other professions are not constituted by law but by generally accepted norms. Engineers need not be licensed or certified, but there are generally accepted norms specifying what they do. For someone to be a lawyer, teacher, or journalist is for that person to occupy a position defined by such a set of norms.

Role-related ethical norms refer to a person occupying a role. Usually this is done merely by referring to being a professional—lawyer, social worker, pharmacist—as a characteristic of the persons to whom the norm applies. For example, the norm that lawyers should not personally solicit clients is a role-related ethical norm. It says something about the manner in which lawyers should conduct their activity. Often role-related ethical norms will not explicitly mention a professional role, but the limitation is implicit or understood. Thus, many norms in professional codes of ethics do not explicitly say a doctor or engineer should do so and so; it is understood that the norms in the code apply only to members of the profession.

There are four possible relationships between ethical norms for professional activity and universal norms. Professional norms could be (1) independent of, (2) identical with, (3) specifications of, or (4) functionally related to universal norms.

An Independent Professional Ethic

If professional norms are independent of universal norms and social values, then they can require or permit conduct completely different from that of nonprofessionals. They constitute a distinct ethical system alongside of, and perhaps taking precedence over, the universal ethical system. This view can be illustrated by the similar position of some religious norms. Religious norms concerning baptism, confession, and diet, for example, are not justified by reference to universal norms and social values and do not apply to people who are not members of a particular religious sect.

The view that professional norms are independent of universal norms and social values is a version of ethical relativism.[4] As such, it is subject to the criticisms of that position. Meaningful disagreement becomes impossible, and one cannot justify the norms. One might think that professional norms could be justified by a perhaps tacit agreement or social contract among professionals, but this view has two problems. First, it presupposes a nonrelativist norm, namely, that contracts should be adhered to. Second, it would not justify norms concerning conduct toward clients and other persons who are not members of the profession and thus not parties to the agreement or contract.

The independence of professional norms is also inadequate for conduct toward others in society.[5] Religious norms, such as Jewish dietary laws and priests' vows of chastity, do not apply to others. However, whenever religious duties affect people who do not belong to the sect, universal norms may limit them. Because professional activity almost always affects nonprofessionals, some broader-based ethic would limit any independent ethic.

Universal Norms

Professionals are people, universal norms apply to all people, so universal norms apply to professionals. For example, professionals should not assault or defraud others. Some complaints against professionals are for violations of such universal norms in professional activity. Earlier it was shown how, by appeal to a norm about promise keeping, a student might justify a complaint about a professor dropping an exam or changing the weight assigned to exams. The norm requiring people to keep promises is universal, and it applies to professors in their professional activity. Complaints are also made about lawyers appropriating clients' funds for their own use. These situations do not often cause ethical perplexity.

I have suggested justifying universal norms by their acceptability to reasonable persons for a society in which they expect to live. Many other theories exist about how to justify them, but almost all justify basic norms that are widely shared, such as those against lying and theft. For the most part, these are the types of universal norms considered in this book, so the absence of a full justification for each of them should not create difficulties. Such norms would be justified by any acceptable theory.

Other professional norms are specifications of universal ones. A *specification* of a universal norm usually identifies particular situations (S in the logical form of a norm) to which a universal norm applies. Professional norms that are specifications simply make universal norms more concrete by indicating a type of situation a professional encounters. For example, that a lawyer should "not knowingly . . . make a false statement of material fact or law to a tribunal" simply specifies one type of situation in which one should not lie.[6] It applies with equal force to lawyers and nonlawyers; indeed, whether the other party is a tribunal makes no difference because lawyers should not lie to any third party.[7]

Sometimes norms apply to professionals because features that make conduct wrong for anyone are almost always present in professional conduct. These are also basically specifications of universal norms. A universal norm is that sexual intercourse requires the free consent of both parties. This norm is justified by the interest in bodily integrity and the social value of freedom and self-determination. Because the dominant position of a professional makes free consent of a client questionable, applying the universal norm to the psychiatrist–client situation results in a specific prohibition of sexual activity with a client.[8] However, the same point applies to the employer– employee relation and is the basis for the prohibition of sexual harassment (including of professional employees). Also, because sexual conduct between psychotherapists and clients is detrimental to the therapy, the social value of protection from injury (to mental integrity) also applies.[9]

One must distinguish ethical relativism from professional norms being specifications of universal ones. A specification merely states that a broader norm applies to a type of situation. It does not deny that the norm applies to everyone. Nor does it claim that the norm is correct because most professionals accept it. To hold that the same norm justifies different actions by people in different situations is not ethical relativism.

Role-Related Norms

A major issue in professional ethics is whether justifiable role-related norms can require conduct different from that required by universal norms. (Specifications cannot do so, for they only apply universal norms to particular types of situations.) Unlike specifications of universal norms, role-related ethical norms make essential reference to the actor being a professional. That is, the norm applies only to persons who have the characteristic of being a member of one or more professions. Can and how might this make a difference?

Role-related norms might differ from universal ones in three ways. (1) Universal norms might permit acts, but role-related norms require or prohibit them. (2) Universal norms might require acts that role-related norms permit or prohibit. (3) Universal norms might prohibit acts that role-related norms permit or require. The first difference is not significant because the role-related norms do not require conduct that is wrong by universal norms. It simply amounts to professionals having additional duties due to their being professionals. All jobs entail people having duties that other people do not have. However, in both (2) and (3), role-related norms permit or require conduct that is wrong by universal norms.

One common approach to justifying professional norms is likely to justify role-related professional norms permitting or requiring conduct that is wrong by universal norms. Some writers suggest that professional norms can be justified by the social value or ideal of a profession.[10] For example, the medical professions promote health. The fundamental norm, many physicians contend, is "First, do no harm."[11] To heal and avoid doing harm, confidentiality of professional–client relationships is essential. Other norms can be similarly derived from the social value a profession serves. These norms are justified as means to the social value. Consequently, physicians are justified in lying to clients whenever they think doing so is better for their clients' health. The same applies to lawyers in winning legal cases, and so on for other professions.

There are two major objections to this approach. First, the precise social value or aim of a profession is controversial and imprecise.[12] One view of medicine's goal is to produce health; another is to prevent disease. The concept of health is often so broad—a state of physical and mental well-being—that little can clearly be ruled out as part of medicine. One cannot, as some people have wanted to do, rule out sterilization or artificial insemination as not producing health. If the aim is prevention of disease, it is not clear why all diseases should be treated, for example, a subclinical case of depression. Moreover, what is a disease often depends on what people think doctors should try to correct. At one time, masturbation and homosexuality were considered diseases, and alcoholism was not; now alcoholism is considered a disease, and the other two are not. Some doctors even contend that hypochondriacs, who come to them when they are not ill, are ill because they have the mental problem of thinking they are sick.

One cannot derive norms as means to vague and controversial ends, especially because controversies over ends occur just when one tries to defend a controversial norm. Consider people who have been voluntarily sterilized and now want to have the sterilization reversed, usually because they have divorced and remarried. One might say that the value of health, or prevention and cure of disease, implies that physicians should not treat this condition. The people are healthy; they are not diseased. But this begs the question about what health and disease are and what the aim of medicine is.

The second major objection to this approach is that it insulates role-related professional norms from other social values. Each profession predominantly serves only one or two social values—lawyers, legal justice; teachers, knowledge; architects and engineers, beautiful and safe structures. To found role-related norms on one or two such values is to ignore the other social values in determining the norms.

The institution or general practice of medicine or law—having the roles of physician or lawyer in society—might be justified by appeal to a predominant social value served.[13] That is, the value served justifies having physicians or lawyers. It indicates their function in society. But that institution or practice can be better or worse, depending on how it fits with other social values. Thus, one must examine each role-related norm in light of other interests and social values affected.

The justification of the criminal justice system provides a striking parallel. The criminal justice system serves the social value of preventing injury; that is its function. Just as there is dispute about the precise aim of medicine, there is dispute about the precise aim of criminal justice, whether to deter wrongdoing or to punish wrongdoers. This dispute can affect particular norms of the criminal justice system, for example, whether capital punishment is appropriate. Moreover, the criminal justice system does not single-mindedly pursue preventing injury. In various ways, its effectiveness is restrained to preserve other social values. To protect privacy, police are not permitted to search wherever and whenever they wish. To protect knowledge and physical integrity, police are not permitted to beat confessions out of suspects. Although the criminal justice system is generally justified by one social value, the justification of each specific rule must also consider other social values and norms.

Similarly, the predominant social value served by a professional role is central to justifying role-related ethical norms. The professionals have tasks to promote that value. The value thus has more significance in determining what they ought to do than it does for most people. For example, lawyers are to promote legal justice, and one aspect is that the state must prove by its own efforts that a person has committed a crime. To fulfill their role of forcing the state to make its case, lawyers must keep confidential their clients' admission of guilt. Plausibly, however, if a client told an ordinary citizen information indicating his or her guilt, the ordinary citizen would have a duty to report it to the police. Here we have a strong conflict between a universal norm and a role-related professional norm. The universal norm requires reporting the information; the role-related norm requires not reporting it. However, if the client's statement is of an intent to commit a future crime, then the value of making the state prove its case does not apply, and the prevention of injury does; so a lawyer should not keep such information confidential. This example is controversial, and some people disagree with the claims. The point is not to settle the issue of lawyer–client confidentiality, but to show how other values are relevant to justifying role-related norms.

To sum up this discussion, role-related ethical norms might require conduct contrary to that required by universal norms. The social value predominantly served by a professional role is important in justifying role-related norms because it is usually significantly affected. Nevertheless, role-related norms cannot be justified by appeal to that predominant value alone. Consideration must be taken of other social values. Thus, role-related norms are justified in the same way universal ones are—by their promoting and preserving justifiable social values and being acceptable to reasonable persons living in a society in which they operate. When role-related norms permit or require conduct that is wrong by universal norms, they can be viewed as exceptions to the universal norms.[14] As such, they must be justified in the same ways other exceptions should be justified—by appeal to justifiable social values and acceptability to reasonable persons.

NORMS

So far the discussion has suggested that conduct is evaluated by norms, norms are justified by values, and values are justified by ethical theories. At this point, a further complication must be introduced. Different types of norms exist, and some of them can be used to justify and evaluate others. This has already been implicit in discussing norms that are specifications of universal norms; specifications are justified by the universal norms they specify.

The first distinction is between obligations and permissions. Some norms express *permissions*—what one may do or not do as one wants. For example, professionals may refuse to accept potential clients. The term *obligation* is used here to express the requirements of professional norms. Obligations state that something is not permissible. If one has an obligation to perform an act, then it is not permissible to omit it. Obligations state that one must act or forbear or (not) be a kind of person. Obligations prescribe or proscribe actions or character traits. Most of the concern in professional ethics is with what professionals are obligated to do, for they are permitted to do what is not prohibited or prescribed.

Table 2.1   Kinds of Professional Norms

OBLIGATIONS

    Standards of virtue and vice

    Principles of responsibility

    Rules of duty

PERMISSIONS

Standards, Principles, and Rules

As indicated in Table 2.1, obligations can be divided into three types: those prescribing standards of virtue, principles expressing responsibilities, and rules expressing duties.[15] Each of them has a somewhat different function.

Standards of Virtue.   Standards, which are used to evaluate persons as good or bad, better or worse, virtuous or vicious, can be fulfilled to different degrees.[16] They refer to character traits of professionals. Teachers can be good or bad, better or worse. One obvious standard is that a professional be competent, for example, that a professor know the subject matter. Obviously, professors can be more or less competent in this respect. However, a professor might know the subject matter quite well but not be very fair in grading. Norms of professional ethics prescribe that professors be competent (know their field), fair, able to communicate to students, and so on.

Standards guide human conduct by presenting desirable traits (virtues) to be sought or undesirable ones (vices) to be avoided. The virtues of professors include knowledge, fairness, and clarity. The lack of these characteristics is the vices of ignorance, unfairness, and obscurity. Professors can guide their conduct to try to develop desirable characteristics. Others can use the standards in evaluating professionals, as in deciding to award tenure to a professor. Among the virtues that we argue professionals should have are competence, loyalty, discretion, honesty, diligence, and candor (see Chapter 4).

Principles of Responsibility.   Other norms prescribe responsibilities. Responsibilities concern conduct, but they leave room for professional discretion and judgment. For example, a commonly accepted principle is that engineers "hold paramount the safety, health and welfare of the public."[17] This principle does not, however, say how safe a structure must be. Must a building be able to withstand an earthquake of 5 or 7 on the Richter scale? Judgment considering the past record of earthquakes in the area, the cost of added strength, and so on is required.

Principles can help explicate standards and be justified by them. Professionals should have the virtue (meet the standard) of honesty. The principle that professionals have a responsibility to protect their clients' money is partially justified by the standard of honesty, at least in protecting it from their own theft. Other principles are directly justified by social values. The principle of engineers holding paramount the safety, health, and welfare of the public can be justified by the social values of well-being and protection from injury.

Because principles are broad in scope, they can come into conflict. Another plausible principle is that engineers act as "faithful agents or trustees" of their employers.[18] This principle can conflict with holding paramount the safety of the public. Suppose an employer directs an engineer to design something that the engineer thinks does not protect the public safety as much as it might—a less expensive building that will not withstand very severe earthquakes. In determining what to do, an engineer will have to balance the responsibilities. How strong is the responsibility to the employer? How much risk does the building pose? Here the weighing and balancing of principles can be used to justify particular acts.

Rules of Duty.   Rules prescribing duties specify particular conduct and do not leave room for judgment or discretion by professionals. For example, a rule prescribes that professionals experimenting on human subjects have a duty to obtain informed consent. A professional does not have discretion to decide whether informed consent is needed for a particular experiment or subject. Because rules are determinate, they cannot be balanced against one another. They apply in an all-or-nothing fashion; that is, if they apply to a situation, they determine the appropriate conduct and leave no leeway for a contrary judgment. Of course, rules can have exceptions, which are often stated as separate permissions. Sometimes it is difficult to decide which rule applies to a situation. But once it is decided that a rule applies, it settles the matter.

It is possible to have rules only for situations in which people should always, with a few possible exceptions, act the same way. Rules cannot always be formulated because whether one should act one way or another varies too much with the circumstances. Although in many situations it might be difficult to determine whether particular conduct endangers the public or is dishonest, some conduct is clear. Thus, it is a rule that engineers not sign any plans or documents that were not prepared under their direction and control.[19]

Rules are usually justified by principles. Rules specify the conduct that principles require for certain types of situations. Rules can often reconcile conflicting principles by containing exceptions. For example, an accepted rule is that lawyers follow clients' decisions about the aims of representation, except for counseling to engage in criminal or fraudulent conduct.[20] The first part of the rule—to follow client aims—can be derived from a principle of loyalty to clients grounded in respect for clients' freedom and self-determination. The exception for criminal and fraudulent conduct stems from a principle not to assist in injuring others grounded in the social value of protection from injury.

Some professional codes of ethics are roughly organized along the distinctions between principles and rules. The Engineers' Council "Code of Ethics" has Fundamental Principles and Fundamental Canons, most of which are principles. The ABA *Model Code of Professional Responsibility* has Canons and Ethical Considerations, most of which are also principles. The AMA *Principles of Medical Ethics* are also mostly principles. These organizations' codes also have more specific statements, variously called guidelines, Disciplinary Rules, and Opinions of the Judicial Council, that are mostly rules. Clearly not all of them are; some are simply more specific principles.

One reason for this distinction is that it is easier to discipline professionals for violations of rules of duty than of principles. Rules prescribe specific conduct with no leeway, and one can determine whether a professional has engaged in the prohibited conduct. Principles can conflict with others, so it is often difficult to determine whether the conduct is wrong. It depends on a weighing and balancing of the conflicting principles, and the professional has discretion. However, discipline for violations of principles can be justified, especially for repeated conduct beyond the bounds of reasonable discretion.

Figure 2.2 Justification of Standards, Principles, and Rules

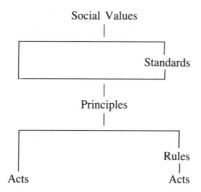

Figure 2.2 illustrates the relations between social values and standards, principles, and rules. Of course, some of the norms are universal, and some are role related. That does not affect the general structure, but only duplicates it for each type of norm. Specifications of principles are either subprinciples or rules.

Obligations of Professions and Professionals

Although codes of professional ethics claim to be fairly complete statements of professionals' ethical obligations, they chiefly comprise statements of obligations of individual professionals. This constitutes a fundamental defect because such codes fail adequately to cover obligations of a profession as a whole.[21] It is important to recognize obligations of professions as a whole and not to confuse them with the obligations of individual professionals. For example, some professions are said to have an obligation to provide services to all who need them. However, individual professionals do not have an obligation to serve all those who are in need.[22]

Obligations of a profession as a whole cannot be directly reduced to similar obligations of each member—that is, obligations of the same kind specifying the same conduct, such as an obligation to provide service equally to all. An obligation of a group (military) not to kill members of another group (innocent civilians) is reducible to obligations of each member of the first group (soldiers) not to kill members of the second (civilians). An obligation of the medical profession to provide services equally to everyone is not so reducibile to a similar obligation of each physician. It is an obligation of the profession as a whole or of all physicians together, not of each individually. Nonetheless, obligations of a profession as a whole can support some obligations of individual professionals—for example, to work for some disadvantaged client who would otherwise not receive services.

SUMMARY

This chapter is complicated because reasoning about professional ethics is a complex matter. Although there are simpler theories of ethics and professional ethics, the claim here is that they simplify at the expense of adequacy. When in doubt, the guide suggested here is to ask what norms reasonable persons would accept for a society in which they expected to live.

There are several levels of justification. An ethical theory is used to justify social values. These values can be used to justify norms. The norms can be either universal (applying to everyone) or role related (applying only to persons in the roles). Roles are defined by norms indicating the qualifications for persons occupying them and the type of acts they may do, such as represent clients in court. Norms can then be used to justify conduct.

Professional ethics includes all the ethical norms about professional activity. Some of these norms are universal ones that apply to professionals simply because they apply to everyone. Others are specifications of universal norms specifying types of situations that frequently arise in professional practice. Other norms are role related and are justified by the effect on the predominant value served by a profession, taking into account all other justifiable social values. If role-related norms permit or require conduct that would be wrong by universal ones, they must be justified as in effect exceptions based on the predominance of the value served by the profession. They are thus justified by the special function of the profession.

Norms of obligation require conduct or character traits. Norms of permission indicate that one may or may not do something as one wishes. Norms of obligation are of three types. Standards of virtue prescribe desirable character traits or virtues; their opposites are vices. Principles are usually general norms prescribing or proscribing conduct. They leave leeway for individual judgment in applying them. They frequently conflict, and one must then weigh and balance them to determine what is correct. They can explicate standards and be used to justify rules or acts. Rules of duty prescribe or prohibit specific types of acts. If a rule applies, unless one's conduct falls within an exception to the rule, one must act as the rule directs.

Finally, most obligations concern individual professionals. However, some apply to professions as a whole—the collective members of a profession. Obligations of professions cannot be reduced to similar obligations of individual professionals. Codes of ethics focus on obligations of individual professionals and tend to ignore obligations of professions.

NOTES*

1. See Paul W. Taylor, *Principles of Ethics: An Introduction* (Encino, Calif.: Dickenson Publishing, 1975), pp. 18–23; John Hospers, *Human Conduct: Problems of Ethics,* shorter ed. (New York: Harcourt Brace Jovanovich, 1972), pp. 36–38.

2. Levy, *Social Work Ethics,* p. 82.

3. See *Report of the Professional Organizations Committee,* p. 8.

4. Veatch, *Theory of Medical Ethics,* pp. 94–96; Veatch, "Medical Ethics," pp. 543–549.

5. Veatch, *Theory of Medical Ethics,* pp. 96–97; Veatch, "Professional Medical Ethics," p. 12.

6. ABA, *Model Rules,* Rule 3.3(a)(1).

7. Ibid., Rule 4.1(a).

8. American Psychiatric Association, *Principles of Medical Ethics with Annotations,* sec. 2,1.

9. Bouhoutsos et al., "Sexual Intimacy."

10. See, for example, Freedman, "A Meta-Ethics," pp. 14–17.

11. But see Veatch, *Theory of Medical Ethics,* pp. 159–164.

12. See John Ladd, "The Internal Morality of Medicine," in *The Clinical Encounter,* ed. Shelp, pp. 218–221.

13. The analysis here has benefited greatly from Gewirth, "Professional Ethics," although he would probably strongly disagree with the way I present it.

14. Compare ibid., p. 299.

15. Bayles, *Principles of Legislation,* pp. 42–44; Ronald Dworkin, *Taking Rights Seriously* (Cambridge, Mass.: Harvard University Press, 1977), pp. 22–28.

---

*See the bibliography at the back of the book for complete references.

16. Technically, standards alone do not constitute norms; they must be prescribed.

17. Engineers' Council, "Code of Ethics," Canon 1; National Society, "Code of Ethics," Canon 1.

18. Engineers' Council, "Code of Ethics," Canon 4; National Society, "Code of Ethics," Canon 4.

19. National Society, "Code of Ethics," Rule 2(b).

20. ABA, *Model Rules,* Rule 1.2(a) and (d).

21. See R. M. MacIver, "The Social Significance of Professional Ethics," in *Cases and Materials on Professional Responsibility,* ed. Pirsig, p. 50.

22. ABA, *Code of Professional Responsibility,* EC 2-26; AMA, *Principles of Medical Ethics,* sec. 6.

STUDY QUESTIONS AND PROBLEMS

1. What is ethical relativism? How might someone think that it applied to professional ethics? What objections can be made to it in general and as a basis for professional ethics?

2. In many foreign countries, it has long been engineers' practice to submit sketches and bids for engineering work. In the 1960s, many foreign projects funded by the United States Agency for International Development asked for bids. However, the codes of ethics of many U.S. professional engineering societies prohibited bidding on projects. Should engineering firms have followed the practice of the countries in which the projects were done? Or should the U.S.A.I.D. have required those countries to follow ethical codes of the U.S. societies for projects they funded? Why?

3. What are the levels of justification in professional ethics?

4. Why is it important that social values be justifiable?

5. Which of the following are role-related norms and which are universal ethical norms? Why?

    a. Children should honor their parents.

    b. Teachers should keep students' grades confidential.

    c. Do not steal.

    d. Abortions are wrong.

    e. Physicians should not perform capital punishment by lethal injection.

    f. Do not embezzle from employers.

6. Can role-related norms permit or prescribe conduct that would be wrong by universal norms? If so, how can one justify such norms? If not, why not?

7. What are the differences between standards, responsibilities, and duties? Which are the following?

a.   If the other party does not do so, a lawyer should advise the court of a precedent in the jurisdiction directly contrary to a legal claim he or she is advancing.

b.   Social workers should be courteous to clients.

c.   It is unethical for a psychiatrist to have sexual intercourse with a patient.

d.   Journalists should be objective.

e.   Dentists must have the informed consent of their patients before performing services.

f.   Nurses should be obedient.

g.   Architects should charge reasonable fees.

8.   Distinguish obligations of an individual professional from those of a profession as a whole. Give two examples of each.

3 Obligations and Availability of Services

The average citizen faces three potential problems in obtaining professional help—economic, racial, and geographic maldistribution of services. This chapter emphasizes the first problem—obtaining professional services at a reasonable price. The value at stake is equal availability of professional services. With some qualification, the professions do recognize a responsibility to establish equal opportunity for or equal access to their services.[1] The central problems that must be overcome are (1) that this obligation belongs to professions as a whole and cannot be directly reduced to a similar obligation on the part of individual professionals and (2) that various traditional professional norms have hindered equal access to professional services.

Two related arguments support the obligation to make professional services equally available. First, because legal privileges are granted for the benefit of society, if professions have a legal monopoly on the provision of services, they should be equally available to all citizens. The government should act for all citizens, so the benefits of a legally created monopoly should extend to all of them.

The second argument is more general. The argument from monopoly assumes that the state should act for all citizens. One reason for that assumption is the value of equality of opportunity; this value, however, directly supports the equal availability of professional services regardless of the existence of a legal monopoly. Thus, denial of equal opportunity to secure competent professional services directly infringes on a fundamental social value.

Many professionals provide their services on a fee-for-service basis, which distributes professional services by the potential clients' ability to pay. This is true for almost all self-employed professionals and for some employed by organizations. For example, the services of an engineer employed by a consulting firm are available only if one pays the firm's fee.

Does availability on the basis of ability to pay satisfy equality of opportunity? The answer varies with the profession and people's ranking of interests and values. Strong arguments exist for making at least some educational, health, and legal services available independent of ability to pay. Basic education—functional literacy—is a practical necessity for any significant opportunities in modern society. Further, to prevent unjust deprivations of freedom, legal counsel is necessary for a reasonable defense to criminal charges. The government thus provides these services regardless of a person's ability to pay. Legal services beyond criminal defense can also be crucial for securing such important interests as divorce, child support payments, or compensation for injury. Health care is also crucial for equal opportunity and minimal well-being.[2] The government also provides some legal and health care services to the poor.

The services of other professions—accounting, architecture, engineering, social work, and so on—are less obviously essential to general equality of opportunity and minimal well-being. One might argue that accounting services and advice for income tax preparation are important for general equality of opportunity. Moreover, engineering and scientific services are important at a general level of providing infrastructure and safety.[3] Nonetheless, it is unclear that these services should be generally available to specific individuals or groups regardless of ability to pay. Equality of opportunity does, however, require that they be available on equal terms.

Some people contend that educational, health, and legal services not only should be equally available, but they should also be of equal quality. Unfortunately, equal quality of services is not achievable. First, there are many disputes about specifying and measuring quality. Second, so long as professionals have different levels of skill, variations in quality will exist. Consequently, here the concern is only with competent services—those that would not be considered bad or incompetent.

Even though people should have general educational, legal, and health services regardless of ability to pay, it does not follow that they should have all such services from which they might benefit. Cosmetic services such as hair transplants should perhaps be distributed on the basis of ability to pay. Similarly, although most services of other professions need not be available regardless of ability to pay, some specific services perhaps should be. For example, social work services might be necessary for some poor persons with domestic and health-related problems to have minimal well-being and equality of opportunity, even access to other professional services.

The values of equality of opportunity and minimal well-being can help determine which services should be available regardless of ability to pay. Some services are more important for opportunities in society than others. Lack of basic mathematics is a greater handicap than lack of introductory philosophy, despite the Socratic claim that the philosophically unexamined life is not worth living. Similarly, some services are more central for minimal well-being than others. Vaccination for polio is more important than vaccination for flu because polio is a more serious threat to well-being. Of course, other considerations should also be taken into account, such as the benefit gained per dollar spent in providing various services.

These arguments support the claim that people have positive rights to certain health, education, and legal services, but only negative rights to other professional services. *Negative rights* imply noninterference; that is, without good cause, neither the state nor other people may interfere with a person obtaining services from professionals willing to provide them. *Positive rights* are to the services themselves. They are sound claims that the services be available.

These distinctions can be briefly illustrated by the history of the availability of abortions. For about a century, most states prohibited abortions except in limited circumstances. In 1973, the U.S. Supreme Court held that, with some restrictions, women have a right of privacy to abortions during the first and second trimesters of pregnancy.[4] This is a negative right to noninterference by the state. Under the Medicaid program, poor women have a limited positive right to medical care. That is, the government will pay for certain services. The negative constitutional right to an abortion does not automatically confer a positive right to have abortions paid for by Medicaid.[5]

Even when positive rights to legal, education, and health services exist, they do not directly affect the obligations of individual professionals. Such rights obligate only the government or perhaps the professions to provide the services. Thus, a patient does not have a right to have a particular physician perform an abortion for her. Similarly, for a number of years, criminal defendants have had a constitutional right to counsel, but except when assigned by a court, individual lawyers have not had a duty to represent criminal defendants. Individual professionals merely have a responsibility to assist the profession in fulfilling its obligation (see Chapter 7).

Ensuring the equal provision of professional services requires a social organization. The legal and medical professions have not only failed to promote such a delivery organization, they have often actively opposed adoption of policies to do so. (For years, the AMA opposed what it called socialized medicine, that is, national health insurance.) Moreover, traditional norms of professions concerning economic matters such as fees and advertising have hindered equal opportunity for services in all professions.

Before examining these traditional economic norms, I shall mention the other two types of maldistribution of services: racial and geographic. They have been more of a problem for the provision of health, education, and legal services than for other kinds of professional services. Except perhaps for education, blacks and other racial minorities receive fewer professional services per capita than whites. This racial maldistribution results partly from economic maldistribution because a larger percentage of the black population is poor, but its fundamental source is racial and ethnic prejudice. Discrimination in employment has contributed to the disproportionate poverty of minorities, and thus to their inability to pay for services. Discrimination by professions has also played a role—for example, by excluding minorities from the professions. A white friend of mine, accompanying a black physician seeing black patients, found that the patients assumed he was the doctor. Lack of minority professionals does not necessarily affect the distribution of services to members of that minority, although it may. For example, women have been underrepresented in professions in the United States, but that has not affected their access to professional services as much as it has the quality of the services they receive. Although few white male professionals serve predominantly black clients, many serve female clients.

Discrimination on grounds of race, sex, and ethnic origin can also subtly influence the quality of professional services. Male physicians have probably not adequately assessed the needs and interests of female patients in such areas as childbirth and mental health. Psychotherapists have been shown to have a bias toward young, attractive, verbal, intelligent, and successful patients.[6] Verbal skills can be quite important for various services. If receptionists and professionals speak only

English, then Spanish-speaking persons will not be able to take advantage of their services. Contrarily, a concern in Florida has been that professors and teaching assistants speak English well enough for students to understand them.

The third maldistribution of professional services, in addition to economic and racial, is geographic. The bulk of professional services is centered in the more affluent urban areas. Many rural communities lack basic health and legal services. Some counties have few or no lawyers. The reasons for the lack of professional services in rural areas are only partly economic. Although many rural areas are poor, sufficient economic demand for professional services often exists. One reason professionals might not wish to practice in rural communities is the absence of facilities. A poor rural county might not have a hospital, and even if it does, it will not have all the modern equipment found in large urban hospitals. Similarly, lawyers in rural communities might not have access to libraries large enough to help them keep abreast of the law. Further, as a group, professionals are often more interested than the average citizen in cultural activities, which are scarce in rural communities. Whatever the reason, it is widely recognized that rural and remote areas are often short of professional services, and some rich urban ones have more than are needed. Similarly, many central urban areas with predominately black or Hispanic populations lack services due to poverty, discrimination, and other factors.

The extent to which health and legal services are unavailable is subject to considerable dispute. Obviously, the answers depend partly on what services one thinks people should have. Nonetheless, many people lack basic health and legal services. Probably around 10 percent of the population—20 million people—lacks any form of health insurance, even Medicaid.[7] The poor who cannot afford legal services constitute a large group. During the 1980s, government programs to provide health and legal services to the poor through Medicaid and the Legal Services Corporation have been decreased. Both programs have deleted some services. Thus, even as the percentage of unemployed persons has decreased, the number of persons without adequate services has probably remained constant due to program cutbacks and population increases.

ECONOMIC NORMS

Several traditional professional norms have hindered availability of professional services. These are largely concerned with economic matters of self-employed professionals, although they have usually been defended by ethical-sounding considerations. The general impact of such norms on access to services is as follows. The professions recognize an obligation to prevent unauthorized practice (provision of services by nonprofessionals), and thus they maintain a monopoly. Norms about fees and publicity prevent competition among professionals and deny potential clients information relevant to choosing a professional intelligently. Finally, norms about specialization may further increase costs. Potential clients then face unnecessarily high fees that prevent some from receiving services and prevent many of those who can afford them from being able to choose high quality services.

Unauthorized Practice

A traditional obligation of the legal and medical professions is to prevent unauthorized practice—that is, the unlicensed provision of professional services.[8] This norm has not been as strong for other professions, such as psychotherapy, because unlicensed provision of those services is usually not illegal. Nonetheless, even those professions that have not had a legal monopoly of the provision of services have often fought to prevent their practice by persons without credentials.

Both the legal and medical professions are currently under pressure to (1) use paraprofessionals to assist in providing services and (2) accept provision of services by others outside of the profession. Paraprofessionals have been providing a growing range of services in medicine, as have other persons in law. In health care, physicians' assistants, nurse practitioners, nurse midwives, nurses, and various therapists can and have taken over provision of some services. A recurrent issue is the extent to which they should have physician supervision. Similar competitive situations for the legal profession are realtors completing real estate contracts, groups such as H.&R. Block preparing income tax returns, and title companies checking property titles.

The fundamental moral guide in the area of unauthorized practice should be the public or social good.[9] The appropriate method of analysis was developed years ago by Karl N. Llewellyn: "For the men of law are a monopoly, and monopoly is subject to regulation. The ground for monopoly is that it makes possible better service; this holds of the bar. The condition of monopoly is that it serve; this does not hold of the bar."[10] For example, lawyers' organizations fought the provision of legal services by unions for injured workers, which helped more people receive services. The same point applies to other professions. In another paper, Llewellyn outlines four steps to be followed in considering the justification of prohibitions of unauthorized practice.[11] (1) Determine the proposed areas of monopolization. (2) Ask of each area why society needs to make it a monopoly. (3) Consider what is gained, if anything, for people other than the monopolists. (4) Finally, if there are complaints about unauthorized practice, consider who is complaining and why, specifically, whether it is the public or members of the profession.

The public concern in prohibiting nonprofessionals from performing certain services is to protect people from injury due to inadequate or incompetent performance.[12] This implies that a professional and only a professional possesses the requisite skills and abilities to provide the services. One legal ethics text modestly claims that the special privilege of lawyers stems from their superior competence, dependability, and breadth of view.[13] Even taken with a grain of salt, such sweeping claims are hardly plausible. Services must be examined individually. Indeed, the same text suggests the following reasons for nonlawyers handling such matters as real estate transactions and tax preparations: (1) easier access to these nonlawyers, (2) equal or superior value of the nonlawyer's expertise, (3) economy and lower cost, and (4) speed in business transactions.[14] Tax accountants or realtors can better handle such matters because they routinely process large numbers of them. Similarly, abortion clinics with medical technicians rather than physicians might provide better service at a lower cost. Concentrating on the provision of one type of service, they become more efficient. At least in early pregnancy, abortions can be performed by medical technicians as well as, or better than, by physicians.[15] The superior competence of professionals cannot justify monopolization of many traditional services simply because in some cases this superior competence does not exist.

Even if professionals are more competent, one should also consider the freedom of the client to choose a lesser service at a lower cost. To justify limiting this freedom, one must show that a reasonable consumer would not knowingly choose to have the services performed by a less competent person in exchange for some other benefit such as lower cost. If informed persons are willing to risk an unclear title to property or a medical complication from an abortion or childbirth in order to save money or secure some other value, any prohibition of unauthorized practice limits their freedom. Many of the restricted services are much less significant, such as filling out forms for no-fault divorces. However, the Florida Supreme Court has held that nonlawyers may serve as typists filling in such forms, provided they use only written information provided by clients and do not ask clients questions for information to put in the blanks.[16] This restriction is especially burdensome on persons who do not speak English well—many Hispanic immigrants.

If a nonprofessional providing a service would pose a risk of injury to others, that is certainly a reason for restricting the service to licensed professionals. Thus, good reasons exist to prevent companies issuing stock with a legal opinion letter from a nonlawyer. If reasonable clients knowingly and voluntarily risk only their own well-being, however, no reason exists for prohibiting unauthorized practice.

Prohibiting nonprofessionals from rendering services is also overly restrictive of their freedom. One need only hold them to the same standard of competence as professionals. Even this requirement has been used to try to prevent competition. When an amendment to the state constitution overturned the Arizona Supreme Court's prohibition of realtors completing purchase agreements, deeds, mortgages, and so on, the court announced that realtors would be held to the same ethical standards (including competence) as attorneys.[17] The point was to discourage them from exercising their constitutional rights by requiring them to have the same legal competence as lawyers. A study of complaints about unauthorized practice of law found that it was lawyers, not consumers, who were complaining. Of 1,188 instances, only 2 percent were from complaints by injured consumers.[18] A federal judge recently found that the American Medical Association has engaged in a long-term attack on chiropractors.[19]

When a profession claims that large recognized occupations, such as realtors, title insurance companies, and chiropractors, provide unauthorized or incompetent practice, their purpose is probably to protect their own monopolistic source of income. Such claims deserve special scrutiny. Prohibition will probably only increase the cost of services and make them less available.

Another approach is for two professions, such as engineering and architecture or law and accounting, to agree which services are appropriately provided by each. One might think that such an approach would result in each profession offering what it is best skilled to provide. Unfortunately, these arrangements are often simply a division of the client pie. Clients might discover that instead of having to hire only one professional, they will require the services of two. A couple in a relatively simple divorce can end up hiring four professionals, one lawyer and one accountant each. Were grocery stores and fast food restaurants to agree what service each would provide, everyone would perceive it as an anticompetitive agreement in restraint of trade and obviously detrimental to consumer interests. In many areas, open competition between professions is also the best way to decide which services different professionals should provide. Those who provide a service most efficiently will eventually dominate in its provision.

Only certain core services should be restricted to specific professions. The two reasons for this are that (1) no reasonable person would want an untrained person to provide the service or (2) an untrained person providing the service might burden the public. The first condition holds for only a few services, but few reasonable people would want a nonprofessional to perform open heart surgery or defend them on a murder charge. Restrictions are less likely to be justified for other services. For example, a reasonable person might be willing to have a person who is not an architect design a house. Of course, as this condition says, no reasonable person would want the important services in question to be provided by nonprofessionals, so restrictions are hardly necessary.

The second condition applies to more services. For example, people who are not lawyers practicing in court might take up so much time as to increase seriously the public's costs in running the courts.[20] Untrained accountants preparing financial statements to be filed with the government could impose heavy costs on the government, which has to review the filed materials. Untrained engineers designing large structures like buildings and dams could cause serious injuries to many persons if the structures were unsafe. Similarly, bungled medical care could drain public resources when others tried to correct the resulting problems.

Greater restrictions than these two conditions allow would unduly limit the freedom of clients to choose, and of nonprofessionals to render, services.

Fees

Professional norms concerning fees have often prevented price competition among professionals. The issues of fee schedules, competitive bidding, and fee splitting arise in most professions. Contingent fees, paid only when the outcome is successful, and percentage fees, paid as a percent of the amount involved, are an issue for some professions in the United States. Examples of contingent fees are those paid only when a plaintiff recovers damages or when a community approves a construction project.

Fee Schedules.   Traditionally, many local professional groups issued minimum fee schedules that were sometimes obligatory and sometimes merely recommended. The argument for them was that they prevented poor performance at a lower cost. However, these schedules operated to decrease competition and thus keep prices higher and to deny consumers a choice between full service at a high price and less service at a lower one.

Professionally set minimum fee schedules are a thing of the past. In *Goldfarb* v. *Virginia State Bar,* the U.S. Supreme Court held that the Sherman Anti-Trust Act prohibits minimum fee schedules for "services performed by attorneys in examining titles in connection with financing the purchase of real estate."[21] A couple had found that nineteen different attorneys all quoted the county bar's recommended fee or a higher one for searching the title to a house. The Court held that this constituted price-fixing. This decision is limited. The antitrust law does not apply to commerce within a state or to state governments, so it is possible for minimum fees to be set for professional services not affecting interstate commerce or by local governments.

Mandatory minimum fees have been dropped by those professions that had them. Nonetheless, full price competition is still often not available. For example, anyone wishing to list a home with a realtor multiple listing service will find that all the realtors charge the same rate, about 6 percent. They will, however, bargain over other terms of the contract, such as its length.

Maximum fee schedules can also affect the availability of professional services. These fee schedules are likely to be set by third party payers, insurance companies, or the government. In the Medicare program, the federal government has instituted diagnostic-related group (DRG) reimbursement to hospitals. Hospitals are paid a fixed amount for each patient with a certain diagnosis. The amount is supposedly set to reflect the average cost of treating such a patient. The aim is to force hospitals to develop more cost-effective methods of treatment so that their costs are below average, and they make money. A similar program might be introduced for payment of physician fees.

Although this program has not existed long enough to evaluate its effects fully, it might result in decreased access to health services.[22] Hospitals, doctors, and other professionals, like all businesses, have some clients who do not pay. The standard method for covering these uncollected bills is to factor the expected losses into charges of all patients. Thus, hospitals and professionals could provide care to poor clients who cannot pay by spreading the costs over those who can pay. With DRGs, this method will not be possible. Moreover, hospitals will want to avoid patients whose expenses are likely to be above average. These often turn out to be poor persons because their general health is likely to be worse than average. Consequently, hospitals are more reluctant to treat sicker patients and those without health insurance. A practice of "dumping" has developed in which hospitals refuse to admit such patients in the emergency room and send them to public hospitals.

Three values are at stake here.[23] One is equality of opportunity of access to health services. Another is freedom of providers to accept or reject clients. The other is efficiency or wealth in keeping costs reasonable. In a fee-for-service health care system, people are often willing to pay whatever they can for services. Consequently, health care providers have no incentive to be efficient because they can always pass on costs to consumers. Maximum fee schedules are intended to force such efficiency. However, when not everyone is in the system and providers have freedom to accept or reject clients, the result can be decreased access.

Competitive Bidding.   A second, and closely related, issue concerns prohibitions of competitive bidding by professionals. The National Society of Professional Engineers' (NSPE) "Code of Ethics for Engineers" used to contain an explicit prohibition of competitive bidding for contracts. The underlying fear was that clients would choose engineers on the basis of price alone, ignoring such factors as experience, training, and so on. The net result, it was thought, would be less competent work that might even cost clients more. To ensure safety, engineers' designs might call for more extensive materials and work than a more careful design would require. Other professions did not explicitly prohibit competitive bidding, but it was, nevertheless, not actually practiced. For example, if a school board needed routine and regular legal services during a year, it would not advertise for law firms to submit bids for the work; and lawyers would not have bid on it had the board done so.

The effect of prohibiting competitive bidding is to deprive prospective clients of an opportunity to secure services at as low a cost as possible. It enables professionals to maintain fees at a higher rate than might otherwise be the case. In short, it restricts competition, and the restriction is broader than necessary to prevent the feared evil of poor or shoddy work due to deceptively low bids. For these reasons, the U.S. Supreme Court has held the NSPE prohibition to be an illegal suppression of competition under the Sherman Anti-Trust Act.[24] Thus, like minimum fee schedules, restrictions on competitive bidding are now illegal.

Because the illegality of competitive bidding is not constitutional, but merely a matter of federal law, both the federal and state governments are exempt. Moreover, professionals do not have to engage in competitive bidding if they do not wish to. The federal government and many state governments, such as Florida, do not engage in competitive bidding. Instead, they receive proposals from various firms and rank the firms by their ability.[25] They then negotiate with the top ranked firm. If an agreement is not reached, they next negotiate with the second ranked firm and so on until a contract is made. Agreement is usually reached with the first firm. Moreover, most professionals would still refuse to submit bids if, for example, an organization asked for bids on legal or accounting services. Bookkeeping by small organizations, however, might be a different matter.

Fee Splitting.   A third general issue concerns fee splitting, the division of fees between a professional and another person. Many professions condemn or restrict fee splitting or commissions.[26] Some also restrict sharing fees or being in business with people who practice another occupation or profession.[27] But in Canada and a few states, a referring lawyer is entitled to part of the fee of the correspondent. The reason given for allowing such fee splitting in Canada is that the amount of fees is regulated. Both those for and against fee splitting argue on the basis of the client's interests but disagree as to the effects it has on them.

Four reasons support the prohibition of fee splitting except in proportion to services. First, if professionals must split their fees with referring professionals, they will have to charge more to cover costs and make a profit. Second, the judgment of referring professionals might not be objective and independent if they have an interest in referring the client to the professional paying the largest referral fee. As the professional's and client's interest conflict, the first professional might not refer the client to the best qualified professional. Third, if the referring professional cannot take the case because it would violate professional ethics—a conflict of interest or lack of competence, for example—then the person should not receive a fee.[29] Fourth, the referring professional should not receive a fee for no work.

The argument for fee splitting is that it should provide clients access to more competent professionals at lower cost.[30] Professionals who do not consider themselves competent to handle a case can attempt it anyway to collect a fee, associate with another and charge a higher fee, or refer the client and receive nothing. Because the latter option is contrary to professionals' economic interests, they are more likely to choose one of the first two options, thus causing incompetent service or a higher fee. Were fee splitting permitted, a professional could refer a client and still receive some compensation. To ensure referrals to competent professionals, the referring professional can be made legally liable for the second one's performance or, what amounts to the same thing, responsible for all the services rendered.[31]

This argument is not sufficient. The second professional's fee might be increased to include the payment to the referring professional, so cost saving would be limited. Moreover, charging in excess of services rendered cannot be justified; it is simple theft.

Consulting with and referring a client, however, is a service that does deserve some compensation. If a client pays directly for the referral, the judgment of the referring professional then is not affected by personal gain. Further, increased malpractice suits are likely to ensure that professionals do not attempt to provide services they are incompetent to render. Of course, professionals can associate with others to do part of the work on a case. Physicians call in specialists for particular aspects of patient care; lawyers sometimes consult with others for specific purposes, such as to determine tax implications; and engineering designs often involve various professionals working on different aspects of the design—structural, electrical, and so on. Allowing professionals to charge a modest fee for a referral seems most likely to help clients receive competent service and allow professionals appropriate compensation for their efforts.

Fee splitting prohibitions do not prevent referral abuses. One of the major scandals in the Medicaid and Medicare program is "ping-ponging." In this practice, each physician charges only for the services he or she renders, but the patient is referred from one physician to another for different, but usually unneeded, specialized services. Physicians know that if they refer patients to other physicians, those physicians will refer patients to them. The AMA *Principles* do not address directly the problem of ping-ponging. The only statement about consulting is that a physician should do so when indicated.[32] Professionals clearly ought not suggest that clients obtain unneeded services, whether to be rendered by themselves or by someone else. Doing so violates an obligation of candor to the client.

"Kickbacks" are rather widespread in the professions. Three major areas may be mentioned. First, title insurance companies frequently return part of a fee to a referring attorney. Second, physicians often receive kickbacks from laboratories to which they send specimens for analysis. Third, engineers sometimes receive compensation from supply companies for ordering or recommending their products. Clients then pay more than the services are worth. If a professional charges a proper amount, a kickback is extra compensation. This difficulty could be remedied by requiring professionals to note the reimbursement in their bills and deduct that amount. Professionals would then have no incentive to recommend products or services from which they receive the largest kickback rather than those best for the client because they would receive the same total compensation in either case.

An interesting parallel problem can arise with professors using their own textbooks in courses. The underlying problem is possible conflict of interest because the professor will receive royalties from the book. At least one professor reimburses students the amount of the royalty if they present a receipt for purchase of a new copy. However, it is unclear that such a practice is necessary. The concern is that a professor will choose a book on the basis of expected income rather than its merits. If the book was designed for just such a course, then the professor supposedly designed it as well as possible. In short, the professor believes it is the best possible book; otherwise he or she would have done it differently. However, there should be some scrutiny by others, such as the department chair, to ensure that the book really is appropriate for the course.

Contingent Fees.   The difficult issue of contingent fees arises chiefly with respect to lawyers in personal injury cases. The American Bar Association (ABA) prohibits contingent fees only for representing a defendant in criminal and domestic relations cases, but most professions prohibit all contingent fees outright.[33] The British legal system does not allow contingent fees; instead, the losing party pays all legal fees. One objection to contingent legal fees is that they deprive a victorious party of full compensation for an injury. Damages are awarded for medical expenses, loss in income, pain and suffering, and so on. If a client suffers a $100,000 loss, the lawyer is likely to receive 33 percent or more, leaving less than $67,000. In the British system, the client receives the full $100,000 plus the lawyer's fee.

Over a century ago, George Sharswood disapproved of the general practice of contingent legal fees because of three undesirable consequences.[34] First, contingent fees change the attorney–client relationship. The attorney has a stake in winning by any means and can become blind to the merits of the case. Second, such fees encourage litigation. A client who loses is out only court costs, a rather small amount. A client who wins might receive a substantial award. Thus, clients might risk cases they would not were they required to pay attorney fees regardless of the outcome. Third, contingent fees have a bad effect on professional character.

Other considerations contradict each of Sharswood's points. First, although the attorney–client relationship is changed, the change need not be for the worse. Because attorneys will be paid only if they win, they are apt to pursue the case more zealously. This reason, however, is sufficient to prohibit contingent fees for accountants. As auditors, accountants are not to work zealously to show a corporate profit but to provide a fair statement of the corporation's financial condition. Second, one must consider what type of litigation is encouraged. Contingent fees are unlikely to encourage frivolous litigation. Because attorneys are paid only if they win, they are not apt to undertake hopeless cases.[35] Third, Sharswood's claim that contingent fees have a bad effect on an attorney's character adds nothing. If contingent fees are morally permissible, then accepting such cases will not harm an attorney's character. Presumably, the bad effect is that such fees encourage lawyers to try to win by any means. However, ethical lawyers will not accept a case unless they believe they have a reasonable chance of winning by fair means. This third consideration, then, either begs the question or is the same as the first.

The main argument in favor of contingent legal fees is that they increase equality of opportunity by enabling indigent persons to defend their rights. Poor persons are often unable to pay a lawyer unless they recover. Without a contingent fee, they cannot afford to sue even if they have good grounds. Contingent fees are unlikely to encourage persons to litigate for rights not previously recognized by the courts because such cases are unlikely to be won, and attorneys are reluctant to accept them on a contingent basis.

This argument has little plausibility for engineers and architects, for they are not likely to work for indigent clients. For them, the contingent fee is most likely to be a means of preventing other professionals from having the opportunity to be considered for a project. For example, an engineering firm carried out free studies under one government administration on the understanding that it would receive the full contract should a bond issue pass.[36] The issue failed, and a subsequent administration, after a new bond issue passed, awarded the contract to other firms. The first firm then complained that these firms were supplanting it. Obviously, the first firm provided the contingent work primarily to get an edge on the contract. Such a practice gives an advantage to large firms that can afford to provide work without compensation until later.

One must compare the contingent fee system with alternatives. One alternative to contingent legal fees is for the losing party to pay both attorneys' fees. If plaintiffs must pay both attorneys' fees should they lose, poor persons will be unlikely to sue for their rights. Should they be unsuccessful, they will owe legal fees they cannot pay. Justice does not necessarily require a losing party to pay all legal fees.[37] In cases that go to trial, something can usually be said for each side; that is, neither party is clearly right. If losing parties must pay both legal fees, they must shoulder the whole financial burden of litigation even though their position was reasonably defensible.

Finally, the argument that contingent fees enable indigent persons to bring justifiable cases assumes that legal services are not otherwise available. If legal representation were generally available to them, the argument would collapse. Legal aid programs usually refuse cases in which representation can be obtained on a contingent fee basis. Were legal aid provided for such cases, victorious plaintiffs would receive the full compensation to which they are entitled.

Percentage Fees. Sometimes professional fees are a percentage of the amount involved in a professional service, such as a probated estate or construction project. The amount of money involved in such cases is not necessarily related to the amount of work professionals perform. In engineering, the work is more apt to be related to project costs than in other professions, but it need not be. (An engineer hired on a percentage fee will receive more if there is a cost overrun, no matter what the reason for the overrun.) With very large estates, lawyers with a percentage fee might receive compensation quite disproportionate to the work involved. To some extent, the rich might subsidize the poor. Rarely would the truly indigent benefit because they do not inherit, sell, or purchase anything of great value. If they must probate a worthless estate, legal aid might be available. Percentage fees give rise to "windfall profits" in these areas. These profits can be maintained only by a near monopoly of services and agreed fee schedules. Consequently, with the abolition of minimum fee schedules, they too have tended to wither away.

However, percentage fees ranging from 25 percent to as much as 50 percent are customary in legal cases taken on a contingent fee basis. A percentage-based contingent fee is justifiable in a way it is not for legal services not provided on a contingent basis, such as title searchers. Because lawyers are not compensated in contingent fee cases they lose, clients who win such cases subsidize those who lose. Contingent fees are a way of pooling the resources of those who have plausible cases. They increase equality of opportunity. In real estate and probate cases, lawyers rarely receive less than the value of their services and do not have previous losses to recover.

This last argument also supports professionals giving expert testimony on a contingent fee basis. The practice would also enable them to recoup losses incurred in cases lost. The law, however, usually forbids compensating expert witnesses on a contingent basis. The fear is that experts will be biased; yet, as one commentator notes, experts on retainers or generally employed by large corporations are just as apt to be biased.[38]

A contingent percentage fee is also possible in engineering. An engineering firm might agree to supervise a project on the basis of receiving a percentage of costs saved. Such an arrangement is unlikely to result in windfall profits because to earn the fee, engineers must work at cost cutting. They will receive what their services are worth to the clients. However, it gives engineers an incentive to permit or require less expensive materials or methods that might not be as sound. Consequently, it does not seem appropriate.

Publicity

Traditionally, most professions severely restricted publicity—advertising and solicitation.[39] As will be discussed shortly, the restrictions on advertising were greatly liberalized during the 1970s. The restrictions on personal solicitation have not been liberalized nearly as much. The restrictions have probably been most detrimental to urban citizens seeking lawyers and perhaps physicians. The potential clients of accountants, engineers, and architects often have considerable knowledge of professional activities and a means for identifying competent professionals and reasonable costs.[40] Individuals and small businesses in large urban centers experience the most difficulty learning about lawyers.[41] Because advertising is the standard method by which people find out about available services and products, restrictions on it tend to prevent average citizens having equal access to professions.

Advertising.   The traditional reasons for limiting advertising rest on a conception of professionals as devoted to public service rather than to mere money making. Advertising, it is claimed, would change that image and undermine public confidence in the professions. Three policies underlie the traditional condemnation of publicity for lawyers: (1) to prevent stirring up litigation, (2) to permit wise selection of counsel, and (3) to protect the public image of the bar.[42]

The concern with stirring up litigation basically refers to an increased burden on the legal system. A similar concern might apply to advertising by physicians; it might increase demands on the health care system. Increased burdens on the legal and health care systems must be balanced by a concern for the health and legal status of potential clients. Only frivolous demands on the system should be discouraged. Without publicity, people who might significantly benefit from professional services might not receive them. Unless people recognize the appropriateness of professional services and know they are available, they will not seek or receive them. Undoubtedly, fewer people fail to recognize health than legal needs, but people are still reluctant to see physicians and dentists for routine preventive care.

How preventing publicity promotes a wise selection of professionals seems an esoteric piece of knowledge available only to professionals. The traditional premise is that a professional builds a practice by gaining a reputation in the community. Although this assumption still generally applies to the limited group using accounting and engineering services, it does not apply to professionals providing services to individuals in an urban environment—physicians, lawyers, accountants, and architects. The net effect of the prohibition on advertising was to provide better access for the upper class than for the middle and lower classes. The policy thus fostered inequality of opportunity.

Advertising is also claimed to lead to boastfulness and self-laudatory statements. Because the public lacks a basis for evaluating the quality of professionals, it can be misled in selecting professionals. However, even if correct, this contention does not support a total ban on advertising, but rather supports only restrictions to prevent misleading and untruthful claims.

Finally, most charitably interpreted, protecting the public image of the professions means preventing people acquiring unrealistic expectations. One can imagine professionals advertising miraculous cures for cancer, how to sue businesses and obtain million dollar judgments, or how to receive large income tax refunds. This legitimate concern, however, does not support a total ban, but only limitations on the content of advertising. People who mistakenly believe that nothing can be done for cancer or nothing can be done to obtain repairs of defective merchandise can also become disillusioned with the health care and legal systems.

The basic argument against bans on publicity, especially advertising, is that it infringes freedom of communication or speech. Freedom of communication rests not simply on the value to speakers in expressing themselves, but also on that to the potential audience (the public) in receiving information.[43] The wise selection and use of professionals depend on full and accurate information about their availability, cost, and quality. Implicit in this justification is the limitation that the public has no interest in false, deceitful, and misleading communications. Total restrictions on publicity are incompatible with the values of freedom of communication and equal opportunity to secure health care, legal justice, and other values promoted by professional services.

Some restrictions on advertising are not only compatible with social values but promote them. Specifically, false, deceptive, and misleading advertisements do not further the interests of the audience and can lead to their being harmed. The interests of potential speakers to communicate such information are thus outweighed. Largely for these reasons, the Supreme Court has struck down as violating the First Amendment most professional restrictions on advertising that is not false, deceptive, or misleading.[44] This does not mean that no restrictions are possible. For example, a lawyer can be required to state in an advertisement whether contingent fees are based on the amount awarded before or after costs are deducted.

One of the more difficult questions concerns advertising the quality of services. Is the use of favorable outcomes of professional services misleading? For example, may lists of former clients be used? To protect the privacy of clients, their consent would be necessary. Even if the relationship is a matter of public record, clients should have control over the use of their names. If the outcome were unfavorable, it is unlikely that professionals would use clients' names or that clients would consent to their doing so. A simple list of clients, however, might provide useful information and not be deceptive. More likely to be deceptive would be pictures of engineering projects in which the firm had only a small role. Similarly, statements of the percentage of cases won or of cures brought about for given diseases could be quite misleading. For example, to build a reputation, some physicians beginning in transplant surgery operate only on patients with the best chances of success. Even without success rates, though, comparisons with other professionals might be objectionable.

Probably the chief objection to such comparative advertising is that it would demean the profession; prospective clients would consider choosing professionals in the same way they consider choosing detergents. Yet some professionals are more competent than others, just as some detergents clean better than others. Consequently, the AMA permits such advertising if the claims can be factually supported and do not imply that one has a unique skill.[45] The ABA permits comparisons with other lawyers if the claims can be factually supported.[46]

Solicitation.   The issue here is direct, personal contact with a prospective client. The traditional concern among lawyers has been with "ambulance chasing"—lawyers contacting persons immediately after accidents and suggesting that they be retained to sue, often on a contingent fee basis. This form of solicitation has not been a problem for the other professionals. And at least one commentator applauds such solicitation as helping people recognize their needs for professional service and gain access to it.[47] The ethical concern with this type of solicitation is that people might be approached when in vulnerable circumstances and might hire a lawyer without adequate reflection or consideration of alternatives. In short, undue influence and overreaching can occur, depriving people of a free and informed choice of professional services.

A classic example of the validity of this concern is exhibited in a U.S. Supreme Court case. The Court upheld the constitutional validity of restrictions on types of soliciting that pose a threat of fraud, undue influence, intimidation, and other forms of vexatious conduct.[48] After hearing of an automobile accident, Ohio attorney Albert Ohralik contacted the parents of an eighteen-year-old woman driver injured in it. He then approached her in the hospital offering to represent her. After again visiting the parents, he visited her in the hospital a second time, and she signed a contingent fee agreement. He also went to the home of the driver's eighteen-year-old woman passenger, who was also injured. With a hidden tape recorder, he secured her verbal consent to represent her. He explained that the young women would not have to pay him anything and would receive two-thirds of the insurance settlement. When both young women fired him, he sued them for breach of contract and received part of the proceeds from the insurance settlement to the driver. Eventually, Ohralik was suspended indefinitely from the practice of law.

Although solicitation of this sort takes unfair advantage of prospective clients, personal solicitation can help serve some of the functions of advertising. Some clients are not aware of their legal rights, and solicitation can inform them. In particular, disadvantaged persons might not know of their constitutional and other legal rights. If these rights are not secured, people lack equality of opportunity and legal justice. In light of similar considerations, the U.S. Supreme Court has held that solicitation by mail on behalf of nonprofit organizations using litigation as a means of political expression and association is constitutionally protected.[49] However, this argument is not likely to hold for other professions. Other professions are not usually engaged in political expression, and the mere fact that speech is involved in solicitation does not provide strong First Amendment protection.

The objection to solicitation is primarily the possibility of prospective clients lacking the opportunity for wise choice. This lack can be due to pressure tactics or simply absence of time to reflect. An unresolved issue is direct mail solicitation by lawyers for a particular case.[50] Suppose a lawyer sends all the victims and relatives of dead victims of a mass disaster a letter indicating that he or she is available to represent them and believes they have a good case. Should this fall under a ban on solicitation or the freedom of advertising? Provided the communication is not false, deceitful, or misleading, there is no objection on that ground. However, the lawyer has reason to believe that the persons, at least the victims, are especially vulnerable. This raises the concerns underlying cases like *Ohralik* and might be considered improper for such persons.

Lawyers, engineers, accountants, and other professionals, unlike health professionals, often do not have individual human beings as clients but corporations, government agencies, and so on. When they do, the concerns about solicitation seem remote. Although the ABA prohibits it, there seem little basis for objecting to soliciting sophisticated clients, including other lawyers.[51] Engineers often make "cold calls" on firms to indicate their availability.

Another concern with solicitation involves professionals taking clients from other professionals. Prohibiting such solicitation primarily limits competition among professionals. However, there are four legitimate concerns. First, a professional might attempt to attract clients by criticizing other professionals. Such tactics could drastically reduce the trust essential to the professional–client relationship and undermine the value of the services. Second, professionals might suggest that people need professional services when they do not. Third, solicitation should be fair and not based on exaggerations or false statements about the ability of either professional or other matters. Fourth, it is difficult to police such inappropriate conduct. However, something less than a total ban on solicitation might suffice to prevent these problems. One must be careful in restricting solicitation because restrictions both limit professionals' and clients' freedom and decrease the availability of services to potential clients.

Specialization

The net effect of specialization on access to, and the cost of, professional services is unclear. Physicians and teachers have long had certified specialties, but lawyers and engineers are only beginning to adopt them formally. Some of the general disadvantages of specialization are as follows. First, too many people enter some specialties, and not enough people enter others. For years, too many physicians specialized in surgery and too few in other fields. Second, with specialization, fewer people tend to enter general practice. Many specialists do not provide comprehensive service, and often no professional is available to provide a total view of a client's needs. Third, when specialization combines with solo practice, services become diffuse. A client of health services must often travel from one place to another to receive complete service. Fourth, cost is likely to increase. Because of their expertise and extra training, certified specialists feel justified in charging higher fees.

The legal profession has been reluctant to adopt certification of specialties. One reason is a fear that potential clients will no longer go to the general practitioner. This reason rests on the personal interests of general practitioners. Another reason concerns certification of those professionals who have been practicing for a number of years. A third reason is a romantic conception of the lawyer as omnicompetent, able to advise clients on all aspects of the law.

Specialization develops when a field becomes too large for one person to master. Law and engineering have developed to that point. In practice, lawyers and engineers do specialize. Engineering education credentials engineers by granting degrees in specialized fields. Many lawyers are specialized by the areas in which they do most of their work. Large law and engineering firms are collections of specialists. They often provide better service for complex or large cases than a solo general practitioner because they can draw on the many different specialties of their members.

Properly organized, specialization can reduce the cost of service. A lawyer who handles many divorce, workers' compensation, or real estate cases becomes familiar with the relevant law and need not do the extensive research—at the client's expense— that one who only occasionally handles cases in those areas must do. In short, specialization can have the economic advantages that division of labor has in other fields, and it need not lead to a reduction in the quality of services.[52]

The problems of practitioners who have worked in an area for a number of years can be reasonably resolved. They may be "grandfathered" into the specialty. Alternatively, if specialists are not given the exclusive right to practice in fields, then other practitioners can still take routine cases in these fields. More complex cases simply raise the problems of fee splitting discussed earlier.

Engineers have had more practical specialization through education and membership in professional organizations—civil engineering, electrical engineering, and so on—than lawyers have. There are good reasons against certifying these specialties and giving them a monopoly of services in their areas.[53] In Ontario, less than 1 percent of engineers bothered to qualify for specialty designation. Given the cost of administering such programs and the likelihood of disputes as to what services can be exclusively rendered by members of specialties (unauthorized practice disputes), such a program is of little benefit to professionals or clients. These considerations apply to lawyers as well. Thus, permitting professionals other than physicians and teachers to designate fields of practice and specialized training should be sufficient. Other norms prohibit them from undertaking work they are not competent to perform.

Even if all the traditional norms of professional ethics were revised, they would not completely solve the problems of maldistribution of services, especially legal and health services. The changes would improve services to the middle class, but they would neither provide for the poor nor solve the geographic maldistribution of services. They would not even make services completely available to the middle class. Thus, by themselves, such changes would be insufficient to realize equality of opportunity. The next section briefly reviews some recent proposals that go beyond changes of traditional economic norms to make legal and health services equally available. These proposals are more directly aimed at the social structure of professional services than the norms considered in this section, which primarily pertain to the conduct of individual practitioners.

PROVIDING MEDICAL AND LEGAL SERVICES

As discussed at the beginning of this chapter, basic education, health, and legal services ought to be equally available to all. Basic education through high school is provided at government expense. Governments also significantly contribute to the cost of college education through state colleges and universities and student grants and loans. Although considerable debate exists as to whether enough is done, basic health and legal services are clearly less equally available than educational services.

The possible approaches to the provision of professional services are limited only by people's imaginations and their ability to organize activities. Attention here focuses on five methods of funding legal and health services to render them equally available. These approaches are not mutually exclusive. Some approaches are more appropriate to one of these professions than to the other.

1. Private insurance mechanisms can be used to fund services.
2. The government can subsidize the costs of services for specific groups.
3. Group practice based on a capitation fee can be used.
4. A national insurance system can be used to finance services.
5. Mandatory national service by professionals can be required for varying lengths of time.

Private Insurance

Insurance is a classic method of pooling risks and spreading costs. Insurance schemes of various sorts have been used or proposed to make professional services economically available. Private health insurance programs have existed for a long time. Rates are somewhat adjusted for risk, although not as much as in life or automobile insurance, and people who are less healthy often pay higher rates. Because the poor, especially the elderly poor, have more than the average health problems, the costs to them are higher and they might be unable to afford it. People in different risk categories pay the average cost of medical services for people in their group plus the costs of administration. In return, they can spread their payments over time and avoid extra expenses should they be greater than average. People still generally pay the costs of services they receive, and as medical costs have risen, so have private insurance rates.

Private insurance has not existed for legal services except insofar as automobile and other liability insurance provides for legal defense. Private insurance is beginning to be used to make legal services available to the middle class.[54] In the early 1970s, the legal profession did not wholeheartedly support such a development. Concern was expressed about the interposition of a so-called lay intermediary between the lawyer and client. Most of the concern was whether panels are "open" or "closed." In open panels, the insurance pays for a lawyer's services, and the potential client may choose any qualified attorney in the area. The argument on behalf of this procedure is that it ensures the client's freedom to choose counsel. In closed panels, a number of lawyers are designated to handle cases for persons in the insurance program. Although clients may choose among these lawyers, they must take one on the panel. As of about 1980, roughly five million families had some form of legal insurance.[55] This number is quite small compared to that of families having private health insurance. Private legal insurance is not designed to attack the problem of costs. It assumes that middle-income people can afford legal services but that they wrongly fear the costs and do not know how to select attorneys. Thus, it does not attack the underlying economic cause of maldistribution of services.

Government Subsidies

As part of its general "War on Poverty" during the 1960s, the U.S. government began to subsidize professional services for the poor. Medicare and Medicaid programs were instituted to provide health care to the elderly and poor. The Office of Economic Opportunity developed legal services programs, which later became the Legal Services Corporation. These programs were not well received by the medical and legal professions despite their ostensible commitment to making services available to all. The medical profession, which had long campaigned against "socialized medicine," resisted more than the legal profession. The lesser resistance by the bar was largely due to the leadership of then ABA president Lewis Powell.

An extended discussion of these programs is not needed or appropriate here, but a few points should be noted. First, they are primarily directed to the poor who previously did not receive services. Second, although professionals did not at first realize it, they promote the economic interests of the professions. Physicians are paid to treat patients whom they previously had not treated or had treated for free. The legal services program does not make payments to the poor or to private lawyers who serve them, but it does increase employment opportunities for lawyers. Also, the Supreme Court decisions in the early 1960s and 1970s requiring that defense counsel be provided for all persons charged with crimes and unable to afford counsel supplied crucial service to the poor and employment for lawyers.[56] Third, these programs are tailored so as not to interfere with services previously provided by professionals. For example, legal services to the poor do not accept cases that lawyers would otherwise take on a contingent fee basis. Thus, the programs do not cut into the existing business of professionals.

Although these programs greatly increase professional services for the poor, middle-class access to services did not improve significantly during the 1970s. Many factors are involved, and somewhat different ones pertain to different services. The basic problem is the increased cost of both health care and legal services. High rates of inflation play a significant part in these increases, but the costs have increased faster than the general rate of inflation. During the late 1970s, the costs of health care increased at one and a half to two times the rate of inflation. The net result was that as health and legal services became more accessible to the poor, they became less accessible to the middle class, especially to those just above the poverty line required for government subsidized services. During the first half of the 1980s, costs of health care and probably legal services continued to increase faster than inflation. Moreover, as noted earlier, significant cutbacks occurred in Medicare, Medicaid, and legal aid under the Legal Services Corporation. In short, the situation deteriorated for both the poor and the middle class.

Group Services

Group practice has been proposed in conjunction with, or independent of, private insurance to attack the cost problem and make services more available. The idea of professional group practice has existed in the legal profession for more than a quarter of a century.[57] Group practice can be combined with either a fee-for-service or a capitation payment method. With capitation payment, each person pays the same fee for a period of time and is provided all or most services.

The benefits of group practice derive from specialization, preventive services, and concentration. If a group has enough professionals and clients to allow specialization, the benefits discussed in the previous section can be achieved without the undesirable effects of costs and referrals. However, the cost claim assumes all professionals will receive roughly the same income. This assumption is not well founded if there is a shortage of specialists, for then specialists will be able to demand and receive substantially higher incomes than others. If clients pay on a capitation basis, professionals have an incentive to provide preventive services that are often less costly than corrective ones. If payments are on a fee-for-service basis, then mere group practice does not encourage preventive practice. Also, concentration cuts the overhead costs of equipment and support staff and saves clients the costs of traveling from one specialist to another. However, solo practicing professionals already sharing a suite of offices and staff have the cost-saving feature of concentration.

Generally, lawyers are not opposed to group practice; large and middle-size law firms actually are group practices. Large law firms have specialists in various areas—corporate taxes, securities, regulations, mergers, and so on—but they operate on a fee-for-service basis and primarily serve corporate clients. A shift to a capitation payment system and group practice for individual clients would be a significant change. Capitation payment would work just like an insurance system; clients would pay a flat fee each year in return for all needed legal services of certain types.

Legal clinics can be viewed as a form of group practice. They do not operate by capitation but by fee-for-service, and clients are not members of the group. Nonetheless, the lawyers are in group practice. They primarily operate by providing standardized basic services—no-fault divorce, personal bankruptcy, transfer of real property—on a mass basis. By providing routine services on a mass scale, they can reduce costs and provide the services cheaper. The ability to advertise and "store front" locations have made their growth possible. Some of them are now large, multistate operations. They do make services more available to the middle class.

More physicians than lawyers seem to prefer solo practice, although medical groups do exist, and many lawyers are engaged in solo practice. Many clients are concerned about group medical practice because in some groups they are sent to whichever physician is available at the time. As a result, they lose freedom of choice and a developed relationship of trust. They at least feel they do not receive the individualized attention they desire. But in other medical groups, patients can choose a primary physician whom they will always see unless they are referred to a specialist. People's attitudes about having one primary physician probably differ from their attitudes about having one primary lawyer because the average citizen has more frequent contact with a physician than a lawyer. People are likely to go to their physician several times a year, but to a lawyer only several times during their life. With either profession, group practice need not prevent client freedom to choose the professional. In large groups, more freedom of selection exists than among solo practitioners in small communities. If group practice preserves this freedom, reduces costs, and improves the quality of service, then society should promote it to make services more available.

National Insurance

So far, national insurance has been proposed only for health care. A practical problem confronts a similar proposal for legal services. Although all health care is rendered to individuals, most legal services are rendered to companies and corporations. However, were national legal insurance restricted to individuals, such a proposal would be more plausible. Borderline cases such as an individual doing business as a company would arise, but programs could be designed to resolve these problems.

There have been many different proposals for funding national health insurance and determining the types of services to be covered. These details are not relevant here. Only three points need be noted about a national insurance system. First, unlike the proposals discussed previously, national insurance would ensure that everyone has access to professional services regardless of financial status. It combines government subsidies for the poor with insurance for the middle class. Unlike private insurance for the middle class, national insurance would cover everyone and realize the value of equal availability of health care for all citizens irrespective of ability to pay. Second, national health insurance need not, as critics frequently claim, limit clients' freedom of choice of professionals and professionals' freedom of choice of clients. Medicare and Medicaid do not significantly limit such freedom of choice, and a comprehensive national insurance plan need not do so either. It does not do so in Canada.

Third, considerable debate exists about whether an ideal national health insurance would be a one-tier or two-tier system. In a one-tier system, all services are provided under national health insurance, so everyone gets the same services. One cannot "buy out" of the plan by paying privately for extra care. In a two-tier system, basic services are made available to all, but additional services are available to those willing to pay or otherwise able to obtain them. This chapter has implicitly assumed a two-tier system. A one-tier system must deny health care professionals and clients the freedom to deal with one another, and the values of equality of opportunity and minimal well-being do not require maximal or equal care for all.[58]

Recently, the primary criticism of national health insurance has been its cost. National health insurance alters only the method of payment, and by itself does not reduce the overall costs of medical care, although it might redistribute them. If everyone paid the same premium, then those people requiring less than average care would subsidize those requiring more than average. Also, were payments proportional to income—for example, by a social security scheme with a progressive tax rate—upper-income groups would subsidize medical care for lower-income groups. Because people's payments would be independent of the amount of care received, they would lack an economic incentive to forgo desired health services. Some authorities believe that demand for medical care would increase. Out-of-pocket expenses would no longer deter people from going to physicians for minor or imaginary ailments. Costs might be reduced in other ways. For example, the DRG payment system would have less negative impact on access to services were everyone covered. Hospitals would not have to recover the costs of indigent clients through charges to others. The central issue is whether society holds equality of opportunity and minimal well-being of enough value to pay the costs of making basic health care equally available. However, not even national wealth insurance corrects the geographic maldistribution of professional services.

Mandatory Service

By this proposal, professionals would be required to work on government salary for a period of time. Although the time might be a percentage of one's regular working time, say 10 percent, the discussion here is restricted to full-time employment for a number of years. Two variations of this proposal are (1) mandatory service for a few years at the beginning of one's career and (2) a total employment by the government—a national service.

In the American political context, the most plausible suggestion is for a few years of service at the beginning of one's professional career.[59] The professionals would be salaried at a reasonable rate considering their experience and training. Medical residency would not suffice as a professional's service commitment.

Such a program has advantages and disadvantages. It would provide inexpensive services for those who need them. The costs with salaried professionals are usually less than with a fee-for-service system. Professionals could be assigned to parts of the country where they are needed, and fees could be charged to those who are able to pay but who were previously without services because of their geographic location. In short, it would go a long way toward providing equal access to services. One disadvantage of such a program is that the professionals would be young and inexperienced and perhaps provide less competent services than those that others in society would receive. The plan would in effect provide job experience for beginning professionals who would then move to higher paying private employment. One should not make too much of these claims, however. Highly motivated young professionals with recent training frequently provide more competent service than complacent, middle-aged professionals who have not kept up with their field. Many young professionals now take government positions to gain experience, and one might require that some or all professionals devote two years in later life to such service, although that program would be much more difficult to implement. The primary objection to such a program, however, is the restriction on the freedom of professionals. What is proposed is simply a draft of professionals. Without a military draft, many people believe it would be hard to justify a draft of professionals. Four reasons can be offered to support such a draft.

1.   The government underwrites much of the cost of professional training, especially in health, but also in law. The service can be viewed as compensation for the training. Because the government also underwrites training in many other professions and fields without exacting a similar repayment, the "deal could be sweetened" by providing more support for students in the health and legal professions.

2.   Everyone has an obligation to contribute a fair share to society. Nevertheless, the burden might fall more heavily on those entering the health and legal professions. Some people believe a military draft is appropriate only during a national emergency, and a national emergency does not clearly exist with respect to health and legal services. The restrictions on freedom involved in compulsory service would be justifiable only were there no other way to solve the problem. If the government were willing to pay enough, it could recruit career professionals to provide the services. However, if a volunteer army is too expensive and inadequate, a similar program in these professions is unlikely to succeed.

3.   Professionals can be distinguished from most other people in society by their governmentally protected monopoly privileges of licensing and by the prohibition of unauthorized practice. Because they receive benefits from society in the protection provided them, they have a special obligation to compensate society.

4.   The compulsory aspect of such service can be overemphasized. No individual would be required to provide such services. One could always avoid it by not entering the health or legal professions. Viewed in this light, the required period of service is more a cost of entering the profession, like the years of education, than a compulsion. No one has a right to be a professional. Rather, it is a privilege, and the period of service is part of the price of that privilege.

These arguments assume that others are not being drafted. If a universal national service is required, as some people have proposed, then no special arguments are needed for requiring such service of health and legal professionals.

The second variation of mandatory service is that, instead of spending a few years, all professionals could be employed by the government on salary, that is, there could be a national health (or legal) service. National health services exist in many countries, such as England and the European socialist countries. Sometimes private practitioners exist alongside the national service system, and sometimes they do not. In Britain, physicians in the system are allowed to spend part of their time in private practice. For the legal profession, a large private practice would be needed to provide services to businesses and corporations. Indeed, by far the larger number of lawyers would be so employed.

There are many arguments for and against such a system, and some are quite complex. Such a system has not been vigorously proposed for the United States and is not likely to be adopted in the foreseeable future. Perhaps the major arguments in favor of such a system are the alleged cost efficiency of a salaried system and the ability easily to ensure the distribution of services throughout society. However, it would significantly limit the freedom of professionals. Another argument against it is that it results in less competent service because professionals lack financial incentives to provide effective service for their clients. This argument assumes that professionals are chiefly motivated by financial gain, something professionals have denied for centuries. Some people claim that clients would be deprived of freedom of choice among professionals, but that need not be the case any more than with group practice. Indeed, freedom of choice by patients need not be any more restricted than at present. Because about as many professionals would be in geographical areas as at present, clients could be allowed to choose the professionals they desire, subject, as at present, to the professionals' willingness to accept them.

The adversarial legal system, based on two opposed sides presenting their cases to be resolved by an impartial third party (judge or jury), makes a national service more questionable for lawyers than for physicians. Attorneys are supposed to represent their clients' interests *against* those of others. If the attorneys on both sides are ultimately paid by, or work for, the same organization, their devotion to their clients might be less. In suits against the government, a special conflict of interest would exist. A similar situation arises with public defenders in criminal cases and lawyers funded by the Legal Services Corporation. Examination of the general level of efforts by public defenders, even allowing for the fact that they are overworked, suggests that their devotion to clients is less than that of private attorneys. Clients of public defenders get more and longer sentences than comparable clients of private attorneys. Moreover, the Office of Economic Opportunity lawyers had special political difficulties in suits against state governments. Consequently, as long as the adversarial legal system is retained, a national legal service poses a threat to lawyers exercising independent judgment on behalf of their clients.

The point of this section has not been to argue for any particular approach to providing equal access to health and legal services. Instead, it has merely been to review briefly the major proposals and the main arguments for and against them. Some of the proposals appear more plausible than others. A profession as a whole has an obligation to make services equally available to all. Because the past organization and practices of the health and legal professions have failed to fulfill this obligation, a new organization and practices ought to be adopted to realize equality of opportunity.

Society should devise a system for delivering basic health and legal services that both makes them equally available and preserves as much freedom of choice as possible for clients and professionals. National insurance or service systems are the only ones that ensure service to all. However, a national insurance system fails to correct the geographic maldistribution of services, and a national service system significantly limits the freedom of professionals. A combination of the two, though, might best realize social values. National insurance would ensure that no one is denied basic services for financial reasons. A national service system, much like a college ROTC program, could supply professionals for service in needy areas. In exchange for individual financial support through professional school, persons would agree to serve where needed for a period of years. Such a program would also help poor students who otherwise would not be able to afford professional education. Whatever form the program takes, however, it should ensure everyone equal availability of basic medical and legal services to realize general equality of opportunity and minimal well-being.

ACCEPTING IMMORAL CLIENTS

The preceding sections of this chapter have focused on traditional norms imped-
ing equal access to professional services and the possible social arrangements that
might render health and legal services equally available to all. One other aspect of
making services available should be examined, namely, the freedom of professionals
to refuse to serve clients, especially those proposing what the professionals consider
immoral conduct. One of the fears physicians have about national health insurance is
that they might lose the freedom to decide which clients they will serve. Traditionally,
professionals have been free to refuse work offered to them, except for lawyers
assigned to cases by courts and physicians, who are obligated to treat people in
emergencies. Are there ethical constraints on this freedom?

The general problem of accepting or refusing clients can be broken down into
four specific questions.

1. To make services equally available, especially to provide health and legal
    services, should professionals accept all clients?
2. If they do not have an obligation to accept all clients, is it ethically permissible
    for them to do so?
3. Under what conditions, if any, do professionals have good reason to refuse to
    accept immoral clients?
4. If a professional refuses to accept a client whose conduct seems immoral, should
    the professional refer the client to another professional who will accept him or
    her?

These questions are taken up in order.

Professional Freedom

Should professionals accept all clients subject to their having the time to handle
the cases adequately? In the past, professionals, like most other people in society, have
discriminated against potential clients on the basis of race, religion, ethnic origin, and
sex. Equality of opportunity implies nondiscrimination on such grounds; so it is not
ethical for professionals to refuse to accept clients on them. Interestingly, few codes of
professional ethics contain such a norm. Perhaps they do not do so because it is a
universal norm applicable to all businesses, or perhaps because to so discriminate is
now illegal.

The argument for professionals being permitted to refuse such clients is on the
grounds of their freedom.[60] To require professionals to serve any and all clients who
come to them, even subject to their having the time and, perhaps, to the clients' ability
to pay, eliminates their freedom of choice as to whom they may serve. Their work
would largely be dictated by others. Most people in society are in this position—they
do not have complete freedom to do the work they wish (they are often assigned
disagreeable tasks by supervisors), but they are free to quit their jobs. A professional's
freedom to accept or reject clients is a similar freedom to accept or not accept
employment. Besides, in a pluralistic society, another professional is often available.

For example, although many physicians believe abortions are wrong except to save the life of the woman, many others ethically approve of abortions on request.

This argument is not as persuasive as might first appear. Consider the case of an eighteen-year-old male college student in Boston who became convinced that, due to overpopulation of the world and the responsibility involved, he did not want to have any children. He decided that a vasectomy would be the most prudent and effective contraceptive measure. All the physicians he contacted in the greater Boston area refused to perform a vasectomy on him. A similar case was a poor twenty-three-year-old nursing assistant in a small town in the 1960s who had three children and two miscarriages and wished to have a tubal ligation. Her physician refused, and as a result, she had two more children. In both of these cases, the physicians believed sterilization was unwise for the particular patients; they might have thought it was unethical. Although the wisdom of sterilization in these cases is debatable, a decade or two later few people think it unethical. In this way, professionals can prevent clients having access to services that the clients believe are morally permissible.[61] In a pluralistic society, professionals are imposing their own views on clients, perhaps to the detriment of the clients.

Nonetheless, this last argument is not strong enough to support a norm requiring professionals to accept all clients subject to time to serve and, perhaps, ability to pay. The freedom of professionals would be greatly restricted, and the restriction is more detrimental than the few cases in which clients would be deprived of appropriate services. The argument does imply that professionals should give clients the benefit of the doubt and provide services unless they are strongly opposed to the clients' course of conduct.

Assuming that society reasonably pursues justifiable values, is it ethically permissible for a professional to accept any client whose proposed course of conduct is legally permissible? Charles Fried argues that a lawyer may always do so. For clients to be unable to achieve their ends due to ignorance or misinformation about the law would violate their rights. Consequently, assisting clients to achieve their legal rights is, he claims, "always morally worthy."[62]

This argument faces several difficulties. First, it mistakenly assumes that because conduct is not legally prohibited, one has a right to pursue it. This confuses legal and ethical rights. Moreover, one does not have a legal right to pursue all conduct that is not legally prohibited. A legal right to conduct implies that others have a duty not to interfere; the fact that conduct is not legally prohibited establishes only that the conduct is permissible, that one has no duty not to engage in it. It does not establish that others have a duty not to interfere, and certainly not that one has a positive right to assistance in performing it. Second, sometimes conduct is not made illegal because legal enforcement would be difficult, unduly punitive, or otherwise cumbersome. Some such conduct may be grossly unethical.

Immoral Clients

Barring discrimination on the basis of race, ethnic origin, religion, and sex, the argument from freedom provides strong support to professionals being permitted to accept or reject clients. However, it is not yet clear that their freedom should extend to immoral clients. The category of morally repugnant clients includes a variety of possibilities that are rarely distinguished but seem important.

First, one should distinguish whether the client's immorality is connected to the service. Treating a mobster for pneumonia or completing a house purchase for a fascist is not related to the client's immorality. Performing disguising plastic surgery on an escaped convict or defending him or her on a charge of murdering a guard during the escape is related to the client's immorality. Of course, this is not a sharp distinction. It is unclear whether assisting a racketeer on a charge of income tax evasion in a "legitimate" business is related to the client's immorality. Nonetheless, the distinction can be used and is relevant to whether one is contributing to the person's immorality.

Second, the client's immorality can be connected to the case in several ways. (1) The immorality might be involved in the means the professional must use to assist the person. For example, manipulating a corporation's books to show large gains or destroying the credibility of a truthful witness involves professionals in actions they might consider unethical. (2) The moral repugnance of the client might relate to the ends sought. A physician might object to prenatal diagnosis for the purpose of sex selection or an engineer to projects detrimental to the environment.

Third, one can distinguish between helping the client do something and protecting the client. Designing inexpensive and unsafe buildings or setting up a dummy corporate shell for drug smugglers is facilitating the clients in achieving ends; treating a robber for strep throat or defending the robber against a robbery charge are protecting the client. Again, although some cases will be unclear, this distinction can often be made and be useful. It cuts across the others.

These distinctions help clarify the issues. If the client's immorality is unrelated to the case, then professional freedom should be permitted. It is permissible to accept such a client. Indeed, it is not appropriate to reject the client because of the immorality. Sanctions for the client's immorality should be directed to the immoral conduct. If a person has committed a crime, it is not appropriate to refuse to sell the person clothes. Granted, one does not have to associate socially with the person, but it is another matter simply to engage in commerce with him or her. Moreover, the concern to make legal and health services available gives a reason for lawyers and health care professionals to accept the client. However, any good reasons for not accepting a moral client (such as not liking that kind of case) apply to an immoral one. Finally, the professional freedom applies whether the service is facilitating or protecting the client.

When the client's immorality is related to the case, the situation is more complex. The issue of immoral means largely relates to obligations to third parties and is considered in Chapter 5. The focus here is on the client with an immoral end. However, in medicine, the distinction between means and ends is often difficult, so situations such as performing abortions are included.

One type of case needs to be noted and ruled out. It involves a client with an immoral end and a professional with a morally valuable end that can be served at the same time. A striking example is a black civil liberties lawyer who represented the Ku Klux Klan after it was denied a parade permit.[63] In this case, the lawyer's end is protecting freedom of speech, which here plausibly outweighs the client's immoral purpose. Consequently, the lawyer can view the activity as moral, everything considered.

Freedom and equality of opportunity cannot morally obligate professionals to help clients achieve immoral ends. Clients do not and cannot have an ethically justifiable freedom to perform unethical acts or pursue unethical ends. If it is unethical for clients to pursue an end, then it surely cannot be morally obligatory for professionals knowingly to assist them. Consequently, clients' freedom cannot be unethically restrained if professionals refuse to aid them. It is only freedom or equality of opportunity for ethically permissible purposes that is ethically required.[64]

Fried's argument for the permissibility of helping clients achieve all legally permissible ends (considered previously) and others for the duty to do so rest heavily on the legal profession's role in protecting clients' rights.[65] At best, the argument applies only to those services essential for minimal well-being or equality of opportunity. It does not apply to those professions whose services are not fundamental. Moreover, it does not apply to facilitating a client's ends, only to protecting them.

The Integrity, Rescue, and No Difference Views

Under what circumstances do professionals have a good ethical reason to refuse a client whose ends they consider immoral? This issue is too complicated to consider in detail here, so the opposing positions are only briefly outlined. The moral integrity view holds that if another professional will provide the services because he or she does not consider the proposed conduct wrong, then it is better for that person to perform them, and the ethically opposed professional has good reason to refuse. The ethically opposed professional would be violating his or her moral integrity, whereas the other one would not. Violating one's own moral integrity is likely to have negative personal effects, such as guilt feelings. However, if no other professional is available, as in the example of a physician in Alaska asked to perform an abortion, then making services equally available sometimes justifies providing the service. This last consideration primarily applies to medical and legal services because there is a positive right to them, whereas accountants, engineers, and architects are unlikely to practice in a region where no other professional is available.

The rescue view holds that professionals are permitted to refuse potential clients with immoral means or ends, except when the service is necessary for minimal well-being or equality of opportunity.[66] The availability of other professionals is irrelevant in this view. It is based on an analogy to the moral duty to rescue persons. If at small cost to oneself one can save a drowning person, one has a moral duty to do so. However, if the threat to the other person is not great (basic values like life are not at stake) or the risk to oneself is significant, then one does not have such a duty. By analogy, if the immoral client has a basic value at risk and one can, without significant sacrifice, assist or save that person, then one ought to do so.

The no difference view maintains that professionals violate their moral integrity only if it is wrong for them to provide the services.[67] However, if another professional will provide the services, then it is not wrong for them to do so, and they would have no reason for guilt. The wrong occurs if the client succeeds in completing his or her course of conduct, for example, by constructing a plant that damages the environment, filing a harassing lawsuit, or having an abortion. Because this wrong occurs regardless of what the professional does (for by hypothesis another will do it if he or she does not), the professional's conduct makes no difference to the occurrence of the wrong. If it makes no difference, then it is not wrong. Consequently, the professional has no good reason to refuse to provide the services so long as another will. If the client cannot obtain another professional to provide the services, then the first professional's conduct does make a difference. If the professional provides the services, then the wrong occurs; if he or she does not provide the services, the wrong is prevented. Thus, if no other professional will provide the services if he or she refuses, the professional should refuse because that will prevent the wrong from occurring.

This last argument assumes that another professional definitely will or will not provide services, and usually that is not completely clear. In the moral integrity view, this consideration is also relevant to what the professional ought to do. Thus, the uncertainty affects both it and the no difference view, so it cannot be an argument for one over the other. This uncertainty is probably irrelevant to the rescue view because anyone who can help should do so. If one does not make this claim, then one adopts an aspect of the no difference view, only in reverse. One does not have a moral obligation to do something because someone else will do it, so one's doing it makes no difference.

An objection to the no difference view is that it implies one should cooperate with a Nazi society. Suppose a professional in a Nazi society is asked to prosecute a Jew, medically terminate the life of a Gypsy, or design a gas chamber to look like a shower stall. Could not professionals argue, as many did, that if they do not do it, someone else will?

The reply is that the no difference argument assumes that the professional is not justified in taking steps coercively preventing the prospective client pursuing the course of conduct he or she desires, as by holding a pregnant woman hostage until she delivers. However, in some cases, that is not correct. In the Nazi examples, professionals were justified in using coercion (joining the resistance) to overthrow the government. After all, it was the antithesis of a society based on justifiable values. Similarly, sometimes a professional is justified in using coercion to prevent a prospective client from performing certain actions. For example, a psychiatrist is justified in having a psychotic committed if he or she is likely to kill someone.

Perhaps the central objection to the no difference view is that it denies the wrongness of producing otherwise wrongful effects, albeit in one limited type of case. The situation is one of causal overdetermination; that is, two different lines of causation are possible and will bring about a result. Suppose two different sets of explosive charges are set at someone's house, and a person is ready to set off one of the charges. Further suppose you have the other detonator and know that the other person will set off a charge. If you set off your charge first, would you do anything wrong? You would be held legally liable, and most people would think the conduct wrong. Although the no difference view agrees that you are causally and morally responsible, it denies that you have done anything wrong. In this case, the wrong is committed by the other person, who set up the situation resulting in the damage to the house. Had that person not been ready to blow it up, it would not have been permissible for you to do so. In the professional situation, the wrong is committed by the client and other professional, who will produce the wrong if one does not.

Finally, if professionals refuse to provide services because they consider the prospective client's proposed conduct immoral, should they refer the prospective client to another professional who will provide them? This issue arises only in the moral integrity view. In the rescue view, either one has a duty to assist, or the prospective client does not need rescuing, so there is no reason to refer. In the no difference view, whenever a professional has good reason to refuse, no other professional is reasonably available. Although many people think professionals should refer such clients, they cannot consistently do so. If a professional is convinced that the conduct is unethical, he or she must think that referring the prospective client is assisting in wrongdoing. No one would think it proper for an individual to refuse to help commit a crime, such as armed robbery, but then refer the would-be robber to someone who would assist. Consequently, if a professional sincerely believes the prospective client's conduct is strongly unethical, he or she cannot consistently refer the person to another one.

SUMMARY

This chapter has focused on the implications of equality of opportunity for making professional services equally available to all citizens. Because of the central importance of educational, legal, and health services in achieving general equality of opportunity as well as minimal well-being, people have a positive right to these services being equally available irrespective of ability to pay. Other professional services need only be available on equal terms. Legal and health care services have been maldistributed economically, racially, and geographically.

A number of traditionally accepted professionally economic norms have contributed to denying the equal availability of professional services. Monopolistic prohibitions of unauthorized practice have prevented services being offered by non-professionals. Such restrictions are justifiable only if no reasonable person would want an unlicensed person to provide services or if an unlicensed person doing so might burden the public. Minimum fee schedules and prohibitions of competitive bidding have restrained competition and kept the price of services high; they are illegal violations of the antitrust laws and are ethically objectionable for the same reasons they are illegal. Fee splitting for referrals is not justifiable, but professionals should be permitted to charge a modest fee for them. Contingent fees in all professions except law are usually unethical, and even those in law could be reduced if legal services handled such cases. Restrictions on advertising and solicitation have been greatly reduced during the last two decades. Restrictions on advertising are justifiable only to prevent false, deceitful, and misleading claims. Norms restricting solicitation are justifiable for situations likely to involve overreaching and undue influence. Finally, licensed specialization, except in teaching and medicine, is not worth the effort and might unduly increase costs.

Various proposals for making legal and medical services equally available to all were quickly surveyed. Private insurance does not address the economic maldistribution of services. Government programs for the poor still leave the middle class, especially the lower middle class, with inadequate services. Group services can help make services available at lower cost, but they do not address the geographic maldistribution. National insurance does address the economic maldistribution and can preserve client and professional freedom of choice, but it does not significantly solve geographic maldistribution. A general national service unnecessarily limits the freedom of professionals, although a limited service is probably justifiable as part of the cost of the privilege of practicing law or medicine. However, the best scheme might be national health insurance supplemented by a voluntary service program to rectify geographic maldistribution.

Questions arise concerning the ethics of professionals refusing to accept clients, especially those whose conduct they deem unethical. It would unduly restrict the freedom of professionals to require them to accept any and all clients on a first-come, first-served basis subject to time to take cases and, in some professions, ability to pay. Because this means clients might sometimes be unable to pursue ethically permissible but unwise courses of conduct, professionals should give clients the benefit of the doubt about the ethics or wisdom of their proposed conduct. It is useful to distinguish services unrelated to the client's immorality from those that are and facilitating clients' pursuit of goals from protecting them. Even in a society reasonably pursuing justifiable social values, it is not ethically permissible to assist clients in all legally permissible conduct. Their moral claims to freedom cannot extend to unethical uses of it, so professionals have no duty to facilitate such conduct.

Three views exist as to when professionals have good reason to refuse to accept clients whose ends they think are unethical. The moral integrity view is that they should refuse if another professional will provide services, but probably should not refuse if no other professional is available. The rescue view is that professionals have good reason to refuse to accept immoral clients unless the services are necessary to protect their basic values. The no difference view is that professionals do not have a good reason to refuse to accept such clients if other professionals will provide the services anyway, but they do if no one else will provide the services, and they can then prevent wrong from occurring. Finally, if a professional refuses to accept a client on ethical grounds, he or she cannot ethically refer the client to someone else who will provide the services.

NOTES*

1. AMA, *Principles of Medical Ethics,* sec. 1; ABA, *Code of Professional Responsibility,* Canon 2, EC 2-16, EC 2-26.

2. See President's Commission, *Securing Access to Health Care,* pp. 16–17.

3. See Baum, "Access to Engineering Services."

4. *Row* v. *Wade,* 410 U.S. 113 (1973).

5. *Harris* v. *McRae,* 100 S. Ct. 2671 (1980).

6. Pope and Winslade, "Unequal Access to Mental Health Services," p. 151; see also Mūnoz, "Commentary."

7. President's Commission, *Securing Access to Health Care,* p. 3.

8. ABA, *Code of Professional Responsibility,* Canon 3; AMA, "Current Opinions," 3.01.

9. Patterson and Cheatham, *Profession of Law,* p. 372.

---

*See the bibliography at the back of the book for complete references.

10. Llewellyn, "The Bar Specializes," p. 190.

11. Llewellyn, "The Bar's Troubles and Poultices," pp. 244–245.

12. Orkin, *Legal Ethics,* p. 249.

13. Patterson and Cheatham, *Profession of Law,* p . 370.

14. Ibid., p. 371.

15. Benjamin N. Branch, "Out-Patient Termination of Pregnancy," in *New Concepts in Contraceptives,* ed. Malcolm Potts and Clive Wood (Baltimore: University Park Press, 1972), p. 183.

16. *Florida Bar* v. *Brumbaugh,* 355 So. 2d 1186 (Fla. 1978); *Florida Bar* v. *Furman,* 376 So. 2d 378 (Fla. 1979), *appeal dismissed* 444 U.S. 1061 (1980).

17. Lieberman, *Crisis at the Bar,* pp. 124–125.

18. Deborah L. Rhode, "Policing the Professional Monopoly: A Constitutional and Empirical Analysis of Unauthorized Practice Prohibitions," in *The Legal Profession,* ed. Hazard and Rhode, p. 310.

19. "AMA Tried to Destroy Chiropractors, Court Rules," *Tallahassee Democrat,* 29 August 1987, p. 3A.

20. Thomas D. Morgan, "The Evolving Concept of Professional Responsibility," in *1977 National Conference on Teaching Professional Responsibility,* ed. Goldberg, pp. 283–284.

21. 421 U.S. 733, 780 (1975).

22. See generally, Dolenc and Dougherty, "DRGs."

23. Macklin, "Equal Access to Professional Services," pp. 4–5.

24. *National Society of Professional Engineers* v. *United States,* 435 U.S. 679 (1978).

25. See Florida, "The Consultants' Competitive Negotiation Act," and Florida Engineering Society, "Suggested Key Steps in Administering the Consultants' Competitive Negotiation Act," in *Engineering Professionalism and Ethics,* ed. Schaub and Pavlovic, pp. 122–131.

26. ABA, *Model Rules,* Rule 1.5(e); ABA, *Code of Professional Responsibility,* DR 2-107; AICPA, "Rules of Conduct," Rule 503; AMA, "Current Opinions," 6.03–6.05.

27. ABA, *Model Rules,* Rule 5.4; ABA, *Code of Professional Responsibility,* DR 3-102; AICPA, "Rules of Conduct," Rule 505.

28. Orkin, *Legal Ethics,* p. 153; Halstrom, "Referral Fees," p. 40.

29. See Franck, "Referral Fees," p. 42, for this and the next point.

30. Halstrom, "Referral Fees"; Morgan "Concept of Professional Responsibility," (see n. 20 above), pp. 292–294.

31. ABA, *Model Rules,* Rule 1.5(e), Comment.

32. AMA, *Principles of Medical Ethics,* sec. 5; see also AMA, "Current Opinions," 3.04.

33. ABA, *Model Rules,* Rule 1.5(d); ABA, *Code of Professional Responsibility,* DR 2-106(C); AICPA, "Rules of Conduct," Rule 302; Engineers' Council, "Suggested Guidelines," 5, e; National Society, "Code of Ethics," Obligation 7, a.

34. Sharswood, *Essay on Professional Ethics,* pp. 160–161.

35. This claim has empirical confirmation. See Rosenthal, *Lawyer and Client,* p. 91.

36. Alger, Christensen, and Olmstead, *Ethical Problems in Engineering,* p. 58.

37. Patterson and Cheatham, *Profession of Law,* p. 265.

38. Lieberman, *Crisis at the Bar,* pp. 130–132.

39. See, for example, Engineers' Council, "Suggested Guidelines," 5, d, f, g, h.

40. *Report of the Professional Organizations Committee,* p. 189.

41. Ibid., p. 192.

42. Patterson and Cheatham, *Profession of Law,* p. 357.

43. See Bayles, *Principles of Legislation,* pp. 85–86; *Virginia State Board of Pharmacy* v. *Virginia Citizens Consumer Council,* 425 U.S. 748, 756–57 (1976).

44. *Zauderer* v. *Office of Disciplinary Counsel,* 471 U.S. 626 (1985); *In Re R. M. J.,* 455 U.S. 191 (1982); *AMA* v. *FTC,* 138 F.2d 443 (1980), *affirmed by an equally divided court,* 455 U.S. 656, *reh'g denied* 456 U.S. 965 (1982); *Bates* v. *State Bar of Arizona,* 433 U.S. 350 (1977); *Virginia State Board of Pharmacy* v. *Virginia Citizens Consumer Council,* 425 U.S. 748 (1976).

45. AMA, "Current Opinions," 5.01.

46. ABA, *Model Rules,* Rule 7.1(c).

47. Freedman, *Lawyers' Ethics,* chap. 10.

48. *Ohralik* v. *Ohio State Bar Association,* 436 U.S. 447 (1978).

49. *In re Primus,* 436 U.S. 412 (1978).

50. See generally, Moss, "Ethics of Law Practice Marketing," pp. 673–682; Ringleb, Bush, and Moncrief, "Lawyer Direct Mail Advertisements."

51. ABA, *Model Rules,* Rule 7.3 (including direct mail); Note, "Soliciting Sophisticates."

52. *Report of the Professional Organizations Committee,* p. 200.

53. Ibid., p. 190.

54. For a simple survey of this type of proposal, see Jim Lorenz, "State of Siege: Group Legal Services for the Middle Class," in *Verdicts on Lawyers,* ed. Nader and Green, pp. 144–157.

55. Lori B. Andrews, "Regulation of Group Legal Services Under State Ethics Codes," in *Problems in Professional Responsibility,* ed. Kaufman, p. 666.

56. *Gideon* v. *Wainwright,* 372 U.S. 335 (1963); *Argersinger* v. *Hamlin,* 407 U.S. 25 (1972).

57. See Llewellyn, "The Bar Specializes," p. 189.

58. For further support of a two-tier system, see Engelhardt, *Foundations of Bioethics,* pp. 354–365. It is also implicit in the President's Commission emphasis on an "adequate level of health care"; *Securing Access to Health Care,* p. 20.

59. See Lowell E. Bellin, "Quality and Equality in Health Care—What Can We Do About It?" in *Moral Problems in Medicine,* ed. Gorovitz et al., pp. 490–491; and Lieberman, *Crisis at the Bar,* pp. 223–224.

60. Charles Fried, "The Lawyer as Friend: The Moral Foundations of the Lawyer–Client Relation," in *1977 National Conference on Teaching Professional Responsibility,* ed. Goldberg, p. 152.

61. Alan Goldman claims that if lawyers accepted only clients whose aims they considered morally legitimate, due to the moral pluralism among lawyers, only clients whose purposes were blatantly immoral would be unable to obtain services (*Moral Foundations,* p. 131). The past practice of physicians makes this claim questionable, although differences in attitudes of physicians and lawyers toward providing services for immoral purposes could be important in this context.

62. Fried, "Lawyer as Friend," (see n. 60 above), p. 144; Fried, *Right and Wrong,* pp. 181–182.

63. See Schneyer, "Moral Philosophy's Standard Misconception of Legal Ethics," p. 1541.

64. The ABA, *Code of Professional Responsibility,* DR 2-109(A), prohibits lawyers accepting clients who wish to harass or maliciously injure someone or to present totally unwarranted claims or defenses; see also ABA, *Model Rules,* Rules 1.16(b) (1) and (3) and 3.1.

65. Newman, "Representing the Repugnant Client," p. 24, assumes that lawyers are defending clients' liberty.

66. See Charles W. Wolfram, "A Lawyer's Duty to Represent Clients, Repugnant and Otherwise," in *The Good Lawyer,* ed. Luban, pp. 214–235; see also ibid.

67. See the exchange between Bayles and Davis, in *Ethics and the Legal Profession,* ed. Davis and Elliston, pp. 428–464.

STUDY QUESTIONS AND PROBLEMS

1. Arthur Brown is a very busy and successful attorney. Ace Retailers has hired him to defend them in a suit by a customer. The complaint was filed twenty-seven days ago, and Brown has not yet filed an answer, although he has had the case for over two weeks. When the president of Ace phones Brown, he tells him that he will not file an answer until he receives a $20,000 retainer. State law requires that answers be filed within thirty days or parties will be considered to have admitted all allegations of fact in the complaint. The president of Ace thinks the fee is high even for a trial, and the case may be settled before going to trial. But because he does not have time to find another attorney, he sends Brown the check by courier. Is Brown's conduct unethical? May professionals ethically withhold services until they are assured of receiving their fee? May hospitals ethically refuse to admit patients until assured that they have insurance or are otherwise able to pay?

2. Reconsider question 2 in Chapter 2. Does the fact that the engineers' no bidding principle has now been declared illegal in the United States make you want to change your answer from what it was before?

3. Management consultant Claudia Debbs contacts Edmond Forbes's accounting firm to suggest a joint venture. She is contacting local businesses to obtain employment. Her proposal is that she will study the businesses and make suggestions for improvements in their methods of operation. If she finds that changes are needed in their accounting procedures, she will recommend Forbes's accounting firm to design and assist in setting up new accounting practices. Forbes will then pay Claudia a percentage of the fee he receives. Would it be ethical for Forbes to make such an arrangement? Why or why not? Suppose Debbs told the businesses of the arrangement when she was hired. Would that make any difference to the ethics of the arrangement? Why or why not?

4. In a Mexican-American community in Texas, Gina Hernandez is with her friend, a recent immigrant from Mexico who speaks little English, when her friend phones the local mental health agency for an appointment. She is having an emotional crisis, brought on in part by the culture shock of moving to the United States and various other difficulties she and her family are having. Gina is glad that she has finally convinced her friend to make an appointment and get help. After a brief exchange, her friend asks Gina to take the phone and explain. The receptionist does not speak Spanish. Gina briefly describes the situation to the receptionist and asks for an appointment with a Spanish-speaking social worker. The receptionist replies that they do not have any Spanish-speaking social workers because there is so little demand for them. Why is there little demand for Spanish-speaking social workers? Should they be made available? Why? Is there a responsibility to make the services of social workers available? Whose responsibility is it?

5. The scene in the television commercial depicts a courtroom with a judge announcing a verdict for the plaintiff in the amount of $150,000. The attractive female plaintiff jumps up and hugs her attorney. A small print caption on the bottom of the screen says "Dramatic Presentation." In the next scene, an elderly couple is shown, and the man gives his name and says that Mr. Ivan Jackson has represented him in several legal matters, and he was completely satisfied with the competence and timeliness of the service. The last scene shows the interior of a well-furnished law office. The voice-over gives the following: "Many people and firms have retained Ivan Jackson, Esquire, to represent them in legal matters. Among the firms Mr. Jackson has successfully represented are the First Bank of Nowhere and Casualty Insurance. If you have been injured in an accident, Mr. Jackson will be pleased to consult with you. You need pay no legal fees unless you win the case. You will be responsible for legal costs. For wrongful injury or any other legal problems, the firm of Ivan Jackson is ready to assist you. There is no charge for the initial consultation." The address and phone number are then given. Is this commercial ethical? Why or why not?

6. Nurse Kay Lewitt has a toe that needs minor surgery—a fusion of the bones so that it is not so easily dislocated. She has just started a rotation of seven days of work followed by seven days off.

She is hoping to get the surgery done without having to take sick leave, but she is not sure how long it will be after surgery before she can return to work. One day she asks a colleague if she knows how long one must be off work for such surgery. Dr. Michael Natwick, an orthopedic surgeon, overhears the question. He asks why Kay wants to know, and she tells him. He says he would be glad to do it for her. Ms. Lewitt tells him that she planned to have Dr. Octavia Peterson, a well-known hand and foot surgeon, do it because she used to work at Dr. Peterson's small private hospital and still occasionally does substitute work on her days off. Consequently, she receives a 50 percent discount on what her insurance does not cover. Dr. Natwick says, "I can do it cheaper than that. I can arrange it so that you do not have to pay anything out-of-pocket."

Is Dr. Natwick's offer ethical? Is this soliciting a client? Is he trying to take a patient away from Dr. Peterson? Do the answers to these last questions make any difference to the ethics of the conduct? Would it make any difference if Ms. Lewitt's problem were a nofault divorce, and lawyers rather than doctors were involved? What differences, if any, are there between personal solicitation by engineers, physicians, and publishers seeking manuscripts? Is it ethical for Dr. Natwick to accept the insurance payment in full when the insurance company requires a deductible to help deter patients from overuse of medical services? Suppose Dr. Natwick provides his services free, and the insurance pays outpatient surgery in full?

7. Ralph Stiles is a counselor at a high school in a remote community. He has a very emotionally disturbed student, and the nearest referral center is a hundred fifty miles away. Although Ralph is not trained for such therapy, he tries to provide it for the student. Is it wrong for him to do so? Why or why not?

8. Try to design the broad outlines of a national health insurance scheme. What services would be included and excluded? How should the scheme be financed? What objections could be made to your proposal?

9. Would a draft of physicians and lawyers for two years of service at modest salary be just? State at least two arguments for and against such a proposal.

10. Computer specialist Tamera Urban is asked by a large company to design a program containing all possible data about its employees. The company wants to include all health information, supervisor's reports, financial information, and criminal records it obtains, as well as informal information about the employees' families. Should she accept the job? Why or why not?

11. Lawyer Van Ward is contacted by a divorced woman. She tells him that her exhusband has not paid any child support for the past two years. He has sent her an occasional check but not through the court, so the money has not been credited to him. She realizes that suing for all the back support will drive him close to bankruptcy, but she maintains, "The bastard deserves whatever he gets." Should Van take the case? Why or why not? If he does, is it ethical for him not to include the informal payments as credits to the husband?

12. Engineers Xenia Yntema and Alonso Blanton are having a disagreement over whether to accept a new client. Cass Dedge, the largest residential developer in the city and affectionately and not so affectionately known as "Big Momma

Cass," came to the office this morning and asked them to do the engineering work on a new development. Their new firm has not been doing as well as expected because of the downturn in construction due to the new tax law. They are surprised that Momma Cass even considered them for the job. Xenia claims that it is the break they have been waiting for. A job this size will mean a big fee and about two years of work; it will also make them well known and bring in other clients.

Alonso says that the marsh Momma Cass wants to develop is a wildlife area, that there are few salt marshes left, and that this project will destroy the environment. There are lots of other places she could put the development that would be just as attractive. The only reason Momma Cass wants to build there is because she got the land cheap a year ago when it was rumored the state would buy it. He does not think it right to build the project.

Xenia agrees that the project will damage the environment, but she counters that whether it is environmentally sound is not for them to decide. The Water Management District must approve it, and it also has to receive other environmental approvals. If those agencies approve it, it is not up to them to impose their moral views. Besides, some other firm will get the job if they turn it down. What would be the point of their refusing?

What, ethically, should Xenia and Alonso do? Why?

4 Obligations Between Professionals and Clients

Securing the services of a professional, as difficult as that can sometimes be, is only a preliminary to the professional–client relationship. This chapter considers the ethical nature of the professional–client relationship and the obligations of professionals to clients and vice versa that arise therein. In the compass of this chapter, it is impossible to provide a complete and detailed analysis of these obligations, and important differences arise in applying these obligations to different professional situations. Therefore, the emphasis is on the standard or normal situation of a competent adult client. Modifications are needed for other situations, such as physicians treating small children and unconscious patients. On the basis of this analysis, a standard is offered to systematize obligations of professionals to clients. General obligations are then briefly developed. Finally, obligations of clients are considered.

THE PROFESSIONAL–CLIENT RELATIONSHIP

Many analyses have been offered of the professional–client relationship. Some of these are empirical, describing the relationship as it normally exists. That is not the purpose of this section. Rather, the purpose here is to develop an ethical model that should govern the professional–client relationship. However, ethical models and norms often assume certain facts. For example, an ethical model of the appropriate relationship between parent and child makes certain assumptions about a child's abilities. A model of full equality would not work for very young children simply because they lack the physical and mental abilities to engage in such a relationship. Similarly, an ethical model of the professional–client relationship can be inappropriate because it makes false empirical assumptions about one or the other parties.

The impulse of philosophers is to generalize. My aim here is to develop general statements of obligation that can require different conduct, depending on the situation. The obligations to keep promises and make preparations for past injustice remain constant, although the required conduct varies with the situation. There is no a priori reason why general obligations between professionals and clients cannot be established even though their application to particular cases requires different conduct in different situations. This does not imply ethical relativism.

An ethical model of the broadest scope will not be based on unusual situations, such as a defendant charged with a capital crime or an unconscious patient. Unusual situations are so simply because they lack features of the usual or have additional features. An analysis based on unusual situations is therefore likely to distort normal situations. Professional ethics should be based on the usual sort of contact average clients have with professionals. Individual citizens are most likely to see lawyers in connection with real estate transactions, divorces, making wills, and personal injury negligence cases. Lawyers also spend much time drafting commercial contracts and advising about business matters. The average client will probably have a physician's attendance during a fatal illness or injury, but most physician–patient contacts are for more mundane matters such as a bacterial infection or a broken bone. Only gross neglect by the patient or physician—for example, the failure of a patient to take any medicine at all or of a physician to ask whether the patient is allergic to penicillin before prescribing it—is apt to turn these matters into seriously life-threatening illnesses or injuries. Engineers are apt to be consulted by companies or governments that want a project designed. Similarly, certified public accountants are usually hired to audit the books of a corporation. Both accountants and architects also deal with individuals for such purposes as income tax preparation and designing houses.

The central issue in the professional–client relationship is the allocation of responsibility and authority in decision making—who makes what decisions. The ethical models are in effect models of different distributions of authority and responsibility in decision making. One can view the professional–client relationship as one in which the client has the most authority and responsibility in decision making, the professional being an employee; as one in which the professional and client are equals, either dealing at arm's length or at a more personal level; or as one in which the professional, in different degrees, has the primary role. Each of these conceptions has been suggested by some authors as the appropriate ethical model of the relationship. Each has some commonsense support.

Although the argument in this section supports one model over the others, it is not the only one that is ever appropriate. The others might be so for certain specialized types of situations. Indeed, a relationship between a professional and a client might move back and forth between two or more models as the situation changes. It does not follow, as one author has objected, that one can generate any number of models or that they are merely matters of style.[1] They are based on the logically possible divisions of responsibility and authority between professional and client. The models set a framework for determining what obligations pertain and so are not mere matters of style.

Agency

According to this view, the client has most of the authority and responsibility for decisions; the professional is an expert acting at the direction of the client.[2] The client hires a professional to protect or act for some interest; the professional provides services to achieve the client's goal—purchase of a house, marriage counseling, design of a building. According to this conception, not only does the professional act for or in behalf of the client, but also acts under the direction of the client, as in bureaucratic employer–employee relationships. This conception is especially plausible for lawyers. In filing a complaint or arguing for a client, a lawyer acts for and in behalf of the client. According to some people, a lawyer is merely a "mouthpiece" or "hired gun." This is not a plausible view of accountants performing public audits, for they are supposed to provide an independent review and statement of the clients' financial conditions.

In some contexts, professionals are prone to adopt the agency view of the professional–client relationship. Professionals are sometimes "identified" with their clients and charged with the clients' alleged moral failings. Lawyers offer the defense that, in representing clients, they do not thereby ascribe to or support clients' goals or aims.[3] They are merely employees hired to perform a specific task. If the projects are bad or immoral, the fault lies with the clients, or perhaps with the legal system for permitting the projects.

The agency model most clearly exemplifies what has been called the "ideology of advocacy." This ideology has two principles of conduct: (1) that the lawyer is neutral or detached from the client's purposes and (2) that the lawyer is an aggressive partisan of the client working to advance the client's ends.[4] This ideology is readily applicable to physicians, architects, social workers, and engineers. A physician, for example, should not evaluate the moral worth of patients but only work to advance their health. The second element of the ideology does not apply to accountants performing audits, for they are to present independent statements of clients' financial conditions. It applies in other accounting activities though. For example, an accountant preparing a client's income tax statement should try to take every plausible deduction on behalf of the client.

Some aspects of this ideology appear inescapable in professional ethics. If professionals accepted only clients whose purposes they approved of and did not consider clients' interests any more than those of others, many persons with unusual purposes (such as wanting an architectural style of a building that is completely inconsistent with those nearby) might be unable to obtain professional services. And even if they did, the services might not be worth much because no special considera-tion would be paid to their interests.[5] The chief problem with the ideology of advocacy, where it does become an ideology, is that devotion to a client's interests is sometimes thought to justify any lawful action advancing the client's ends, no matter how detrimental the effect on others.

The agency view of the professional–client relationship is unduly narrow. Four considerations indicate limits to a professional's proper devotion to a client's interests, and consequently to a client's authority in decision making.

1. As discussed in the next chapter, professionals have obligations to third persons that limit the extent to which they may act in behalf of client interest.

2. The agency view arises most often in the context of defending professionals, especially lawyers, from attribution of client sins. This focus is too narrow to sustain a general account of the professional–client relationship. It best pertains to an adversarial context in which two opposing parties confront one another. In counseling, a lawyer's advice "need not be confined to purely legal con-siderations. . . . It is often desirable for a lawyer to point out those factors which may lead to a decision that is morally just as well as legally permissible."[6]

3.   Professionals emphasize their independence of judgment. Unlike soldiers, who are not expected to think for themselves but to do things the army's way, professionals should exercise their training and skills to make objective judgments. The agency view ignores this feature.

4.   Except in cases of dire need—medical emergencies, persons charged with crimes—professionals may accept or reject specific clients. With a few restrictions, they may also cease the relationship. Consequently, the agency view is too strong. Professionals must also be ethically free and responsible persons. For their own freedom and the protection of others, they should not abdicate authority and responsibility in decision making.

The agency view of the professional–client relationship is more plausible when the client is a large corporation or government agency. Indeed, a recent analysis suggests that law firms hired by large corporations tend more to be hired guns.[7] Corporate counsel now hire and direct outside law firms, and the firms might be fired for failure to take direction.[8] Although professional independence is greatly reduced in such a relationship, the first and fourth considerations in the previous list still hold. The professionals still have obligations to third parties that limit their activities, and they can accept or refuse clients.

Contract

If a client ought not to be viewed as having the most authority and responsibility, then perhaps the authority and responsibility should be shared equally. In law, a professional–client relationship is based on a contract, and the ethical concept of a just contract is of an agreement freely arrived at by bargaining between equals. If the relationship is a contractual one, then there are mutual obligations and rights, "a true sharing of ethical authority and responsibility."[9] Because it recognizes the freedom of two equals to determine the conditions of their relationship, the contract model accords well with the values of freedom and equality of opportunity.

However, no gain results from treating as equals people who are not relevantly equal in fact or from assuming a nonexistent freedom. The history of contracts of adhesion (the standard forms offered by monopolies or near monopolies such as airlines) indicates the injustice that can result from falsely assuming contracting parties have equal bargaining power. Many commentators have noted relevant inequalities between professionals and clients, especially in the medical context.[10] First, a professional's knowledge far exceeds that of a client. A professional has the special knowledge produced by long training, knowledge a client could not have without comparable training. Second, a client is concerned about some basic value—personal health, legal status, or financial status—whereas a professional is not as concerned about the subject matter of their relationship. The client usually has more at stake. Third, a professional often has a freedom to enter the relationship that a client lacks. A professional is often able to obtain other clients more easily than a client can obtain another professional. Especially if a potential client has an acute illness, has been referred to a social agency, or has just been charged with a crime, he or she is not free to shop around for another professional. From this point of view, the bargaining situation is more like that between an individual and a public utility.

These considerations are not as important for the usual situation in architecture, accounting, and engineering. The clients of these professionals are often better informed about the subject matter of the transaction than are clients of lawyers and physicians. For example, businesses and corporations have accountants working for them who can give advice about auditors. Firms hiring consulting engineers have often had previous experience working with engineers in that field. Governments, even local ones, frequently have one or two engineers working for them who can advise and help. Moreover, they are freer than the professional to conclude an arrangement with another firm. Thus, in these situations, the factual basis for the contract model is most nearly present. However, the consulting engineer or architect has some special knowledge and ability the client lacks, or else a professional would probably not be hired, so the contract model's empirical assumptions do not quite hold even in these cases.

The freedom of students (clients) to choose teachers (professionals) varies considerably. In elementary school, students are assigned to classes and teachers. In high school and college, students have more choice among courses and teachers. However, for required courses, there is often only one teacher available that semester. Moreover, the disparity in knowledge necessarily applies. Normal classes are not based on a contract between equals; they are more like contracts of adhesion offered on a take it or leave it basis. Only independent study courses approximate a contract between equals.

Friendship

Instead of viewing the relationship as one between two free and equal persons dealing at arm's length, some authors suggest that the relationship is more personal. One does not relate to a professional as one does to a grocer or public utility. The personal element is most closely captured by viewing the relationship as one of pals or friends. According to this view, professional and client have a close relationship of mutual trust and cooperation; they are involved in a mutual venture, a partnership.

Perhaps the most sophisticated version of this conception is that proposed by Charles Fried.[11] He is primarily concerned with the legal and medical professions. Fried seeks to justify professionals devoting special attention and care to clients and sometimes seeking ends and using means that they would not seek or use for themselves. Friends are permitted, even expected, to take each others' interests seriously and to give them more weight than they do those of other persons. Fried suggests that the attorney–client relationship is analogous to a one-way limited friendship in which the lawyer helps the client secure legal rights. The lawyer helps the client assert his or her autonomy or freedom within the bounds society permits. Others have suggested that the physician–patient relationship should similarly be viewed as a cooperative effort of friends or pals to deal with the patient's illness or injury.

The many dissimilarities between friendship and the professional–client relationship, however, destroy the analogy. First, as Fried recognizes, the professional–client relationship is chiefly in one direction; the professional has a concern for the client's interests but not vice versa. Second, friendship is usually between equals. Even in friendships between employer and employee, the employer's superiority in the office is changed to a position of equality in the bar for a drink. As the previous discussion of the contract model indicates, professionals and clients are not equals. Third, the affective commitment of friendship is usually lacking.[12] Professionals accept clients for a fee, not out of concern for individuals. Thus, one commentator concludes that "Fried has described the classical notion, not of friendship, but of prostitution."[13] Fourth, in the contemporary health care system, clients often meet physicians as strangers, not as friends.[14] This is especially true for treatment by specialists and in hospitals, but it also applies to family physicians. Due to geographic mobility, people often live in a community for only a few years, and family physicians do not have an opportunity to establish long-term relationships and come to know these patients well. Fifth, the notion of friendship hardly applies to corporations and government agencies as clients. Because the factual assumptions of this model are incorrect and the analogy supporting it is weak, its ethical implications are unfounded.

The friendship analogy is not needed to justify a professional paying special attention to a client's interests. The role of a professional is to provide services to clients, and the acceptance of a client is sufficient to justify the special attention. A barber who accepts a customer pays special attention to a customer's hair over that of others who need a haircut more. One need not postulate the barber as friend to justify this attention. It is presupposed by any system of hiring services.

Paternalism

Once one abandons models that assume the professional and client are equal and accepts that the professional is to some extent in a superior position to the client, one faces the problem of the proper extent of professional authority and responsibility in decision making. Parents have knowledge and experience that children lack, and it is often ethically appropriate for them to exercise their judgment on behalf of their children. Similarly, because a professional has knowledge and experience a client lacks and is hired to further the client's interests, perhaps the relationship should be viewed as one of paternalism.

Paternalism is a difficult concept to analyze. A person's conduct is paternalistic to the extent his or her reasons are to do something to or in behalf of another person for that person's well-being. What is done can be any of a number of things, from removing an appendix to preventing the person from taking drugs. One can also have a paternalistic reason for acting in behalf of a person—for example, filing a claim for food stamps or asserting a legal defense. The key element of paternalism derives from the agent, X, acting regardless of the person's, Y's, completely voluntary and in-formed consent. X's reason is that he or she judges the action to be for Y's well-being regardless of Y's consent to it. Y might be incapable of consent (a young child or psychiatric patient), Y might never have been asked, or Y might have refused to consent to the act.[15]

Conduct can be paternalistic even when Y in fact consents.[16] For example, if X is prepared to do something to Y regardless of Y's consent, then X's reason is paternalistic even if Y does consent. Parents frequently manipulate a child into assenting to actions, although they were prepared to do them without the child's assent. The key element is that X would have done the action, if possible, even if Y had not consented. Such claims are difficult to establish, but this difficulty is a practical problem and does not affect the conceptual matter. In manufacturing consent, information can be withheld, false information provided, or more emphasis placed on some facts than others. Professionals sometimes manufacture consent when action cannot legally be taken without client consent, such as accepting a settlement or performing an operation.

The concept of doing something to or in behalf of someone includes failure to do something. Suppose Y requests X to do something for him, but X refuses because she thinks it would be detrimental to Y's well-being; for example, a physician refuses to prescribe a tranquilizer for a patient. This also counts as doing something to or in behalf of a person without his consent; Y does not consent to the tranquilizers being withheld.

A voluminous literature exists concerning the justification of paternalism.[17] The brief discussion here will outline only the major arguments. Paternalism requires justification because it involves doing something to or in behalf of another person regardless of that person's consent. It thus denies people the freedom to make choices affecting their lives. They lack self-determination. As argued in Chapter 1, the loss of control over their own lives, especially to professionals, is one reason for people's concern about professional ethics. Thus, paternalism is of central importance in professional ethics.

Three arguments are often offered to justify paternalism.

1. The agent has superior knowledge as to what is in a person's best interest. Because the agent knows better than the person what is best, the agent is justified in acting to avoid significant harm to, or to procure a significant benefit for, the person. This argument is perhaps the central one in favor of paternalism by professionals. As noted before, a professional possesses a relevant knowledge the client lacks, so he or she is better able to perceive the advantages and disadvantages of alternative actions. Consequently, the professional rather than the client should have primary authority and responsibility for decisions.

2. The client is incapable of giving a sufficiently voluntary and informed consent. By "voluntary" is meant without duress, psychological compulsion, or other significant emotional or psychological disturbance. By "informed" is meant with appreciation of the consequences of a course of conduct and its alternatives. If people cannot give such consent, then their decisions will not adequately reflect their reasonable desires and will not be expressions of their "true selves." This argument, which in some respects is a subcase of the previous one, is also popular in the professions, especially medicine and social work. It is often claimed that people who are ill have a strong feeling of dependency, are worried by their illness, and are in a weakened state; so they lack their usual mental command. A somewhat similar argument can be made about lawyers' clients. If charged with a criminal offense, a person is fearful and disturbed. Even in civil suits, a client's emotions might be aroused, preventing an objective view of the situation.

3. A person will later come to agree that the decision was correct. Although the person does not now consent, he or she will later. For example, an unconscious accident victim with a broken limb will agree that a physician was correct to set the bone. Parents often require their children to do things, such as take music lessons, on the ground that later the children will be glad they did—"You'll thank me later!" An engineer might see a way to improve an agreed on rough

design to better serve a client's needs, although it involves a significant alteration from the rough design. She might make the change in the belief that the client will agree when he sees the completed design.

To decide whether these justifications support viewing the professional–client relationship as paternalistic, it is useful to consider when reasonable people would allow others to make decisions for them. First, a person might not wish to bother making decisions because the differences involved are trivial. For example, an executive authorizes a secretary to order any needed office supplies because the differences between brands of paper clips and so forth are not important. Second, the decisions might require knowledge or expertise a person does not possess. For example, an automobile mechanic knows whether a car's oil filter needs changing. One goes to a mechanic for knowledge and service. Third, a person might allow others to make judgments if he or she is or will be mentally incompetent. Some people voluntarily enter mental hospitals. One would, however, want some assurance in this and the previous case that the persons making judgments for one have values similar to one's own. For example, a woman might not want a physician to make decisions in childbirth if the physician believed in saving the fetus' life over the woman's. Often, even usually, one can assume that the values are those of reasonable or average persons in society.

The first of these reasons does not directly relate to the arguments for paternalism, but the second and third do relate to the first two arguments for paternalism. Reasonable persons would allow others to make decisions for them when they lack the capacity to make reasonable judgments. However, most clients do not have sufficiently impaired judgment reasonably to allow others to make important decisions for them. This incapacity argument has little or no plausibility for the common clients of architects, engineers, and accountants. Business and corporate clients are unlikely to have significantly impaired judgment, even if they are biased. Moreover, even with individuals, the view is not plausible for the common cases. A person who wants to purchase a house or make a will, or who has the flu or an infection, is rarely so distraught as to be unable to make reasonable decisions. Consequently, the argument from incapacity does not support adopting a paternalistic conception of the professional–client relationship for most cases, although it supports using that conception in special cases.

The first argument for paternalism, that from superior knowledge, fits with reasonable persons allowing others to make decisions when they lack knowledge. Moreover, clients go to professionals for their superior knowledge and skills; such knowledge and skill is a defining feature of a profession. However, many decisions require balancing legal or health concerns against other client interests. As many authors have noted, crucial professional decisions involve value choices.[18] They are not simple choices of technical means to ends, and even choices of means have a value component. Professionals have not had training in value choices. Even if they had, they might not know a client's value scheme sufficiently to determine what is best for him or her when everything is considered. An attorney might advise a client that he or she need not agree to such large alimony or child support payments, but the client might decide that for personal relations with the former spouse or the welfare of the children, the larger payments are best. Similarly, a physician can advise bed rest, but because of business interests, a client can decide his or her overall interests are best promoted by continuing to work on certain matters. The client might especially need the income or be on the verge of completing a business deal that will earn a promotion. Social workers are often distraught to learn that "bag ladies" and other "derelicts" prefer their life to one with the benefits that a social worker can provide. Physicians sometimes fail to realize that a patient's other concerns, even a vacation trip with the family, can precede health. They write and speak of the problem of patient noncompliance just as parents speak of noncompliance by children. Yet one does not have everything when one has health. Similarly, a client might want an engineering or architectural design to use one type of construction rather than another because its subsidiary supplies such materials.

Although a professional and client are not equals, sufficient client competence exists to undermine the paternalistic model as appropriate for their usual relationship. Clients can exercise judgment over many aspects of professional services. If they lack information to make decisions, professionals can provide it. Sometimes professionals argue that clients can never have the information they have. This is true, but not directly to the point. Much of the information professionals have is irrelevant to decisions that significantly affect client values. The precise name of a disease and its manner of action are not relevant to deciding between two alternative drug therapies, but the fact that one drug reduces alertness is. Similarly, clients of engineers do not need to know the full weight a structure will bear, only that it is more than sufficient for all anticipated stress. To deny clients authority and responsibility by adopting the paternalistic model is to deny them the freedom to direct their own lives. Clients are not capable of determining the precise nature of their problem, or of knowing the alternative courses of action and predicting their consequences or carrying them out on their own. They need and want the technical expertise of a professional to do so. However, they are capable of making reasonable choices among options on the basis of their total values. They need professionals' information to make wise choices to accomplish their purposes.

Finally, when the professional–client relationship is conducted on the paternalistic model, client outcomes are not as good as when the client has a more active role. Douglas E. Rosenthal studied settlement awards in personal injury cases.[19] The actual awards received were compared to an expert panel's judgments of the worth of the claims. The less the client participated in the case by not expressing wants, seeking information from the lawyers, and so on, the more the awards fell short of the panel's estimates of the worth of claims. Other studies have found that in medical care, disclosure of information (and consequent more informed participation of clients) also beneficially affects outcomes.[20] Not only does the paternalistic model sacrifice client freedom and autonomy, but as a result, client values and interests are also often sacrificed.

Fiduciary

As a general characterization of what the professional–client relationship should be, one needs a concept in which the professional's superior knowledge is recognized, but the client retains a significant authority and responsibility in decision making. The law uses such a conception to characterize most professional–client relationships, namely, that of a fiduciary. In a fiduciary relationship, both parties are responsible and their judgments given consideration. Because one party is in a more advantageous position, he or she has special obligations to the other. The weaker party depends on the stronger in ways in which the other does not and so must *trust* the stronger party.

In the fiduciary model, a client has more authority and responsibility in decision making than in the paternalistic model. A client's consent and judgment are required, and he or she participates in the decision-making process. But clients depend on the professional for much of the information upon which they give or withhold their consent. The term *consents* (the client consents) rather than *decides* (the client decides) indicates that it is the professional's role to propose courses of action. It is not the conception of two people contributing equally to the formulation of plans, whether or not dealing at arm's length. Rather, the professional supplies the ideas and information, and the client agrees or not. For the process to work, the client must trust the professional to analyze accurately the problem, canvass the feasible alternatives, know as well as one can their likely consequences, fully convey this information to the client, perhaps make a recommendation, and work honestly and loyally for the client to effectuate the chosen alternative. In short, the client must rely on the professional to use his or her knowledge and ability in the client's interests. Because the client cannot check most of the work of the professional or the information supplied, the professional has special obligations to the client to ensure that the trust and reliance are justified.

This is not to suggest that the professional simply presents an overall recommendation for a client's acceptance or rejection. Rather, a client's interests can be affected by various aspects of a professional's work, so the client should be consulted at various times. The extent of appropriate client participation and decision making can be determined by advertence to the reasons for allowing others to make decisions for one. Professionals do not have expertise in a client's values or in making value choices. Their superior knowledge and expertise do not qualify them to make value choices significantly affecting a client's life plans or style. However, they do have knowledge of technical matters. A patient will certainly let a physician determine the dosage of medicines. A client can reasonably allow an engineer to determine the general specifications of materials for a job. A lawyer may decide whether to stipulate facts or object to testimony.[21] Clients allow professionals to make these judgments because the effects on their values are small, and they do not wish to be bothered. In short, client consent and involvement are not necessary when (1) the value effect is not significant or (2) the matter is a technical one, and the professional's values do not differ significantly from the client's.

The literature on medical ethics is replete with discussions of informed consent, and it has been taken up as important for other professions such as engineering and law.[22] The legal doctrine of informed consent developed from medical malpractice and experimentation. Informed consent is legally necessary before one can perform procedures on a patient. However, informed consent has a strong ethical basis in protecting a client's self-determination. The elements of informed consent are (1) a capacity to understand and choose; (2) an explanation of a proposed course of action, its alternatives, and the risks and potential benefits of each option; and (3) free and voluntary consent.

Informed consent is not itself a model of the professional–client relationship. Instead, it is a method or technique to guard against paternalism and promote shared decision making. Doubt exists about the extent to which it has actually promoted these goals in medicine. The process can become a ritual of securing a patient's signature on a form. One might think that informed consent implies a contractual model of the professional–client relationship. However, as previously suggested, it better fits the fiduciary model. The client consents, agrees to, or accepts the professional's recommendation and explanation of it. The client does not participate in formulating a plan of action or developing alternatives and determining the risks and benefits of each. Nonetheless, the client's self-determination is retained because the client's consent is necessary.

The appropriate ethical conception of the professional–client relationship is one that allows clients as much freedom to determine how their life is affected as is reasonably warranted on the basis of their ability to make decisions. In most dealings of business and corporate clients with accountants, architects, engineers, and lawyers, the relationship is close to a contract between equals or even agency. As clients have less knowledge about the subject matter for which the professional is engaged, the special obligations of the professional in the fiduciary model become more significant. The professional must assume more responsibility for formulating plans, presenting their advantages and disadvantages, and making recommendations. Because of the increased reliance on the professional, he or she must take special care to be worthy of client trust. Thus, although the fiduciary model is appropriate throughout the range of competent clients and services, the less a client's knowledge and capacity to understand, the greater the professional's responsibilities to the client.

Finally, some clients are not competent to make decisions. In this case, the paternalistic model becomes appropriate. These cases of an incompetent client will almost always be restricted to members of the legal, teaching, social work, and health professions. Even then it does not follow that the professional should make the decisions. If a client is incompetent, a legal guardian exists or should often be appointed to make decisions. When there is a guardian, the professional has a fiduciary relationship to him or her. Consequently, the appropriate occasions for professionals to adopt a paternalistic role are restricted to those in which a client is incompetent and a guardian does not exist or the law authorizes it.

OBLIGATIONS OF TRUSTWORTHINESS

The fiduciary ethical model of the professional–client relationship emphasizes a professional's special obligations to be worthy of client trust. Only if a professional deserves a client's initial and continuing trust has the ideal of the fiduciary conception been achieved. As should be clear from the rejection of paternalism, the sense of trust involved is not that of trusting a professional to make decisions for one.[23] One may always pertinently ask, "Trust to do what?" The answer is trust to fulfill the functions that the average client wants and for which a professional is hired. A client wants a professional to use expertise to analyze the problem, formulate alternative plans or courses of action, determine their probable consequences, make recommendations, or carry out certain activities (audit, surgery) in his or her behalf. A professional's obligations to a client are those necessary to deserve the client's trust that these activities will be performed in a manner to promote the client's interests—including the freedom to make decisions regarding his or her life.

This section presents seven general obligations that professionals must fulfill to be deserving of client trust. The criterion for determining professionals' obligations to clients is the standard of trustworthiness, of being worthy of a client's trust. Each obligation can then be justified as one that a reasonable client with ethical purposes would want a professional to fulfill. No hard claim is made that the obligations presented are exhaustive or mutually exclusive (indeed, one has been added in this edition).[24] Although they seem to be distinct, some (for example, honesty and candor) might be combined. Perhaps others should be added. The fiduciary model's ideal of a professional being worthy of a client's trust provides the criterion for determining which obligations should be included or excluded. In short, although no proof is given for the completeness of the obligations presented here, a principle of inclusion and exclusion is used. Of course, one might disagree with the principle.

The seven obligations of professionals to clients can be stated as standards of a good or trustworthy professional. A good professional is honest, candid, competent, diligent, loyal, fair, and discrete. These are virtues of a trustworthy professional. However, these obligations can also be viewed as norms of conduct. As such, they present certain responsibilities. Possession of the character traits and fulfillment of the responsibilities are not the same. A generally candid and discrete professional can fail to be so in some situations and thus violate responsibilities. Contrarily, a professional who is not generally a candid and discrete person has professional responsibilities to be candid with clients and not to reveal confidences. Certain duties require specific conduct to fulfill these responsibilities. However, no list of duties fully specifies any of the responsibilities. Duties are classified under one responsibility, but they are often partially supported or limited by others.

Honesty

Professionals should be honest with their clients. By definition, a dishonest professional is not worthy of a client's trust. Because the obligation of honesty is to the client, it does not directly require honesty toward others. Professionals can be honest with their clients and in acting in their behalf be dishonest with others. If so, they do not violate a responsibility to their client but one to others. Nevertheless, in two ways they can weaken a client's reasons for trust. First, their clients can be tainted by their dishonesty toward others in the clients' behalf. To the extent a professional is an agent of a client, his or her conduct reflects on the client. How much it appropriately does so depends on the extent of the client's knowledge and authorization of the professional's dishonesty. Second, honesty is not an easily divisible character trait. One can be dishonest in certain respects, such as not putting money in parking meters, and still be honest in others. Nonetheless, one who acts dishonestly toward others in behalf of a client is more likely to be dishonest with a client. If dishonesty toward others increases the likelihood a professional will be dishonest toward a client, it renders him or her less worthy of the client's trust.

One duty of honesty is not to steal from a client. A clear form of professional theft is an accountant or lawyer appropriating client funds for personal use. This is one of the more frequent forms of lawyer dishonesty toward a client, and the bar has not generally been very active in punishing such dishonesty. Disciplinary committees rarely act against a lawyer who returns embezzled funds.[25] This lack of action is both detrimental to the status of the bar and prejudicial to future clients of that lawyer. To make restitution, the lawyer might use funds entrusted to him or her by other clients or become financially hard pressed and so more tempted to appropriate the funds of future clients. Professors can also steal from students, especially graduate students, by publishing their papers as their own or failing to give them credit for work on research projects.

Such blatant theft is often not possible for professionals. Physicians rarely handle funds of patients. Nonetheless, forms of theft such as kickbacks are open to them as well as to engineers and other professionals. A subtle form of professional theft is the provision of unneeded services. When physicians perform unnecessary tests or surgery, they are being dishonest with their clients.[26] Professionals can also be dishonest in not providing services. If professionals are compensated by a fixed fee for a problem, such as drafting a will or treating an illness, they may have an incentive to provide less than full care to reduce their costs.[27] Of course, determining what services are needed is difficult. It would be best to cease speaking of needed and unneeded services, because the question usually is how helpful a service might be. A title search going back fifty years is adequate for most purposes, but better protection is provided by one going back seventy-five years. Similarly, some engineers' or physicians' tests are apt to be more useful than others. How far professionals go on these matters depends on their attitudes toward risk and other factors. If they believe that a service is probably of little value but they might as well perform it and be safe because the client can pay, dishonesty is involved. As a check on motives, professionals can ask themselves, "Would I want it done were I in the client's (financial) position?"

Candor

Truthfulness is probably a subclass of honesty. One can be truthful but dishonest; a person could steal or cheat but admit it truthfully when asked. Three reasons exist for treating candor separately from honesty. First, dishonesty is commonly associated with promoting one's self-interest, especially financial interests. Lying by professionals is often not for the professionals' own benefit but in what they believe to be their clients' interest. Second, candor goes beyond truthfulness by requiring full disclosure. One can avoid lying by keeping silent, but in so doing, one fails to be candid. Not all instances of failing to provide information are readily considered dishonesty. Third, the responsibility of candor is so important to professional ethics that it deserves separate treatment.

The responsibility of candor is at the heart of the professional–client relationship. If the relationship is fiduciary rather than paternalistic, then the professional respects the judgments of the client and acts on important matters only with the client's consent. A client might consent to a professional undertaking a range of activities in her behalf; yet this range is limited. She might consent to a professional making judgments in her behalf if the matters do not significantly affect her values or are primarily technical, such as the size of heat ducts adequately to heat a structure. However, because the relationship is a fiduciary one, the client also trusts the professional to consult her and respect her informed judgment in all important decisions. A client enters the relationship to receive information from the professional, so if the professional withholds information he has reason to believe would influence his client's judgment, he alters the agreement. He manipulates the client's information so that the client's judgments conform to his. The professional thus acts on his judgment of the client's interest regardless of the client's informed and free consent, and the relationship is paternalistic.

One form of such manipulation is what lawyers call "cooling the client out."[28] For example, suppose that in negotiating a settlement, the other side offers $5,000. The attorney thinks $5,000 is a reasonable amount, but the client unreasonably expects $10,000. She tells the client that the offer was for $3,000 but that she might be able to get $4,500. In a few days, the attorney phones back and says she managed to bargain the opposing party into offering $5,000 and recommends that the client accept. This example is a clear case of paternalistic manipulation of information to obtain client consent. The motivation for such cooling out is not always so paternalistic; the attorney might desire to reach an early settlement simply to obtain a sizeable fee for little work.

This example involves a professional deliberately lying to a client. A lie can be distinguished from withholding information. The paradigm of a lie is intentionally telling someone what one believes to be false. The intent is to deceive. Withholding information need not be intended to deceive, to produce a false belief, but merely to keep a person in ignorance. The conceptually difficult cases are those in which information is withheld to create a misapprehension on the part of another—for example, not indicating by a note to a financial statement that certain property has greatly depreciated in value. Although these cases are conceptually difficult, they are not morally difficult. The wrong in lying is the intent to deceive. From a client's point of view, she has hired the professional for information on which she can rely, and deceit defeats that purpose whether it results from false information or the mere withholding of it.

The element of trust involved in the professional–client relationship makes truthfulness even more important than in relationships that do not involve such trust.[29] If one purchases a used car, although more truthfulness is now legally required than previously, one does not put faith in all the dealer's claims. In a relationship involving trust, one is more apt to do so. Therefore, a lie is apt to result in greater harm. Moreover, because the relationship itself is one of trust, and a lie indicates that the other person cannot be trusted, the relationship is likely to be irreparably destroyed.

Few people have ever claimed that lying can never be justified. If a great harm might befall a person or others as a result of a truthful disclosure, then lack of candor is justifiable. Although a lie is prima facie wrong, it can be the lesser of two evils.

Physicians frequently believe that an obligation not to harm their patients outweighs that of full disclosure. The argument for nondisclosure is that the information would be harmful to the patient's mental well-being. A serious problem affects this argument. To use the traditional principle that a physician's first obligation is to do no harm merely moves the issue back one step. The issue then becomes whether the psychological distress is harm. Although a patient could be psychologically depressed by the information, he could also want to know. To determine whether the distress is greater than the benefits of being informed involves a complex value judgment for which physicians have not been trained and for which they frequently lack relevant information. An overwhelming percentage of the population believes people have a right to all available medical information, although over half thinks some patients should be told less than others.[30] Nonetheless, 7 percent of physicians report that they withhold information about diagnosis once a week, and 6 percent report weekly withholding of treatment risks.[31]

Oddly, physicians usually discuss withheld information with family members, and almost a majority of the population thinks it appropriate to withhold information from a patient if the family so requests. In Ontario, it is technically illegal to disclose information to others, including family, without a patient's consent.[32] The decision about permitting such family involvement might seem to be a choice between radical individualism and recognition of the family's role in ordinary life. However, if a patient wants a physician to let the family decide whether she is given information or whether the family is told withheld information, she could usually so indicate. A patient who really wants information might decide not to allow the family to have it withheld from her. She might also request that if information is withheld from her, the family be told in the hope that a family member will tell her.

A likely example of justifiable nondisclosure is the following. A forty-year-old divorced woman with two children has a vision impairment that is a somatic reaction to stress resulting from her divorce, a move to a different community, and a new job. In cases like this, vision does not usually improve. If she is told the impairment is probably permanent, her stress will be increased, the chances of recovery decreased, and further impairment made more likely. An ophthalmologist delays informing the patient of the prognosis until he is fairly sure no improvement is possible.

Lack of candor is justifiable in this case in part because disclosure directly affects the cause of the patient's disease. In contrast, mental stress is not the cause of cancer, and untoward results of disclosure depend on rash conduct by the patient. In short, in the ophthalmologist's case, harm is more certain because of the more direct causal link between the information and the anticipated harm. Moreover, the information is not permanently withheld. In this case, a responsibility of candor to the patient is overridden by an obligation to protect and promote the patient's health.

Failure fully to disclose information also occurs in legal practice. In interviewing a client, a lawyer wants to determine the facts so that she can construct the client's case. A client asks for specific information about the legal status of certain evidence. Informing the client of the legal significance might encourage him to "remember" the facts in a way most favorable to his side. For example, suppose a man is charged with murder, and the weapon was his pocket knife. In an interview, an attorney asks the client whether he usually carried the pocket knife. Suppose the client asks, "What difference does it make?" The significance is that if the man did not usually carry the knife, then his having it would be evidence of premeditation; if he usually did carry it, then it is more plausible that he acted in a fit of passion and is guilty only of manslaughter. If the attorney provides this information before the client answers, the client is not likely to say he went and got the knife to have with him on this specific occasion.

Similar situations arise in other professions. For example, a university professor takes a leave of absence to teach at another university for a year as a visiting professor.

If she wants a regular position there, she can have it. She consults a tax accountant to see whether she can claim her expenses for the year as a tax deduction for a job away from home for less than a year. The accountant asks about her intention to remain, and the professor asks why he wants to know. The reason is that if she intends to return, then the expenses are deductible, but if she intends to remain, they are not. If the accountant explains this to the professor, she will amost certainly say she intends to return and generally act in ways to support this claim, even if she has practically made up her mind to accept the new position.

In such situations, failure to inform a client of the significance of facts would not be justified by some other obligation to the client. Instead, it would be by an obligation to others—the government and society. What is at stake is encouraging or contributing to fraud. Withholding the information is not paternalistic, for it is not for the client's benefit but to prevent harm to society.

Failure to explain the significance of such facts to a client might damage the professional–client relationship. A client could feel his attorney or accountant is not being open and is letting the client do himself in. Part of this effect on the trust relation can be mitigated. Unlike a physician's refusal to inform cancer patients of their diagnosis, a lawyer or accountant can explain the significance of facts after she gets the client's statement. She need not withhold the information forever. If providing the information is likely to encourage the client to engage in unethical conduct, a professional is not obligated to disclose the information at that time. These cases must be distinguished from those in which the client simply wants to know the consequences of two alternatives to decide what to do. The tax accountant example borders on a case of that sort, although it is unlikely the professor would refuse a new job simply for the tax considerations.

How information is conveyed is crucial.[33] A typical student complaint is that in lectures professors use words students do not understand and "go too fast." One reason for the difficult words is that most disciplines and professions have a specialized vocabulary. Professionals are familiar with it and use it without thinking. (You have undoubtedly encountered some unexplained philosophical, legal, or medical terminology in this book.) Students cannot comprehend information if they cannot understand the language in which it is presented. Professionals should generally view their communications with clients as teaching. The point is not merely to convey the literal truth, but to produce understanding and appreciation of its significance. Finally, the information can be conveyed in a sympathetic manner or brutally. For example, one could say, "Professor Bayles, an uninterrupted hour of your lecturing bores me to death" or "Professor Bayles, even the most avid student of professional ethics on amphetamines might nod off during your lecture without a break for some humor and time to assimilate the valuable information."

Competence

Although it is not a moral virtue, competence is probably the most crucial of a professional's characteristics. Professionals have an ethical responsibility not to hold themselves out to do or accept work they are not competent to handle. No matter how honest, candid, diligent, loyal, fair, and discreet professionals are, if they are incompetent, they are unworthy of trust, for they cannot do well the job for which they are hired. Of course, clients' beliefs about professionals' competence might not be correct. Reputations for competence, like all reputations, are fickle. Very competent professionals might not have a reputation among potential clients for competence, and incompetent ones might. Generally, the most reliable judgements of competence are those of other professionals.

Almost all professional codes require that professionals undertake only that work they are competent to perform and continue learning to keep abreast of the field.[34] Many professions do not require periodic examinations of competence. When a professional is licensed to practice, the license is good for life unless disciplinary action is taken. A professional's knowledge that was current forty-five years ago is not so now.[35] The pressures of professional work make it very difficult to keep up in a field, especially one in which changes are occurring rapidly. Professionals would be hard pressed to read the flood of periodicals even if that was all they did. Because almost all professionals specialize, they can realistically be expected to remain current in their specialty, whether ceramic engineering, tort law, or pediatrics.

How do professionals know when a client's difficulty is beyond the limits of their expertise? This problem is especially acute when specialization is not certified or persons without a specialty or certification are not prohibited from providing services. For example, general medical practitioners are usually legally free to perform surgery, and many of them do relatively simple procedures. Should a civil engineer undertake the design of a building's electrical system, or should she have an electrical engineer as a consultant? Merely stating that a professional should associate another when indicated or when she is not competent in an area does not settle the problem.[36] Clients are rarely capable of determining when a specialist (or a different type of specialist from the one they consult) is needed in borderline cases. They must trust professionals not to undertake work they are not competent to perform. However, as noted in discussing fee splitting in the previous chapter, professionals have a financial reason for handling cases themselves if possible.

To obtain informed consent, professionals must explain the available alternatives. Because many professionals, especially in health care, have limited domains of competence that overlap those of other professionals, the issues of competence and disclosure of alternatives are important. To what extent, if any, are professionals obligated to be aware of and disclose alternatives available from other professionals? Surgical versus medical treatment of angina (heart pains) is an example. Should an internist note that surgery is available and as successful as medical treatment? A similar point applies to psychotherapy. Some problems that psychotherapists treat (say, depression) are also amenable to other forms of treatment (say, drug therapy). Some psychotherapists are not licensed to prescribe drugs. Should they advise clients that effective, perhaps more effective, drug treatments are available from other professionals?

Three possible claims might be made at this point. (1) Professionals need not present alternatives available from other types of professionals even if they know of them. (2) If they know of alternatives available from other types of professionals, then they ought to present them to clients. (3) Not only should professionals present alternatives available from other types of professionals, but they have an obligation to know of these alternatives.

Position (3) seems the best one. First, it better accords with clients' limited knowledge. It does not assume that a client prefers treatment of the type offered by the professional consulted for all problems, nor does it assume a client knows the exact nature of the problem before seeing the professional. Second, it is plausibly required by informed consent. Consent is not informed if it is based on only some of the alternatives. One does not make an informed decision to purchase an automobile if one does not know that the dealer across the street offers a comparable automobile for $1,000 less. Although consumers have the burden of discovering alternatives in purchasing automobiles, that burden should not rest on them in professional services. Because professionals have special expertise not widely available, clients cannot easily discover alternatives.

Third, the burden on professionals need not be overwhelming. They need not know everything about all other related professions. They need only know about services available for problems that fall within their domain of expertise. Indeed, a psychotherapist who treats depression should, it seems, keep up with the general literature about depression. Moreover, the professional need not know how to do the alternative treatments or their underlying theory, only that they are available and effective. Consequently, the burden does not appear overwhelming. The duty to know of alternative services by other professions has been recognized in at least one ethical code.[37]

Another aspect of the problem is that although professionals are not very familiar with an area, they can often learn enough to handle a case. Professionals frequently have to research a particular problem. If they devote suffcient time to a problem outside their usual practice, they can often do a competent job. However, should a client have to pay for a professional's education, especially if he could obtain a trained specialist for less? At this point, at least the responsibility of candor applies, and the professional should explain the situation to the client. It is the client's money and work to be done, so he should decide the question.

Diligence

A responsibility of diligence or zeal is closely related to, but distinct from, that of competence. One can be supremely competent but not diligent, or diligent and zealous but incompetent. A person who is not diligent can neglect significant matters and turn out a substandard "product." A poorly graded paper, mistaken diagnosis, or badly designed project can result from carelessness or incompetence. Thus, these two considerations are sometimes confused or lumped together.[38] A client is often unable to determine whether the unsatisfactory result in her case was due to neglect, incompetence, or unavoidable error.

A responsibility of diligence clearly follows from the criterion that a professional be worthy of a client's trust. A reasonable person would not entrust his important affairs to someone he thought would not actively and carefully handle them. Diligence is especially necessary when time is important, as it often is in professional activities. Many legal clients have lost cases because their lawyers failed to file claims in time, respond to a complaint, or appear in court. Similarly, if one is ill, one wants diagnosis and treatment sooner rather than later. Also, clients often want engineers to design projects quickly, and many wait until the last minute before taking their income tax to an accountant. Journalists almost always work under severe deadlines. Diligence does not require immediate action but allows for reasonable delays, as for test results or space on a court docket.

Professionals perhaps violate the responsibility of diligence more frequently than any other. Most complaints against lawyers are for neglect.[39] And whether justified or not, one of the most common complaints about physicians is that they do not devote adequate time to patients. One may wonder how many missed diagnoses are due to physicians' lack of diligence in ruling out less likely but more serious diseases. Engineers sometimes consider a problem to be a standard one without thoroughly checking it, and college teachers often fail to prepare for class and to return student papers promptly.

A common complaint by, and defense of, professionals is that they lack time to provide each client the attention they think ideal. This defense is questionable. Self-employed professionals can usually make time. It only requires saying "No!" when asked to undertake yet another task. If they really are too busy to devote adequate time to clients, they can reduce the number of clients or other activities. This will result in decreased income if the professional is paid on a fee-for-service or capitation basis. But, if the professional does not provide diligent service, the fees are not justified anyway and violate the responsibility of honesty.

One can always devote more time to a specific client, but beyond some point, further consideration and attention are unlikely to be justified by expectable benefits. Hence, some professionals' complaints about lack of time are simply claims that further time or attention to a case would not be justified. Is this decision one for the professional or the client? Because it is essentially a value choice of possible benefits and burdens to the client, the fiduciary model implies that the decision is that of the client. At least when hired on a fee-for-service basis, a professional should make clear to a client that further time could be spent on research or examination, but that it would cost a certain amount and have such and such a likelihood of uncovering anything significant. Because the client bears the risks, she should have the option of deciding whether the extra assurance is worthwhile.

Some physicians practice "defensive medicine" and perform tests not likely to provide useful information simply to protect themselves against possible malpractice suits. Were a physician to put the choice of a further test clearly to a patient, and she declined, the physician would also have a good legal defense. "Defensive medicine" could thus be based on talking to patients, which would both be less expensive and fulfill the responsibility of full disclosure.

In one type of situation, it is justifiable to provide a client less attention than a professional considers ideal. If an insufficient number of professionals is available to provide appropriate attention to each client without some potential clients being denied service, then a professional must balance an obligation to provide diligent service with that to make services equally available. This consideration primarily applies in law, education, and medicine, for people have positive rights to such services. In the other professions, client's rights are only to equal availability, and this is not denied if services are provided on a first-come, first-served basis. Physicians in rural communities and emergency rooms and lawyers in public defenders' offices are often in such situations. The issue is one of balancing obligations to clients and to society. The time and attention devoted to the client is less than might be appropriate if conditions of practice were more adequate, but they are appropriate for the context. The professional rather than the client should judge the adequacy of time in this context. Otherwise, self-interested clients might deprive many others of scarce resources. However, professionals must take care that their motivation is in fact making services available rather than ensuring their own pecuniary well-being.

Employed professionals, such as nurses and social workers, often lack time to provide the services they think ideal and must often balance services for one client with those for others. They do not determine their client loads, so they cannot simply take on fewer clients. The problem is often acute in social work agencies and hospitals. If the projected nursing shortage occurs, it will become worse. In such a situation, services should be allocated on the basis of their importance to clients. Social workers can, to some extent, simply provide less assistance and investigate less thoroughly. Nurses, however, often have prescribed services to render—IVs to start and so on. Thus, they cannot simply perform fewer services without threat of dismissal. A limit exists as to how much they can do, and the pressure to get it done is increasing the strain on nurses. Consequently, more are leaving professional practice, increasing the shortage and strain on those who remain.

Loyalty

Clients ask professionals to act in behalf of some of their interests. A professional who disloyally "sells out" a client's interests is not worthy of the client's trust. There are limits to the loyalty clients can properly expect from professionals. They may expect only a loyalty that does not violate a professional's other responsibilities. A client is certainly not justified in expecting a professional to commit illegal acts; the value of protection from injury by others in society would be greatly infringed were this allowed. The most difficult problem is determining the boundaries between a professional's loyalty to a client and other responsibilities. Sometimes other responsibilities must give way to loyalty to clients, and sometimes loyalty must give way to other responsibilities. (These conflicts are discussed in detail in Chapters 5 and 6.) Factors other than responsibilities can affect a professional's loyalty to a client, and a major part of some professional codes of ethics pertains to these factors.

The responsibility of loyalty faces conflict from a professional's self-interest and the interest of third parties. One largely unavoidable conflict is that between a professional's interests in income and leisure and a client's interest in services. If professionals are paid on a fee-for-service basis, then they have an interest in providing services. Higher rates of elective surgery occur when physicians are paid on a fee-for-service rather than on another basis. Rarely would a physician consciously think that although surgery is not indicated, he or she needs some extra money for a new car. Instead, self-interests unconsciously affect physicians' perceptions of patients' needs. A similar consideration applies to engineers designing projects and being paid a percentage of the project costs. The more expensive the project, the greater their fee.

Alternative systems of paying professionals do not remove the conflict but merely reverse the effect on the client. In a capitation payment system, professionals have an interest in having as many clients as possible to maximize their income and in performing as few services as possible to minimize their costs. On a salary system or a flat fee for a case, professionals receive the same income no matter the number of clients or services performed, so they have an interest in minimizing clients or services. These payment systems thus encourage professionals not to perform useful services. Shortages of professionals or clients have effects similar to these payment systems.

This fundamental conflict of interest between professional and client cannot be removed. It is inherent in the professional–client relationship. At best, it can be minimized by making a firm agreement with the client after initial consultation as to what will be done and its total cost. Such an arrangement is possible only for cases in which the total professional work can be reasonably estimated. Although engineers, accountants, lawyers, surgeons, and dentists perform much work on this basis, physicians rarely do so. However, it has been suggested that to contain medical costs, physicians be compensated a flat amount for diagnostic categories, by MDDRGs. For example, a standard fee for a bronchial infection might cover any needed office visits and possible complications. Many physicians and medical ethicists are concerned that this would give physicians incentives to provide fewer services than needed. Fee-for-service payment, however, gives incentives to provide more services than needed. Nor can one claim that providing fewer services risks harm, and providing more does not. Extra diagnostic tests and so on do pose risks of harm, as though paying for unuseful services were not itself a harm.

An important identity of professional and client interests also exists. Generally, in doing a good job for their clients, professionals enhance their professional reputation.[40] One must distinguish between professional and nonprofessional reputation, especially for lawyers. A lawyer who does an excellent job for an unpopular client can lose her reputation in the community while enhancing her reputation among other lawyers. The public does not view favorably lawyers who skillfully win cases for unpopular clients. This consideration also applies to some other professionals; for example, nuclear engineers are not very popular with a significant segment of the public.

The relationship between professional reputation and doing a good job for clients is complicated for teachers.[41] Popularity with students is not clearly related to effective learning. Often one can look back on high school teachers and discover that one learned more from teachers one did not like than from those one did. Similarly, at one university in a large math course, there was reportedly an inverse correlation between student evaluations of teachers and how well students did on the common final exam. That is, students of teachers with better student evaluations did worse than those of teachers with poorer ones. However, judgments of other faculty about a professor's ability are often not good indicators either. Faculty are likely to judge one another on knowledge of the discipline and research rather than on teaching. Moreover, often due to mistaken notions of professional independence and academic freedom, they do not sit in on classes by other faculty and so lack an important basis for judging their teaching.

Besides the irremovable general conflict of interest between professional and client with respect to payment, conflicts of interest are possible with respect to specific professionals, clients, and problems. Such conflicts can usually be avoided or removed. Many professional obligations in codes are aimed at avoiding these conflicts.

The key element of loyalty to a client in specific matters is independence of judgment. Most professional codes mention such a responsibility.[42] The reasons for the obligation of independence of judgment go to the nature of professionalism and the professional–client relationship. Professionals should apply their special skills and knowledge to make judgments on which their clients can rely in protecting or promoting their interests. If these judgments are biased, clients do not receive the type of advice and assistance they are seeking, and actions taken on the basis of such judgments might be detrimental.

Independence of judgment can be lost or interfered with in many ways. An important but often ignored way, especially for psychiatrists, psychologists, social workers, physicians and lawyers, is overidentification with a client. Beginning professionals especially have this difficulty. Overidentification with a client's interests can lead to mistaken judgments and actions that jeopardize the client's and even the professional's interests and violate responsibilities to others. An example of a lawyer indicates the problem.[43] An unemployed client had bought a used car that needed many repairs. After making some free repairs, the dealer charged $400 for the last repairs and refused to release the car until the client paid. The client had no money to pay the bill. Pretending to be a prospective buyer, her lawyer went to the dealer and asked to take the car for a test drive. He then drove the car to the client's house and gave her the keys.

The objectivity that a professional must maintain frequently leads clients, especially of physicians, to view the professional as coldhearted and uncaring. Sometimes these opinions rest not on the substance of professionals' attitudes but on the manner in which they provide advice and comments. Sometimes an attitude of unconcern is necessary for professionals to maintain their own mental stability; for example, pediatric oncologists (physicians specializing in the treatment of cancer in children) simply could not bear the psychological pain if they identified with their patients. Physicians' concern with "bedside manner" indicates awareness of the impression of callousness they can give patients. Despite this aspect of style, however, caring requires a nonidentification of interests to retain independent, objective judgment.[44]

A professional's personal interests can also lead to a lack of independent judgment. For example, a lawyer could own property affected by a client's proposed actions or could be likely to be called as a witness. An accountant could own stock in a client's competitor. A physician could wish to conduct an experiment for which the patient is a potential subject or could have developed a technique or therapy he or she wants to promote. Requirements of informed consent of experimental subjects are designed to ensure that the client is aware of these interests and agrees to participate. Fewer conflicts arise for physicians than for other professionals because a patient's health does not usually adversely affect the interests of others, including physicians.

However, if patients have contagious diseases, treating them risks the health of medical personnel. The widespread fear of AIDS has led some nurses to refuse to care for patients with the disease. Medical residents use a variety of means to avoid caring for such patients, from dumping them on other residents, to not seeing them on rounds, to not applying to hospitals likely to have them.[45] The cause is not simply fear of catching the disease, but the strain of caring for patients for which relatively little can be done. The reaction is understandable, even though partly based on ignorance; yet it does violate the responsibility of loyalty. It also perhaps reflects the success of medicine. Although physicians and nurses today are rarely exposed to such diseases, in the early part of this century, they constantly faced dangers from tuberculosis, yellow fever, and a variety of other diseases, in particular, hepatitis.

At the very least, professionals have a duty to inform clients of their own personal interests that might affect their independence of judgment. Clients trust professionals to exercise independent judgment, and they should be aware of anything that might adversely affect the basis for this trust. Professionals have a responsibility to minimize the influence of such interests on their professional judgments.

One can question whether client consent is sufficient to permit a professional–client relationship in such cases.[46] Given the superior knowledge of professionals, the opportunities for even unintentional exploitation are great. Perhaps clients should be protected from these risks regardless of their consent. Such a policy would not be straightforward paternalism, for the fear is that clients will be misled into consenting to professional employment and thus be exploited or defrauded. Although client freedom of choice is desirable, freedom not based on proper information is a mirage. Client consent is not a sufficient justification, but it is necessary. If the conflict is not great or is only potential, and the client consents, then it is permissible for a professional to undertake a case.

Business dealings between professionals and clients other than for professional services can affect loyalty. For example, an engineer might own a supply company for materials the client uses, and a new production design might eliminate the need for those particular materials. If a lawyer sold her house to her client, it would be unwise for the lawyer to do the title search and contract for the client. Ideally, if everything were fully explained, a mutually satisfactory agreement might be reached. However, should any difficulty arise, the pressure on the lawyer or engineer to conceal information from the client or to misadvise him is nearly overwhelming. The previous argument against the sufficiency of consent applies even more strongly here.

A second factor affecting independence of judgment and loyalty to a client is a conflict of interest between clients. This conflict of interest creates a conflict between the professional's obligations of loyalty to the different clients.[47] This problem can be divided into two types of cases—those in which two or more clients are involved in the same transaction or activity and those in which they are involved in separate transactions or activities. The first type of case is the most obvious. In general, a lawyer ought not represent clients whose interests might conflict. Even though no conflict exists when two or more clients ask for representation, if their interests in the case might conflict, a lawyer ought not represent both. Two persons charged with committing the same crime might believe their interests do not conflict, but the defense of one could be contrary to defense of the other. A husband and wife purchasing a house probably do not have interests that would conflict in the particular case, although a conflict might arise as to whether ownership should be joint or in only one of their names.

In a divorce, a husband and wife do clearly have conflicting interests. As a general policy, conscientious lawyers avoided representing both spouses in fault divorces. Although no-fault lessens conflicts, interests in the property settlement and child custody can conflict significantly. Nonetheless, to avoid the costs of two lawyers, a couple might decide to permit one lawyer to handle their divorce. To prohibit such an arrangement would unduly limit the clients' freedom. They could legally secure a divorce without a lawyer; to prohibit them obtaining legal services to ensure the divorce's validity prevents them minimizing risks of an invalid divorce as they see fit.[48]

An obvious requirement is that a professional fully disclose to both clients a possible conflict of interests.[49] Unfortunately, full disclosure is not such an easy matter. First, sometimes full disclosure might require the revelation of confidences of the other party.[50] If full disclosure is not possible, then an attorney should not accept both clients or an engineer accept payment from two or more parties for a project. A requirement of disclosure to the extent discretion allows is insufficient, for the very facts that cannot be disclosed might be most important. Without full information, client consent does not adequately represent a client's desire to assume risks.

Second, must lawyers disclose what their position will be should an actual conflict arise? They cannot at that point act as an advocate for either. Their options are to act as mediator, arbitrator, or counselor as to the legal effects of alternatives or to withdraw. If a serious conflict were to arise and the lawyer to withdraw, the parties would be subject to even higher legal fees than they would have paid had they originally retained separate lawyers. If clients are not informed of the position an attorney will assume should a conflict arise, then they have not been fully apprised of the consequences of alternatives, and their consent is not fully informed.

One should distinguish the role of a professional as representing two or more clients with a possible conflict of interest and acting as a mediator between two or more persons with an actual conflict of interest. Social workers, clinical psychologists, and lawyers often serve as mediators for spouses having marital difficulties. A mediator's task is not to represent or advocate the interests of either or both parties, but impartially to facilitate discussion and compromise between them. Consequently, the conflict of interest between the parties should not result in a conflict of professional obligations to them. However, the extent of the role a lawyer might have in advising such clients and perhaps drawing up a divorce agreement is unclear.[51] If one party appears to be significantly more naive or vulnerable than the other, then a lawyer should not do so unless that person has separate legal advice. The lawyer-mediator cannot advocate that person's interest, and without a balance between the parties, the resulting agreement smacks of unfairness and unconscionability.

Physicians do not have as many conflicts of interest between clients as lawyers because the health of one does not ordinarily adversely affect the health of others. Such problems do arise in a few types of situations. For example, a family physician recommending a form of contraception to a couple must consider the possible side effects, say, a vasectomy for the male versus a tubal ligation or birth control pills for the female. A more significant conflict arises in organ transplants if the same physician treats both patients. For example, suppose a physician attends both a potential recipient and a potential donor for a kidney transplant. The potential recipient's interest lies in receiving an organ from the best tissue match, usually a relative. However, the removal of a kidney is a health risk to the donor. In such cases, a physician other than the recipient's should discuss the situation with the donor.[52]

Also, legal firms face many problems of potential conflicts of interest between clients not immediately involved in the same case. Various corporations eventually end up in litigation with each other. Other professions confront this problem much less often because, for example, an architectural or engineering project for one client is unlikely to be contrary to the interest of a subsequent client. Also, as illustrated at the beginning of Chapter 1, a law firm can find itself representing two different clients in separate cases and taking opposite sides on the same point of law. Even if different members of the firm work on the cases, can a firm simultaneously take opposing positions in separate cases and retain independence of judgment? A direct conflict could emerge should both cases be appealed and consolidated. Perhaps the best that can be done is to monitor cases for potential conflicts, disclose the possibility of conflict, and leave the decisions to clients. If a client believes a conflict exists, then for all practical purposes, one does.[53]

A common problem for lawyers and to a lesser extent other professionals results from switching sides. In particular, a professional might work for the government and then work privately. Federal law requires that after leaving government people cannot represent a party in a matter in which they personally and substantially participated; it further bars for two years after employment such representation in any matter pending under the person's responsibility.[54] In recent years, several former employees of the executive branch have been charged with violating this law. The underlying concern is to prevent the use of confidential information. The same can apply to lawyers or accountants who switch from one firm to another. For lawyers, the issue is complicated by the fact that if one lawyer in a firm cannot represent a client for such reasons, all other lawyers are also disqualified.[55] Sometimes a firm can avoid this disqualification by instituting a "Chinese wall" isolating the involved attorney from participation and resulting fees.

Finally, a professional's loyalty and independence of judgment can be adversely affected by interests of third parties. The legal and to some extent the accounting professions have tried to insulate their members from third party influences by forbidding them to practice with people not in their particular profession or in a firm in which people not in their particular profession participate.[56] One fear is that nonprofessional interests and considerations will influence their actions. The financial interests of nonprofessionals, however, do not justify such a strong rule because professionals also have an interest in maximizing profit. Consequently, the justification for such a restriction must rest on laypersons directing cases in nonprofessional ways. That concern could be met by less stringent rules prohibiting nonprofessionals directing professionals' judgments in behalf of specific clients. A significant effect of these restrictions has been to prevent the formation of firms of lawyers and accountants that could offer clients more efficient combined services.

Professionals have a responsibility to ensure that third party payers do not influence their professional judgment in behalf of specific clients. It is unrealistic to require that professionals not be paid by nonclients. Parents must pay for medical care for children. With parents paying for services for children, potential conflicts of interest are relatively small. Although parents are usually concerned enough with their children's welfare to want a professional to exercise independent judgment in their children's behalf as much as they would want the professional to do in their behalf, that is not always the case. For example, parents of retarded children sometimes want them sterilized, which can be contrary to the interests of the children.

When a third party pays for professional services for an adult, as when an insurance company pays for services, a couple of duties involved in the responsibility of loyalty can be formulated.[57] First, the professional should receive the informed consent of the client. Because the arrangement can affect the professional's independence of judgment, the client should know of the possibility and who is making the payments. Otherwise, the client is not justified in trusting the professional's judgment. With physicians, this condition is usually met, for clients know who their medical insurer is. Second, professionals have a duty to inform the people paying them that they cannot direct or regulate their professional judgment or conduct. That is, professionals should make their employment conditional on their acting solely on the basis of personal and their clients' judgment of the clients' best interests. They must then, of course, live up to this condition if the payer tries to influence their judgment. Doing so might require considerable personal courage because they can lose future business from a payer, such as an accident insurance company.

The introduction of DRG payment to hospitals under Medicare, health maintenance organizations (HMOs), and other payment systems creates special problems of third party payers for physicians. Should physicians consider the cost of treatment in making decisions and recommendations?[58] When patients pay directly, the financial considerations can be left to them. If, however, the government or employers are paying for services through insurance, then the decision is not clearly one for the patients. The purpose of such cost containment payment systems is not to deprive clients of useful services, but to decrease the provision of unuseful ones. Part of the determination of service utility is its cost. Indeed, cost has been an element of the traditional concept of extraordinary treatment. Thus, because physicians rather than patients should make the decision, it seems appropriate for them to consider costs in their decisions.

In certain types of situations, professionals do not owe loyalty to clients. This occurs when they are hired to further a client's interests only to the extent of properly and accurately representing the client's position to others. Accountants hired to perform public audits and lawyers hired to make an independent evaluation to be provided to someone else serve a client's interests only to the extent that a correct statement is in the client's interest. The client can have interests (not disclosing financial losses or pending law suits) that are contrary to the professional's independent judgment. In these cases, a client in effect occupies the position of a third party payer and must not be allowed to direct or regulate a professional's independent judgment.[59] (The same general problem of employers influencing the judgments of employed professionals is discussed in Chapter 6.)

Fairness

The virtue and responsibility of fairness stem from the value of equality of opportunity. They primarily refer to how a professional treats one client in comparison to others. A professional is unfair when service to one client is slighted for service to another. One might argue that fairness is largely encompassed by the responsibilities of diligence and loyalty. If a professional provides diligent and loyal service to each client, then each is treated fairly. However, diligence and loyalty might not capture all that is included in fairness, and it is worth special emphasis.

One aspect of fairness is impartiality. In discussing the availability of services, I noted that professionals should not discriminate on grounds of race, religion, ethnic origin, or sex. I also pointed out that such considerations can affect not only the provision but also the quality of services. Professionals have acted on the basis of stereotypes. Bias or partiality can also be based on factors such as physical attractiveness. It is simply human for professionals to be attracted to or like some clients more than others. There is nothing unethical about this alone. However, if dislike or revulsion results in a client receiving less attention and service than others, then unfairness is involved.

Fairness is especially crucial for professionals who serve groups of clients, such as group therapists, nurses, and teachers. Nurses, for example, frequently have patients who are whiners and complainers. They constantly ring for service—bring me this, bring me that, help me to the toilet. Nurses are inclined to avoid such patients. When the whiners interfere with the provision of appropriate service to other patients, they should be ignored. Moreover, if nurses have spare time, it is permissible to spend it chatting with those patients they like and enjoy talking to. However, it is unfair to deny appropriate care to even the most ungrateful and complaining patient (for example, by not giving pain medication on time).

Teachers probably confront issues of fairness among clients more than any other professionals. Suppose a paper is due on a given day. Some students might not complete it on time, giving as excuses having other papers due or having to study for an exam. Other students in the class might have been in the same position but completed their papers. To allow extra time for those who did not is unfair to those who either planned ahead or balanced their efforts so as to get their papers in on time. In general, if there are announced rules or deadlines, it is unfair to allow some to violate them on grounds that probably apply to others. Those who do submit papers on time do not have an equal opportunity with those allowed more time. Professors' own lack of diligence might lead them to sympathize with dilatory students, but it does not justify the unfairness of permitting poorly excused late papers.

The more troublesome issue concerns grading. Obviously, it is unfair to grade one student in a class by higher standards than another. The difficult issues concern differences in grading standards between various sections of a course, courses in a department, departments, or even schools. In a large lecture course with several discussion sections, it is unfair if one section is graded by easier standards than another. One might argue that even then each student had an equal opportunity to get in the easier section, that usually it is mere luck of scheduling that determines which section one is in. However, if grades are to measure knowledge and ability, it is unfair if students in the same course are graded by different standards.

The issue of variations in standards between courses, departments, and schools cannot be considered in detail. Here the question of fairness is that between the clients of one professional or group of professionals and those of another professional or group. It is complicated by grades being used for two purposes—to signify mastering certain information or skills and to rank students by their comparative knowledge and ability. Moreover, those who use grades—prospective employers, scholarship grantors, and so on—do not have complete knowledge of their basis. For example, Canadian students have complained about the numerical grading scale on the ground that, in the sciences, with objective tests, one can score in the nineties, but in the humanities, with more essay tests, such scores are rarely given. Consequently, they claim, students in the sciences have better chances of obtaining scholarships and fellowships. If these claims are true, then students in the humanities are denied an equal opportunity for such financial aid.

Thus, fairness can pertain to the adequacy of services to individual clients, comparisons in services rendered to different clients of the same professional, and even to comparisons between clients of one professional and another. One cannot demand that each professional provide service as good as another. Some professionals are bound to be better than others. Nonetheless, professionals should strive to provide services of equal quality to each of their clients.

Discretion

The responsibility of discretion is one of the hardest to reconcile with a professional's obligations. Writers on professional ethics usually speak of "confidentiality" rather than discretion. Discretion is a broader concept than confidentiality, including material that is not confidential. The ordinary sense of confidentiality primarily refers to facts and information learned from a client.

The underlying value is privacy, the control of information about oneself that others have. One can intrude on another's privacy without violating confidentiality. For example, many actions lawyers take in behalf of clients are a matter of public record. However, clients would not be able to trust professionals who constantly spoke to others about actions that they took in their behalf. Clients usually do not want their lawyer or realtor to discuss freely the terms of their divorce settlement or house purchase at cocktail parties, even though the settlement or purchase is a matter of public record. Although such disclosures do not violate any legal right of privacy, the moral basis of privacy is freedom to pursue one's business without scrutiny by others unless one consents or they have a need to know. Being the subject of cocktail party gossip does not satisfy a legitimate need of others. The public might have some legitimate interest in the private affairs of public figures, such as movie stars and politicians. But for the average citizen, the point of a public record of divorce proceedings and house purchases is to provide an authoritative record should any subsequent inquiry arise. Thus, even though the record is public, the purpose and intent is limited to legitimate concerns, and consent to disclosure should be construed as limited to these functions. Professionals who fail to recognize such points exhibit a lack of respect for their clients. They might also carelessly let other strictly confidential information slip.

A more usual element of the responsibility of discretion is confidentiality. It is basic to professional–client relationships. For professionals to make the best possible recommendations and take appropriate actions, they need all possibly relevant information. Clients are often reluctant to discuss matters of a personal nature, whether they affect the body, possibly illegal or simply stupid actions, or business secrets. They might not fully appreciate the significance of facts. This last point is dramatically illustrated by an old lag convicted of burglary and appearing before a judge for sentencing at the Old Bailey in London. When the judge asked him whether he had anything to say before being sentenced, the man replied that it was unjust and unfair that he be sentenced for the crime, that he was completely innocent, and he could prove it. The skeptical judge inquired how he could prove it. The man responded that he could not have done it because he was in prison on the day the burglary occurred. When the startled judge asked why he had not mentioned this before, the defendant replied that he thought the jurors would have a poor opinion of him if they knew he was an ex-convict! To obtain as much information as possible from clients, professionals need to assure clients that what they say will remain confidential.

At the very core of the responsibility of discretion is the professional privilege of client communications. This privilege is a legal doctrine providing that professionals cannot be required to reveal client confidences in a court of law. A major issue in modern law, which cannot be adequately considered here, is the proper extent of this privilege. Most professions do not have such a legal privilege, so it primarily relates to lawyers and to physicians in some jurisdictions.

The most sensitive area of the privilege relates to lawyers. Because of the essential involvement of lawyers in the legal process and their function of representing their clients, they must have some privilege. If all the information a lawyer obtains from a client could be required to be presented in court, clients could not trust their lawyers with any information that they believe might damage their case. In that situation, except for a few minor matters of procedure and admission of evidence, lawyers could only be literal mouthpieces for their clients.

Journalists' position regarding confidentiality is reversed from that of other professionals. Their clients are their audience. When journalists assert confidentiality, it is of their sources. Thus, confidentiality cannot be claimed on grounds of client privacy. Instead, it must rest on the privacy of their sources and the interest of their clients, the public, in information. Journalists argue that without such confidentiality, they cannot adequately obtain information for their clients. The strength of this claim varies with the subject matter. Confidentiality of sources can be quite important if the subject is of major significance, such as the Watergate cover-up, but quite trivial if the matter is the private life of a movie star. In some states, journalists do have a legal privilege not to reveal their sources.

Three kinds of reasons can be given for a professional violating confidentiality: the best interests of (1) the client, (2) the professional, or (3) other persons.[60] Codes often state that confidential information may be disclosed when the client consents. Such disclosure does not break confidentiality, for confidentiality means permitting the client to control to whom information is given, and that condition is met if the client consents.

Other instances of disclosure for the benefit of a client need not be with his or her consent. For example, in negotiating in behalf of a client, it might be advantageous for a lawyer to disclose information to the other party. Similar situations are even more common in the health care professions. A psychologist or psychiatrist might obtain information that would help a patient's regular physician treat him or her, or vice versa. However, as argued in the first section, the professional–client relationship should conform to the fiduciary rather than paternalistic model. If professionals were to disclose confidential information whenever they thought it in the client's best interest, they would be using a paternalistic model. The client's consent and judgment would be ignored. Nevertheless, the threat of very serious injury to a client justifies violation of confidentiality. Consider the case of a nurse who is told by a patient that he is taking a powerful pain killer, but is explicitly asked by the patient not to tell the physician. Suppose the nurse knows that this medication has affected clinical findings (such as blood pressure), making a misdiagnosis likely, and can also interact with another medication the patient is taking. Should the nurse preserve the patient's secret?

Such examples make it unwise never to permit a professional to violate confidentiality. Nonetheless, one must guard against permitting the professional to violate confidentiality simply whenever doing so is likely to benefit the client, even if only minimally. Two rules are possible. First, for some situations (nursing, lawyers negotiating), an understanding can be reached with the client that professionals will disclose confidential information for limited purposes when they believe it is in the client's interest, except for items the client explicitly indicates should not be disclosed. This rule includes all situations in which a group or team renders service, as in a hospital or a legal firm. The client should understand that information will be shared with other members of the team as thought necessary to provide service. Second, in other cases, professionals may disclose information if they sincerely believe failure to do so will probably result in very serious harm to the client's interests. When failure to disclose would merely amount to a missed opportunity to benefit the client, disclosure would not be permissible. Clients have good reason to accept these norms, for confidentiality is secured except when a serious threat of injury to them exists.

Disclosure of confidential information for the sake of the professional is justified in only two kinds of situations: when it is necessary for professionals (1) to collect a just fee or (2) to defend themselves against a charge of wrongdoing. In the first situation, a client should not be permitted to use confidentiality to cheat or defraud a professional. To substantiate the value of their services, professionals often have to explain in some detail what these services were and why they were performed. In the second situation, clients might not wish to have information disclosed because it would show their complicity in wrongdoing. The more difficult problem is when the client has not done anything wrong but does not consent to a professional's disclosure of information. For example, an engineer might be accused of having stolen a production process from a former client, and his present client might refuse to allow information about her new and different process to be disclosed. In these cases, however, protection of the innocent is a more basic value than protection of a client from embarrassment or financial loss.

Finally, disclosure of confidential information can be justifiable because of the interests of others. No one disputes that confidential information may be disclosed when the law requires a professional to do so. The difficult questions are when the law should require disclosure and whether there are other situations in which the interests and values of others ethically justify disclosure although the law does not require it. These issues cannot be considered until professionals' obligations to third parties have been elucidated.

OBLIGATIONS OF CLIENTS

Little has been written about clients' obligations to professionals except for physicians contending that clients should faithfully comply with their directions and pay their bills. One obligation of clients is to keep commitments.[61] The professional–client relationship involves commitments by the client, at least to pay for the services. It does not include a general commitment to follow the professional's recommendations and advice. If it did, one would have agreed in advance to whatever the professional recommends, and informed consent would be otiose.

A client can make specific commitments during the relationship, such as to diet, work with one's spouse to ease difficulties, and so on. However, because these commitments are for the benefit of the client, not the professional, it is questionable how binding they are. If a client does not fulfill them, then primarily the client, not the professional, suffers. Nonetheless, a professional might well conclude that he or she is wasting time with a noncooperative client and so have reason to terminate the relationship. In such a case, a client can hardly claim to have been abandoned without needed services; if the client does not do what is central to obtaining the benefits of the services, he or she must not think they are crucial. Of course, allowance must be made for weakness of will, especially when compliance is unpleasant. Moreover, this obligation applies only if the client makes a specific commitment. A client need not do so. One goes to a professional for advice and help, but one does not have to take it. Clients often do not commit themselves actually to doing what is recommended, only to trying.

A second client obligation is truthfulness. This is merely a specification of the universal norm of truthfulness and subject to the normal exceptions. Note that this obligation is not as broad as the professional's obligation of candor. One could argue that failure fully to disclose relevant information would also be wrong. It would often deceive the professional into thinking that he or she has a better chance of success than is the case and undermine the integrity of professional practice.[62] However, the argument is not completely persuasive. Whether the integrity of professional practice is violated depends on whether professionals have a claim to producing the best results they can from their perspective. It is doubtful that they do because the quality of results should be judged from the client's perspective. Thus, if a client believes keeping certain information secret is worth the risk of less valuable services, it is the client's judgment that counts. Of course, clients' judgments are often wrong. Generally, it is unwise to pay someone in effect to work with one hand tied. Nonetheless, doing so is not clearly unethical, although it prevents the professional from making a fully informed decision whether to accept a client.

One other obligation is worth noting, namely, that of clients not knowingly requesting professionals to act unethically. All professionals confront such clients—

social workers being asked to violate rules in applying for financial aid, physicians to prescribe narcotics, lawyers to put on perjured testimony, teachers to change students' grades, and accountants not to disclose income on tax returns. Where the acts are criminal, such conduct amounts to criminal solicitation. The same underlying principle pertains in ethics.

None of these client obligations to professionals is a role-related norm. Each is merely the specification of a universal norm to the professional–client context. This should not be surprising. The fiduciary model indicates that special obligations apply to the advantaged party—the professional. Otherwise, the situation is like other contractual interactions and governed by universal norms for them.

Finally, clients might have obligations to serve as research subjects or teaching material or to report incompetent or unprofessional conduct. However, any such obligations are not to the professionals but to the public.

SUMMARY

This chapter has concerned the obligations of professionals arising out of the professional–client relationship. Five ethical models of the professional–client relationship were discussed—agency, contract, friendship, paternalism, and fiduciary. The primary issue between them concerns the respective authority and responsibility of professionals and clients in decision making. The agency model falsely assumes that a client has sufficient knowledge to direct a professional in most matters, and it encourages professionals to ignore ethical obligations to others. The contract and friendship models both falsely assume that clients have sufficient knowledge to be full partners in the activities. Although this condition is sometimes approximated when organizations employ accountants, architects, lawyers, or engineers, it rarely holds for individuals employing lawyers, physicians, architects, social workers, and accountants. The paternalistic model deprives clients of freedom to direct their own lives and falsely assumes professionals are able to make complex value judgments in behalf of clients.

The fiduciary model presents the best ethical ideal for the professional–client relationship. It recognizes the superior knowledge that professionals have and imposes special obligations on them in virtue of that superior knowledge; yet it permits clients to make the decisions that importantly affect their lives. Clients must rely on professionals to analyze problems, formulate alternative courses of action, determine the likely consequences of the alternatives, make recommendations, and use their expertise in helping them carry out their decisions. Because clients must rely on professionals, the professionals must be worthy of clients' trust in performing these tasks.

The fiduciary model's implication that professionals must be worthy of client trust provides a criterion for determining professionals' obligations to clients. Seven virtues and responsibilities of professionals to clients are honesty, candor, competence, diligence, loyalty, fairness, and discretion. By definition, a professional must be honest to be worthy of trust. Professionals can be dishonest toward clients by suggesting and providing services that are not useful, as well as by outright theft. Candor is probably a subclass of honesty and includes full disclosure to clients as well as truthfulness. Although lying to clients can probably never be justified, because it effectively destroys a trust relationship, information may be justifiably withheld from clients if necessary to prevent direct harm to them and if they are told as soon as possible.

Competence is not itself an ethical virtue, but the responsibility to keep current with one's field and not to undertake tasks for which one lacks competence is an ethical one. Moreover, to inform clients of alternative approaches, professionals have an obligation to be aware of developments in other professions pertaining to problems they handle. Diligence is the requirement that a professional work carefully and promptly. Self-employed professionals cannot properly argue that they lack time to consider each client's case adequately unless a shortage of professionals means some people would be denied services to which they have a right. Employed professionals such as teachers, nurses, and social workers often have no direct control over the number of clients they have. If they have more than they can ideally handle, they must provide services based on the priority of the value to the different clients.

Because professionals are hired by clients to protect and promote their interests, they must be loyal to their clients. A professional's loyalty can be affected by conflicts of interest between the client and the professional, other clients in that transaction or in other cases, or third party payers. Client consent to a professional acting in his or her behalf after disclosure of an actual or possible conflict of interest is a necessary but not sufficient condition to justify a professional accepting a case. The professional must also be able to exercise independent judgment in behalf of the client. Accountants performing audits, lawyers making independent evaluations, and journalists owe independence of judgment to the public.

Fairness, primarily an obligation to provide impartial service to clients, rests on the value of equality of opportunity. Bias can affect the quality of services professionals provide clients. Professionals should not favor one client over another. This obligation is especially important for teachers in grading.

Discretion rests on the clients' value of privacy in not having information about them conveyed to others without their consent. Even discussion of a client's public activities can be indiscreet. Confidential information about a client may be disclosed for the client's sake if (1) the client has been informed that the professional will do so when he or she judges it to be in the client's best interest and the client has not explicitly refused permission or (2) disclosure is necessary to prevent significant harm to the client. It may also be disclosed by a professional in order to collect a fee or in self-defense against a charge of wrongdoing. Confidential information may be disclosed to protect others from injury when required by law. For journalists, confidentiality pertains to sources of information, not to the audience that is plausibly the clients. Consequently, it does not rest on the privacy of clients, but on the privacy of sources and the interests of clients in information.

Finally, clients have three obligations to professionals. The first is to keep commitments they make to them, including to pay them. Clients also have an obligation to be truthful to professionals, but arguably not to full disclosure. Lastly, they may not request professionals to perform unethical acts. These obligations are all specifications of universal norms, not role-related ones, because in a fiduciary relationship, the special obligations are those of the advantaged party—the professional.

NOTES*

1. See K. Danner Clouser, "Veatch, May, and Models: A Critical Review and a New View," in *The Clinical Encounter,* ed. Shelp, pp. 94–96.

2. See Veatch, "Models for Ethical Medicine," p. 5. Veatch calls this the engineering model of the physician, but this assumes it is appropriate for engineers.

3. ABA, *Model Rules,* Rule 1.2(b).

4. Simon, "The Ideology of Advocacy," p. 36.

5. Simon's proposed alternative to the ideology of advocacy suffers these defects to some extent. He does not allow for professional roles. Thus, all professional obligations are at best specifications of universal norms. "The foundation principle of non-professional advocacy is that problems of advocacy be treated as a matter of *personal* ethics. . . . Personal ethics apply to people merely by virtue of the fact that they are human individuals. The obligations involved may depend on particular circumstances or personalities, but they do not follow from social role or station." Ibid., p. 131.

6. ABA, *Code of Professional Responsibility,* EC 7–8; see also ABA, *Model Rules,* Rule 2.1 and comment.

7. Chayes and Chayes, "Corporate Counsel," p. 294.

8. Ibid., p. 292.

9. Veatch, "Models for Ethical Medicine," p. 7; see also Veatch, *Theory of Medical Ethics,* esp. pp. 134–137.

10. See, for example, Masters, "Is Contract an Adequate Basis," p. 25; May, "Code, Covenant, Contract, or Philanthropy," p. 35; Engelhardt, "Rights and Responsibilities," pp. 16–17; Richard Wasserstrom, "Lawyers as Professionals: Some Moral Issues," in *1977 National Conference on Teaching Professional Responsibility,* ed. Goldberg, pp. 120–122.

11. Charles Fried, "The Lawyer as Friend: The Moral Foundations of the Lawyer–Client Relationship," in *1977 National Conference on Teaching Professional Responsibility,* ed. Goldberg, pp. 129–158; and Fried, *Right and Wrong,* chap. 7; see also Veatch, "Models for Ethical Medicine," p. 7; Pellegrino and Thomasma, *Philosophical Basis of Medical Practice,* pp. 64–66.

12. Edward A. Dauer and Arthur Allen Leff, "The Lawyer as Friend," in *1977 National Conference on Teaching Professional Responsibility,* ed. Goldberg, p. 164.

13. Simon, "The Ideology of Advocacy," p. 108.

14. Engelhardt, *Foundations of Bioethics,* pp. 258–262; Veatch, "The Physcian as Stranger: The Ethics of the Anonymous Patient–Physician Relationship," in *The Clinical Encounter,* ed. Shelp, pp. 187–207.

15. Some authors contend that paternalism does not apply to persons incapable of consent because they define paternalism as limiting a person's autonomy, which

---

*See the bibliography at the back of the book for complete references.

incompetent persons lack; see, for example, Beauchamp and McCullough, *Medical Ethics,* p. 84. Such a definition makes it difficult for parents to be paternalistic and undercuts the grounds for some laws, such as compulsory commitment because persons are a danger to themselves.

16. Cf. Joseph Ellin, "Comments on 'Paternalism and Health Care,' " in *Contemporary Issues in Biomedical Ethics,* ed. Davis, Hoffmaster, and Shorten, pp. 245–246.

17. See especially Feinberg, *Harm to Self;* Kleinig, *Paternalism;* and Van DeVeer, *Paternalistic Intervention.*

18. See, for example, Glenn C. Graber, "On Paternalism and Health Care," in *Contemporary Issues in Biomedical Ethics,* ed. Davis, Hoffmaster, and Shorten, p. 239; Buchanan, "Medical Paternalism," p. 381; and Goldman, *Moral Foundations,* pp. 179–186.

19. Rosenthal, *Lawyer and Client,* chap. 2.

20. President's Commission, *Making Health Care Decisions,* pp. 100–101.

21. See ABA, *Code of Professional Responsibility,* EC 7-7; but see ABA, *Model Rules,* Rules 1.2(a) and 1.4.

22. See Martin and Schinzinger, *Ethics in Engineering,* pp. 59–64. Strauss, "Toward a Revised Model of Attorney–Client Relationship"; and Spiegel, "Lawyers and Professional Autonomy."

23. Cooper, "Trust," distinguishes (1) entrusting someone with something, (2) deeming someone to be trustworthy as honest and so on, and (3) having confidence in abilities and so on. The sense involved in the test is being worthy of trust in senses (2) and (3).

24. See Levy, *Social Work Ethics,* chap. 11, for a similar but distinct set.

25. ABA, Special Committee, *Problems and Recommendations,* p. 117.

26. AMA, "Current Opinions," 2.16.

27. See Capron, "Containing Health Care Costs," pp. 723–724, for a discussion of physician fixed fees—MDDRGs similar to hospital DRGs.

28. Rosenthal, *Lawyer and Client,* pp. 110–112.

29. Bok, *Lying,* pp. 214, 219.

30. President's Commission, *Making Health Care Decisions,* p. 72.

31. Ibid., p. 97, table 2.

32. Christie and Hoffmaster, *Ethical Issues in Family Medicine,* p. 104.

33. See President's Commission, *Making Health Care Decisions,* pp. 89–93; Christie and Hoffmaster, *Ethical Issues in Family Medicine,* pp. 110–114.

34. ABA, *Code of Professional Responsibility,* EC 6-1; ABA, *Model Rules,* Rule 1.1; AICPA, "Rules of Conduct," Rule 201(A); AMA, *Principles of Medical Ethics,* sec. 5; ANA, *Code for Nurses,* sec. 5; Engineers' Council, "Code of Ethics," Canon 2; NASW, "Code of Ethics," Principle I(B).

35. In one case, the license of a seventy-eight-year-old osteopath practicing in 1972 by standards of 1927 was revoked; *Huls* v. *Arizona State Bd. of Osteopathic Examiners in Medicine and Surgery,* 29 Ariz. App. 236, 547 P.2d 507 (1976).

36. AMA, *Principles of Medical Ethics,* sec. 5; ABA, *Code of Professional Responsibility,* DR 6-101 (A) (3).

37. See National Federation of Societies for Clinical Social Work, "Code of Ethics," III(b).

38. See ABA, *Code of Professional Responsibility,* Canon 6, DR 6-101(A) (3), and DR 7-101.

39. Martin Garbus and Joel Seligman, "Sanctions and Disbarment: They Sit in Judgment," in *Verdicts on Lawyers,* ed. Nader and Green, p. 54; and Whitney North Seymour, Jr., *Why Justice Fails* (New York: William Morrow, 1973), p. 17.

40. Patterson and Cheatham, *Profession of Law,* p. 78.

41. See Cahn, *Saints and Scamps,* pp. 38–40.

42. ABA, *Code of Professional Responsibility,* Canon 5; ABA, *Model Rules,* Rule 2.1; AICPA, "Rules of Conduct," Rule 102; Engineers' Council, "Suggested Guidelines," 4, a–f.

43. Bloom, ed., *Lawyers, Clients & Ethics,* pp. 30–35.

44. See also Levy, *Social Work Ethics,* pp. 134–136.

45. See Zuger, "AIDS on the Wards," p. 19.

46. ABA, *Code of Professional Responsibility,* DR 5-101(A), permits client consent to justify such a relationship; ABA, *Model Rules,* Rule 1.7(b), does not permit consent alone to do so, for the lawyer must also reasonably believe the representation will not be adversely affected. See also Patterson, "Analysis of Conflicts of Interest Problems," pp. 589–590.

47. See Kipnis, *Legal Ethics,* p. 40.

48. See generally, Thomas D. Morgan, "The Evolving Concept of Professional Responsibility," in *1977 National Conference on Teaching Professional Responsibility,* ed. Goldberg, pp. 300–301.

49. See, for example, ABA, *Code of Professional Responsibility,* DR 5-105(C); Engineers' Council, "Suggested Guidelines," 4, c.

50. Hazard, *Ethics in the Practice of Law,* pp. 36, 76.

51. See Linda J. Silberman, "Professional Responsibility Problems of Divorce Mediation," in *Ethics and the Legal Profession,* ed. Davis and Elliston, pp. 305–317; see also ABA, *Model Rules,* Rule 2.2.

52. AMA, "Current Opinions," 2.13(1).

53. Hazard, *Ethics in the Practice of Law,* p. 83.

54. 18 U.S.C. sec. 207 (1982). See also ABA, *Model Rules,* Rule 1.11.

55. ABA, *Model Rules,* Rule 1.10.

56. ABA, *Code of Professional Responsibility,* DR 5-107(C); ABA, *Model Rules,* Rule 5.4; AICPA, "Rules of Conduct," Rule 504.

57. See ABA, *Code of Professional Responsibility,* DR 5-107(A) and (B); ABA, *Model Rules,* Rule 1.8(f); Engineers' Council, "Suggested Guidelines," 4, c.

58. See generally, Dyer, "Patients, Not Costs, Come First," and Brazil, "Cost Effective Care Is Better Care."

59. ABA, *Model Rules,* Rule 2.3; AICPA, "Rules of Conduct," Rules 101 and 102.

60. See ABA, *Code of Professional Responsibility,* DR 4-101(C); ABA, *Model Rules,* Rules 1.6, 2.3, and 3.3(a) (2); AICPA, "Rules of Conduct," Rule 301; AMA, "Current Opinions," 5.05.

61. See Benjamin, "Lay Obligations," pp. 96–97.

62. Ibid., pp. 98–99.

STUDY QUESTIONS AND PROBLEMS

1. What is the relation between an ethical model and empirical conditions? What is the purpose of an ethical model?

2. Annette Beaudais is a wealthy real estate developer. The owners of the building next to hers have bought airspace from a city landmark entitling them to construct an apartment building that will block the view from her building. She wishes to stop this construction by challenging the planning commission's approval. Her attorney, Charles Dunkirk, has developed three arguments for a suit, the strongest one being that the landmark law violates the state constitution. However, Annette does not want to use this argument because she plans to purchase some air rights from a landmark and believes the law is a good way to preserve historic buildings. A lawyer friend advised her that no legal provision has been made for someone other than the chair of the planning commission to preside at meetings, and because the vice chair presided during the hearing about the sale of air rights to the building next to hers, she wants to challenge on those grounds. Dunkirk believes such a challenge to be silly. Which arguments should be used? Who should make the decision on such matters? Why? What model of the professional–client relationship underlies your answers?

3. Georgia Hendricks, a seventeen-year-old unwed woman, came to Dr. Ernest Friedman after moving from another city. She was about twenty-four to twenty-six weeks pregnant. She was a Medicaid patient but lived with her mother, who worked. During the examination, she indicated that the baby was not kicking very much. At about twenty-seven to twenty-eight weeks, an ultrasound examination was performed. It revealed a spina bifida lesion (opening) around the middle of the spinal column. It was not possible at this point to determine the extent of the lesion and possible damage.

   Dr. Friedman has three options. (1) He can inform Georgia and perform an abortion should she so desire. However, abortions at this stage of pregnancy are legal only for the physical or mental health of the woman, not for eugenic reasons. An abortion at this point would have to be by hysterotomy, with the probability of a live birth. Premature "delivery" might cause significant stress for the infant and would compound problems. (2) Ms. Hendricks can be informed that it is likely that her infant has a significant defect but that it is impossible at this point to determine the extent of it. Because Georgia has completed only two years of high school, she may be unable to grasp completely the significance of this information. Moreover, the anxiety such information would cause might adversely affect the fetal environment or even bring on premature labor. (3) Dr. Friedman could withhold the information from Ms. Hendricks but arrange for immediate care of the infant on birth. This would involve delivering in a hospital with neonatal intensive care facilities and having a pediatrician on hand at birth.

What should Dr. Friedman do? Why? What obligation, if any, does Dr. Friedman have to the fetus? Is it also his patient? Is there a conflict or potential conflict of interest between patients?

4. Is the contract model of the professional–client relationship appropriate whenever the client is a business firm? Why or why not? Does it make any difference what profession and business are involved? Why?

5. Reconsider problem 7 in Chapter 3. After considering the responsibility to provide competent service, have you changed your mind? Should Ralph Stiles have informed the student of his lack of training? Is the student capable of making a sufficiently voluntary and informed choice to receive the therapy?

6. Irvine Jacobwitz, an engineer, is hired by Kristine Lovell to make some additions to a project he designed and completed a few years ago. In going over the previous work, he discovers some mistakes in the original design that make it less safe than is desirable. He can correct those mistakes as part of the additions without telling Lovell of the original errors. Should he correct them? Is it ethical not to tell Lovell of the original mistakes? Why or why not?

7. Morris Newhouse, a physician, was treating Opal Pierce for a number of years. Opal had been bedridden and treated for cancer. During her treatment, Dr. Newhouse had prescribed a barbiturate sleeping pill for her. After the active treatment, it became clear she had become addicted to the barbiturate. Consequently, Dr. Newhouse arranged for Opal's pharmacist to prepare pills that contained progressively less barbiturate and more sugar as a substitute, until now Opal is completely off the barbiturate. However, Opal is receiving the placebo (sugar pills). Dr. Newhouse is charging a nominal sum for prescribing the pills, and the pharmacist is charging the regular cost of the barbiturate, although the actual cost is greater. Was it ethical for Dr. Newhouse to prescribe the placebos to remove Opal's dependency? Opal is paying for medication that she does not biologically need. Is it ethical for the physician and pharmacist to continue to prescribe and give the sugar pills without informing her? Give reasons for your answers.

8. The local newspaper ran a story saying that the city council had passed an ordinance requiring all bicycles to be licensed. This story was incorrect, for the bill had simply come up for first reading and did not require licensing but only provided for voluntary licensing. For the next two days, city hall was deluged

with phone calls about the "new ordinance." On the third day, the newspaper ran another story about the rash of phone calls, stating the correct facts about the proposed ordinance. It did not mention the errors in the original story or run a correction notice. Was the newspaper's conduct ethical? Did it have an obligation to acknowledge its mistake? Why or why not?

9. Sara Thomas consulted lawyer Quentin Ross about handling her divorce. She and her husband had been separated for two years and had a separation agreement covering all property and support payments drawn up in another state where they had lived. They had no children. She thought the marriage finished. Although her husband did not want a divorce, he agreed not to contest it if she wanted one. Quentin agreed to handle an uncontested no-fault divorce based on the separation agreement for $150.

A week later, Sara phoned Quentin and asked him to cease working on the divorce. Her husband had persuaded her to think about it some more. A couple of months later, Sara went to see Quentin again and asked about various aspects of the settlement and her legal situation if she simply remained separated. About a week later, she phoned and asked a few more follow-up questions. Quentin did not hear from her again for about another four months. Then he had a phone call from Sara saying to go ahead and prepare the divorce papers. The case then proceeded smoothly to a default judgment (her husband did not appear). Quentin then sent Sara a bill for $850 plus court costs. When Sara phoned about the bill, Quentin explained that he charged her his fee for a contested divorce because she had been to see him and phoned several times.

Was Quentin's conduct ethical? What responsibilities, if any, did he violate? How might he have handled the case to avoid difficulties? What if, anything, can Sara do? What should she be able to do?

10. Lawyer Upton Vickers was handling an automobile injury plaintiff's case. Over the past two years, the case had been put on the trial docket four times, and each time it was postponed at the request of the defense counsel. When the case came up the fifth time, Upton was quite busy on other business. Believing that if the case was reached it would probably be postponed again, he did not go to court until 11:30; trial call was usually at 10:00. Much to his surprise, Upton discovered that the case had been called. Because no one appeared for the plaintiff, the case had been dismissed with prejudice so that it could not be brought again. Did Upton act unethically? Why or why not? What happens to his client? What should the client be able to do? Why?

11. When county engineer Wanda Xanthasis got married, the equipment dealers and contractors with county contracts got together and pooled their money. They then bought Wanda and her husband a number of gifts, some of them expensive, and a representative gave them to the couple. Is it ethical for Wanda and her groom to keep the gifts? Why or why not?

12. Yves Zorach, an accountant, is contacted by an employee of an existing client corporation. The employee, Adrianne Bates, tells him that she and other personnel of the corporation are going to form a new company to compete with their present employer. They would like him to serve as their accountant. Can Zorach

ethically do so? Why or why not? Should he preserve Adrianne's confidence, or should he inform his present client? Why?

13. Elaine Feder, a pregnant sixteen-year-old who wants an abortion, visits the local planned parenthood organization. She requests that they not notify her parents. Nurse Clyde Davis phones Elaine at home. When Elaine's mother answers, he does not leave his name or that of the planned parenthood organization, but he does leave the phone number, asking Elaine's mother to have her phone them. Elaine's mother phones the number and discovers it is the planned parenthood organization. She confronts Elaine and forces her to have the baby and marry the baby's father, a seventeen-year-old high school student. Was nurse Davis unethical in leaving the phone number? Why or why not? Do parents have an ethical right to be informed of medical treatment for their children? Was Elaine ethically able to consent to the abortion?

14. George Howard is an activist lawyer with political ambitions. A couple of years ago, he handled a suit that struck down racial and sexual discriminatory practices of a local corporation. He is also vice president of a local environmental organization. The corporation's factory is now being forced to close due to new local regulations on pollution. The local black organization, which considers him its lawyer, wishes to join the corporation's management in attacking the local regulations on pollution so that the factory can remain open. George would represent the blacks who obtained jobs as a result of his earlier case. The suit would probably be opposed by the environmental organization to which he belongs. Would it be ethical for George to take the case? Would there be a conflict of interest? Would it be unethical for him to refuse the case? Could he ethically remain as general counsel to the black organization and refuse the case? How much, if at all, should his political ambitions affect his decision?

15. Iris Jordan, an accountant and professor at the state university, is preparing an audit case for the use of her students. Is it ethical for her to use the actual audit reports of a client that were submitted as evidence in a court case? Why or why not? In teaching, how much effort must be made to disguise actual cases? When should persons be disguised? Do patients in teaching hospitals automatically consent to the use of their cases for teaching purposes?

16. Mary Niles sees a young junior high student, Karl Long, in her job as counselor. Karl is inclined to brag about his exploits. Today he claims he has a bad hangover as a result of drinking almost a fifth of vodka the previous night. Upon questioning by Mary, he reports that it was at the house of a friend whose parents were away for the evening. During the last month, he proudly asserts, he and his friends have gotten drunk on at least three other occasions when the parents of one of them have been away. Mary knows that Karl has been having trouble with his parents, but he trusts her. Should she inform Karl's parents about his drinking? If not, what should she ethically do? If so, what can she say to Karl?

17. Orlando Poyner had a sore shoulder whenever he raised his arm over his head a certain way. He went to his doctor. After examining him and x-raying the shoulder, the doctor determined that there was nothing major wrong. He sent Orlando for ultrasound treatments. The technician used heat pads, which often

make ultrasound more effective, on the shoulder. Orlando thought the pads were awfully hot. During the second treatment, the technician asked Orlando how he had burned his shoulder. Orlando proceeded with the rest of the treatments, but he did not feel any better. Deciding that the treatments were a waste of time and he did not want to bother with another series, Orlando told the technician after the last one that his shoulder felt much better. The technician said she would notify the physician. Orlando then decreased his daily exercise program for a month by omitting those exercises in which he felt the soreness. The shoulder got better.

Was Orlando's conduct unethical? If so, what obligation did he violate? Might such behavior have consequences for others? What would outweigh that obligation? Suppose Orlando did not want to hurt the technician's feelings. Suppose Orlando was afraid the technician and doctor would suggest more ultrasound or other therapy. Is avoiding difficulties with health care workers a sufficient justification for telling "little white lies"?

18. Social worker Quinella Rouise has a dilemma. She has two clients who suffered strokes about the same time and could benefit from being transferred to a hospital in another city. Unfortunately, the hospital can accept only one. She must decide who.

One patient is Saul Tassein, a sixty-five-year-old physician who retired about a year and a half ago from a successful general practice. After retirement, he took up many different activities. He was so pleased with his retired life that he persuaded his wife also to retire just before his stroke. He now has difficulty speaking and is confined to a wheelchair, though he might eventually be able to walk with a cane. He is highly motivated and becomes impatient when he does not progress as much as he thinks he should from treatment. He also becomes frustrated because he cannot express himself verbally.

The second patient is Mrs. Ursula Ventry, a forty-five-year-old black who had just begun taking courses at the community college before her stroke. About twenty years ago, she had worked as a clerk, but she quit to raise a family. With the two children now twelve and sixteen years old, she wanted to go back to work but needed new job skills. She too has difficulty understanding and speaking. She has lost feeling on the right side and has visual difficulties. Since her stroke, she has been depressed and uncooperative in all aspects of her treatment. Several times she has indicated that she would rather be dead than paralyzed.

Which patient should be sent for more intensive treatment? Identify characteristics of the patients that might bias you toward one or the other. Defend your decision as being a fair one.

19. Professor Waldo Xanders is a softie, but he does not want the students to know that because they will take advantage of him. In particular, he thinks it is unfair to students who get their work done on time if he allows lame excuses for late papers. One year one-sixth of his classed claimed there had been a death in the family the week papers were due. Ever since, Professor Xanders has announced at the beginning of each class that only written medical excuses will be accepted

for late papers and missed exams. However, he does believe there are other legitimate excuses, such as a death in the family; so if a student comes to him with such an excuse, he will accept it. Is Professor Xanders lying to the students when he says the only excuse for a late paper is a written medical one? If so, is it wrong to do so? Is it fair to accept excuses that students have been told would not be accepted? What bad consequences might result from his policy? Is there another policy he could follow? How can it avoid illegitimate excuses?

20.   Dr. Yvette Zorn had finally had enough of her patient Aylmer Boggs. She had been treating him with hemodialysis for a year. Aylmer had end stage renal disease, that is, his kidneys were basically not functioning. However, Aylmer would not cooperate in the treatment. He continued to drink alcohol and use drugs, refused to stay on the prescribed diet, and would not cooperate with the psychotherapist. Consequently, Dr. Zorn convinced the hospital authorities to terminate treatment, and Aylmer was given a month's notice so that he could find another source of treatment. Did Aylmer violate any obligations to Dr. Zorn? Did she violate any obligations to Aylmer? Suppose Aylmer does not secure an alternative source of treatment and shows up at the hospital emergency room ill from being several days past due for treatment. Do Dr. Zorn and the hospital have any duty to provide treatment?

5 Obligations to Third Parties

Many of the most interesting, important, and difficult problems of professional ethics concern conflicts between a professional's obligations to a client and to others. For a number of reasons, discussions of these problems often appear to sacrifice society's interests to those of individual clients. Many discussions are written by professionals whose self-interest and training put client interests first and whose arguments tend to reflect that perspective. Codes of ethics focus on obligations of individual professionals to clients, and many discussions unquestioningly accept the existing codes as ethical premises. Also, the American cultural tradition is highly individualistic, emphasizing individual rights more than rights of the public or an individual's obligations to others.

Conflicts between obligations to clients and to others are central to professional ethics. The professional–client relationship requires that a professional devote a special concern to clients that is not given to others. Such responsibilities to clients as loyalty and confidentiality and the weight given to these responsibilities stem from the professional role in relation to clients; the norms are role related. Most of a professional's obligations to others are universal norms or specifications of them; they do not stem from a professional role because there is no special relationship with others. (The chief exceptions to this claim are the relationship of lawyers to courts and of accountants as auditors.) Consequently, when conflicts arise between a professional's obligations to clients and to others, the issue is generally that role-related responsibilities to clients must be limited by universal responsibilities to others. These responsibilities must be weighed against one another and more precisely defined. In weighing these responsibilities, one must produce a balance that best preserves and promotes social values. Sometimes this balance will make it possible to formulate rules that help specify the professional role, but sometimes it provides only general guidance. Before one can attempt to reconcile obligations to clients with those to others, obligations to others must be made explicit.

THIRD PARTIES

The obligations considered in this section are those of a professional to persons (third parties) other than clients and employers. According to the agency model of the professional–client relationship, a professional has few if any obligations to others except those established by law. A professional, as a neutral agent of a client, is absolved of responsibility for a client's immoral but legal actions. However, the agency model has been rejected in favor of the fiduciary model, which states that a professional is not completely directed by the client but offers independent advice and service. To the extent professionals are free moral agents, they are responsible for effects on third parties and subject to obligations to them.

The general argument for professional obligations to third parties stems from the role of professions in society. Professions are licensed or informally authorized by society to provide certain types of services promoting values such as health, welfare, legal justice, financial integrity, and safe structures. The granting of a license and privilege in effect creates a trust for professionals to ensure that these activities are performed in a manner that preserves and promotes values in society. Consequently, professionals always have some obligation to consider whether their activity is compatible with the realization of values by others.

These considerations arise at two levels. One is the level of professional norms; the other is that of particular actions by professionals. In acting in behalf of a client, a professional is permitted to act in a way that best promotes the client's interests within the framework of professional norms. These norms should preserve and promote social values, and so doing requires recognition of obligations to third parties. Protection from injury, equality of opportunity, and so on cannot be fully realized in society if professionals are permitted to act toward others in any manner they or their clients wish. In arguing against proposed changes in recognized norms, professionals often mistakenly assert that they should act in the best interests of their clients and that proposed changes in norms would hinder their doing so. But the issue is what those norms should be; that norms would hinder professionals doing the most possible for clients does not necessarily indicate improper hindrance of their promoting client interests. To claim otherwise is to assume that the extant norms are correct and thus begs the question.

Truthfulness, Nonmaleficence, and Fairness

Truthfulness is one obligation that professionals have to third parties. Because professionals do not have a special relationship of trust to third parties, an obligation of candor would be too strong; universal norms do not require disclosing all information to others in all dealings, especially in such situations as bargaining. Although professionals are as justified in withholding information as their clients are, clients are not ethically entitled to lie or deceive. Because their authority stems from that of their clients, professionals cannot be justified in acting toward others in ways that their clients are not. Although professionals are often authorized to perform actions that nonprofessionals are not, such as prescribe medications, they have no authority to act toward others on behalf of a client in ways the client ought not. Social values are not promoted by institutionalizing a role whose function is to perform immoral actions for citizens that citizens ought not perform themselves. The obligation of truthfulness includes a requirement to provide information that would obviously mislead others should it be withheld.

Another responsibility of a professional is nonmaleficence or not to injure third parties. A fundamental value is protection from injury by others. No social role that permits people generally to injure others can be justified. The crucial notion is that of injury. The actions of a lawyer, engineer, management consultant, or realtor in behalf of a client often result in a financial or opportunity loss for another person. Such conduct does not injure that person provided certain conditions are met. In a competitive society, a gain for one person often means a failure to gain by another. The nonbenefit of the latter is not immoral or unjust, provided it resulted from fair competition. Social rules define fair competition, and as long as competitors act within them, losers are not wronged by winners.

Fairness is thus a third obligation of professionals to third parties. As just noted, fairness often involves following the social rules of a competition. However, that is not all there is to it. The rules of a competition can be unfair. Fairness also includes not discriminating on the basis of race, sex, ethnic origin, and so on. One can also take unfair advantage of another in negotiating and so on. However, the fairness of social rules is crucial in professional ethics. Most generally, fairness involves rules that are based on considering equally the values and interests of all involved.

Illustrations

The application of these obligations to third parties is relatively straightforward for physicians. They have a duty to protect others from dangerous patients. They should isolate or quarantine patients with dangerous communicable diseases, but more controversial situations also exist. For example, psychotherapists have a legal duty to warn third parties if their patients are apt to cause them serious physical injury.[1] The difficulties with this situation do not concern the ethical principle. Psychiatrists and the state may invoke involuntary commitment for the mentally ill who are a danger to others. The central problems are whether something less than commitment suffices and the strength of evidence a psychiatrist should have before warning others.

Similarly, a physician who has good reason to believe that a patient's illness poses a danger to others in her employment has a duty to warn the employer. For example, a school bus driver or airline pilot subject to unpredictable blackouts should be reported to an employer. At a more mundane level, when prescribing drugs that seriously impair reactions, physicians should warn patients not to drive. Physicians have an obligation to the patient in such cases, but they also have one to third parties who might be injured.

Physicians also have duties of truthfulness toward third parties. For example, they should not lie on various health forms, such as life insurance examination forms. The more difficult problems concern withholding information from third parties, especially at the request of the patient. A patient might ask that his or her spouse not be told that an illness is fatal. How can a physician respond to the spouse when asked how the patient is? Another example is a physician who provides an examination of a man applying for work with the city garbage collection. The employment form asks whether the patient is a heavy drinker, which is defined as someone who has more than six beers a day. The patient does, but the physician knows that many of the employees of the sanitation department also do. If the physician indicates this patient is a heavy drinker, he will not be employed. Truthfulness seems to require noting that the patient is a heavy drinker, but one might argue that in this context (for the purpose of determining whether the patient can be as reliable an employee as most others), he is not.

Physicians have to worry about effects on third parties only in some cases, but engineers and architects must almost always do so. In engineering codes of ethics, obligations to third parties are the most fundamental.[2] Almost all architectural and engineering projects have a potential for injuring people. Whether the design is for an automobile, building, electric power system, or sewer system, a faulty design can result in injury to others. Nor should engineers lie to prospective purchasers about the capabilities of equipment they sell.

For accountants and teachers, the responsibilities of truthfulness and fairness predominate because most of the injury they cause others results from a lack of truthfulness or fairness. Auditors certify that financial statements present data fairly, in accordance with generally accepted accounting principles. Failure to be truthful can cause others to make unwise investments. Similarly, lack of fairness in preparing income tax information and forms can injure the government, and thus society. Similarly, teachers should be truthful and fair in providing references to prospective employers or others. A problem is recommendation inflation similar to grade inflation.[3] Glowing letters that do not provide a fair evaluation of the person's strengths and weaknesses are common.

Social workers often represent clients to various agencies and get third parties involved with them. Representations to others about clients should be truthful and fair. When involving others in a client's care, social workers should consider whether the involvement might cause them injury. If these persons are advised of the risks and are still willing to help, then the social workers have not wronged them even if they do end up suffering. The choice to become involved was theirs.

For journalists, because the clients are the audience, duties to third parties primarily apply to sources and subjects of their presentations. Truthfulness is crucial. Indeed, it is in part legally required by the laws of defamation. But fairness is just as important. Fairness requires giving the subject of a negative story an opportunity to respond to charges and presenting the response.[4] Nonmaleficence can also justify not publishing an accurate and fair story if it would seriously injure its subject without producing a greater benefit for the clients. Journalists too readily conclude that the benefits to the audience outweigh the injury to subjects by appealing to the public's right to know. The appeal to the right to know begs the question, which is whether the public has a right to know information when it will do irreparable injury to the subject.

Lawyers must also usually consider effects on third parties. Lawyers represent clients in their relations to others. Even in drafting a will, the beneficiaries and relatives of the client will be affected by it. Consequently, lawyers must always take into account the obligations of nonmaleficence and fairness, and often the obligation of truthfulness as well.

The Adversary System

The traditional ethics of the legal profession have not emphasized obligations to third parties. Lawyers do recognize an obligation not to aid clients in illegal activities, but if the clients' courses of conduct are legal, they recognize few further obligations toward third parties. The rationale for this position rests on the adversary system of law. In court, two parties oppose one another, and each side marshals the facts and arguments as best it can to support its claims. The court determines which view is correct. Attorneys need not be concerned for the interests of adverse parties because they will be represented to the court. In the adversarial context, it is claimed, the obligations of nonmaleficence and fairness are mitigated. About the only applicable elements of nonmaleficence are those not to bring suits merely to harass others and not to badger witnesses maliciously.[5] Fairness to the opposing party consists in simply abiding by the rules of the tribunal with respect to the conduct of a case; if this is done, the lawyer bears no responsibility for whatever the adverse party may lose.[6] If the judge or jury makes a bad decision, the losing party is injured by them, but not by the opposing lawyer.

Most writers on legal ethics treat obligations to the court or tribunal as distinct from those to third parties, but in fact they are simply a subclass of them. The obligation of truthfulness applies to the courts, and lawyers should not lie or mislead judges, and they should correct misapprehensions about the law.[7] Traditionally, lawyers have not been thought obligated to disclose facts adverse to their client's case. Modern rules of discovery, which permit the opposing party to request and obtain information, partially eliminate this difficulty, provided the opposing party knows enough to ask for the relevant information.

Various commentators have attacked the use of the adversary model for determining the obligations of lawyers.[8] In the nineteenth century, most legal work occurred in the adversary context of the courtroom, but during the twentieth century, the focus of legal work has shifted to office counseling about prospective conduct. Many authors now distinguish obligations appropriate to the adversary context from those appropriate to the counseling context.[9] In the latter, other affected parties are not present, and unless the lawyer (or the client) considers their interests, they will not be considered at all.

Some scholars contend that the distinction between adversarial and nonadversarial contexts cannot be maintained. Even in counseling, a lawyer must look forward to possible litigation concerning the matter. Consequently, the lawyer must act to prevent the client being disadvantaged in any possible litigation.

This argument is deficient. First, it fails to distinguish between adopting a position and ensuring that courts will uphold one. Drafting an instrument so that one's position will be upheld by the courts is one thing; adopting an unfair position is another. Second, one must distinguish between preventing a client from being at a disadvantage (taken advantage of) and taking advantage of another party. Third, when drafting a contract that will be reviewed by attorneys for the other party, one is still in a sort of adversarial context. The opposing lawyer will examine the contract from his or her client's point of view. Not all contracts or instruments are so reviewed. In drafting installment contracts to be used for the purchase of automobiles, an attorney knows that most automobile purchasers do not take the contracts to their lawyers for review; no bargaining occurs over any contract terms except price. The same applies to the preparation of legal opinions for the issuance of stock certificates. The adversarial model simply does not fit these situations. Both sides are not represented before an impartial tribunal.

Even when the adversarial model does fit the situation, it does not settle the matter. Some writers on legal ethics frequently argue that adoption of some rule is inconsistent with the adversary system. For example, it might be claimed that an obligation of lawyers to present material facts adverse to their party and not disclosed by opposing counsel is contrary to or will weaken the adversarial system. But even if this is true, it does not follow that the proposed norm is wrong. One must also establish that the adversarial system is ethically required.[10] However, it is doubtful that the adversary system can be shown to be the best form of legal system and required.[11] Moreover, even if adversary systems are generally best or required, it does not follow that the rule is wrong. One must show that the addition of the norm would make the system worse. That amounts to having to show that the norm is not a good one. Consequently, appeals to the adversary system will not settle disputes about obligations.

CLIENTS VERSUS OTHERS

The central problem of reconciling obligations to clients and to others must now be confronted. A common professional position is that so long as conduct is legally permissible, responsibilities to clients take precedence over responsibilities to others.[12] Because professionals have obligations to clients, proper conduct for them often differs from that for nonprofessionals. The frequency with which the following comment of Lord Brougham (from the early nineteenth century) is approvingly quoted testifies to the strength with which this view is held.

> An advocate, in the discharge of his duty, knows but one person in all the world, and that person is his client. To save that client by all means and expedients, and at all hazards and costs to other persons, and, amongst them, to himself, is his first and only duty; and in performing this duty he must not regard the alarm, the torments, the destruction which he may bring upon others. Separating the duty of a patriot from that of an advocate, he must go on reckless of the consequences, though it should be his unhappy fate to involve his country in confusion.[13]

Taken literally, Brougham's comment would be the strongest possible claim to violate universal morality, for he does not even restrict the means used to legal ones. However, in the original context of a thinly veiled threat to expose the king's adulterous affairs should charges be brought against his client, the queen, Brougham implicitly restricted the means to legal ones. And almost everyone agrees that professionals should restrict themselves to legal means, except for rare acts of civil disobedience such as courtroom disruptions.[14]

The Issues

The problem of reconciling responsibilities to clients and to others can be broken into more discrete issues. One issue is how the *law* should balance professionals' obligations to clients and to others. Should accountants who are not auditors be legally required to report cases of fraudulent corporate balance sheets? Should engineers be legally required to report poorly designed products to consumer protection agencies? Should physicians be legally required to report cases of child abuse, gunshot wounds, and venereal disease to authorities? Ought lawyers be legally required to report confidential information received from clients, such as where murderers have left their victims' bodies or their clients' intentions to commit crimes? Simply stating that professionals must act within the law provides no guidance as to what the law should be.

A second issue concerns balancing obligations when the conduct is within legal limits. Can any legally permissible means be used to assist clients, regardless of how well these means conform to the dictates of universal norms? The question is more important for lawyers than other professionals. Lawyers' assistance of clients is more likely than that of other professionals to be adverse to the interests of third parties. Normally, if an engineer, physician, or teacher helps a client, their aid is not adverse to others and often helps them. Nonetheless, all professionals face conflicts between the interests of their clients and those of others.

One difficulty in analyzing these problems concerns the basis for claiming that conduct is contrary to universal norms. If it is illegal, at least a community has clearly judged that it ought not to be engaged in. If it is not illegal, in a pluralistic society, a generally accepted judgment of its morality might not exist. However, the question is not whether the conduct is contrary to what most people believe to be wrong, but whether it is contrary to a rationally defensible ethics applying to nonprofessionals. Furthermore, this aspect is often not in question, because the conduct is detrimental to others and thus violates a norm not to injure others. In a few cases, such as abortion, that is disputed.

A few brief examples will illustrate the type of problems involved in reconciling responsibilities to others with those to clients. Suppose a consulting engineer discovers a defect in a structure that is about to be sold. If the owner will not disclose the defect to the potential purchaser, ought the engineer do so? Suppose a lawyer learns that a client intends to commit perjury on the witness stand. Should the lawyer report the client's intentions to the authorities? May the lawyer morally put the client on the stand? Suppose a physician diagnoses a man as having Huntington's chorea, a fatal genetic disease usually not manifested until after the age of thirty. Further suppose that the man tells the physician that he does not want his wife to know because he wants to have children, and she might not be willing if she knew they could be affected with the disease. Should the physician respect the patient's request?

One argument is that a professional, especially a lawyer, must distinguish between the wrongs permitted by a reasonably just legal system and personal wrongs.[15] A lawyer ought not commit personal wrongs such as lying to a judge or abusing a witness. However, in asserting a technical point, such as a statute of limitations to defeat a legal claim, a lawyer is acting as a representative of the client, for the act is legally defined. When lawyers act as representatives and not personally, they are insulated from responsibility.[16]

Several difficulties confront this view. A major problem is distinguishing between representative and personal acts. That distinction might be based on how the acts are defined. Filing motions and making objections are acts defined by the legal system; lying and abusing persons are not so defined but have meaning independent of the legal system. This distinction is not clear-cut, however; lying to a judge can be defined independent of the legal system, but the act can also be described as committing a fraud on a tribunal. A judge is defined by a position within a legal system, so even "lying to a judge" is not completely specifiable independent of a legal system. Humiliating a witness can also be described as cross-examining a witness, which is a legally defined act. Conduct can be properly described in more than one way, and some descriptions of an act might refer to a legal system and others not.

Even if it can be made, the distinction between wrongs a system permits and those done personally has limited applicability. It best applies to an attorney in a trial situation. In counseling or negotiating, fewer of an attorney's acts are defined by reference to the legal system. Indeed, because negotiation also occurs complete-ly outside a legal context, probably no acts of negotiation are necessarily defined by the legal system. The distinction is also perforce restricted to lawyers. The acts of architects and most other professionals are not defined by similar systems of rules. The analysis will not apply to professional ethics generally, or if it is applied it will confine other professionals to all the requirements of universal norms.

More fundamentally, even granting the distinction, why should the way an act is defined have conclusive weight in determining the morality of conduct? Presumably, the reason is that the legal system allocates rights to settle disputes peaceably and that objections to injustice the system permits should be corrected through the political process. But many ethical constraints limit conduct that is not beyond the realm of legal tolerance; it would be a morally deficient society in which everyone pursued his or her claims to the extent of the law. No argument is given why acts performed in a representative capacity are subject only to legal constraints and not also ethical ones. This analysis places legal rights above ethical considerations. No reasons exist to so exalt legality.

Difficulties might ensue from distinguishing between the conduct of a person in a professional role and as a private citizen. "Costs" are involved in ascribing an amoral character to a lawyer's activities in the professional role.[17] Arguments like the previous ones for allowing such conduct assume that the legal system is just. To the degree the legal institution is not just or wise, such role-related norms can be undesirable. A lawyer's character might also be adversely affected. As lawyers, they need to be competitive, aggressive, ruthless, and pragmatic. Such traits cannot be readily con-fined to the professional role. These character traits usually affect most conduct and are relatively permanent.

At this point, a way is needed to resolve conflicts between a professional's obligations to clients and to others. Just as religious obligations are limited by ethical norms and law when they adversely affect persons outside the sect, so professional responsibilities to clients must be limited by ethical responsibilities to others. A balancing of these responsibilities cannot be done solely on a case-by-case basis, for many detrimental effects of general professional practice do not result from single cases. In short, the issue is how one determines the norms of professional roles. This issue cannot be settled within the perspective of professionals because it is the one that is to be determined. Reference must be made to the broader framework of social values.

A Test

The approach here is to adopt a consumer perspective. The balancing is between what people would want done for themselves as clients and the effect of such conduct on themselves as affected third parties. In particular, the test is to ask what norm that balances responsibilities a reasonable person would accept if he or she had justifiable social values and a general probability of being client or affected person.[18] This is just a particular application of the general method adopted in Chapter 1.

The proposed test has several merits. First, it subjects professionals to universal norms but permits exceptions to those norms that apply only to professionals. Second, the legitimacy of these exceptions is determined by social values that are also the basis of universal norms. Third, assuming that a reasonable person would not have them, the test eliminates irrational or reprehensible desires or interests of persons. Thus, a client's envy or hatred of a third person is not considered. Fourth, the test builds in fairness as equal consideration of the values and interests of all those affected. It does this by requiring one to consider oneself in the roles of both client and affected person. This reflects the idea of universalizability common to many ethical theories.

The procedure has three important steps. First, one must identify and weigh the values and interests of the client against those of others who will be affected. Unlike a standard utilitarian analysis—determining the rightness of actions by their producing the greatest balance of happiness over unhappiness—this evaluation is not done simply on the basis of the happiness of the persons affected. Second, one must consider the general probability of one being in either position—client or affected third party. This consideration is especially important for issues in which many persons are affected. Third, one must remember that one is considering rules for professional roles; one is not deciding a particular case, and one will not be able to give a different answer for a later similar case. In general, the procedure is designed to foster asking whether one would rather live in a society with professionals governed by one set of norms or another. Consideration of examples will clarify the procedure.

The simplest case is that in which only three parties are involved—a professional, a client, and one affected party. An example is a consulting engineer who has found a structural defect in a building that the client, a seller, has not revealed to the prospective buyer. The engineer's report was confidential, and should the prospective purchaser learn of the defect, the price would go down. The client's values involved are confidentiality and financial interests. The prospective purchaser's affected values are financial but can also be physical safety. If the defect makes the premises unsafe, then any occupant could be injured or killed.

To apply the recommended procedure, one should ask whether one would be willing to risk the financial loss and injury for financial gain and confidentiality. Due to the importance of physical safety, a reasonable person would conclude that knowledge of the defect as a purchaser is more important. Therefore, a reasonable person would support a rule that obligates the engineer to inform the prospective purchaser of the defect.

To show the significance of the weighing of values and interests, one can compare this case with one in which an engineer has determined that modification of a structure to the owner's desired use would be prohibitively expensive. In this situation, a prospective buyer would not risk physical safety; however, knowledge of the engineer's report would give the buyer a bargaining advantage over the client. The values to be compared are financial interests and confidentiality for the client and financial interests for the prospective purchaser. A reasonable person would prefer a norm by which the engineer respects confidentiality in this case. Purchasers are capable of protecting themselves from financial loss because they need not offer more for something than it is worth to them, even though a seller might have been willing to sell for less.

More complex cases arise when a large number of persons might be affected by a client's conduct. In these cases, the values of the affected persons must be weighted by the number of persons involved. One way to do this is to weight the values by the general probability of being a client or affected party. An example will clarify this point. Suppose a business consultant hired by the management of a corporation learns that the balance sheet, although done according to accepted accounting procedures, gives a deceptively favorable impression of the corporation's financial strength. The management's values are financial interests, including job security, and confidentiality. The affected parties include all stockholders as well as potential stock purchasers. Although the financial loss to management of the actual financial position becoming known is probably greater than for any particular stockholder, there are many more stockholders. Consequently, to apply the recommended procedure, one must use the general probability of being a stockholder versus that of being a member of management. Because people are much more likely to be stockholders, at least through a retirement system, they will prefer a norm requiring disclosure to one requiring the preservation of confidentiality. Thus, the consultant should break confidentiality in this case.

Lawyer–Client Confidentiality

Probably the most discussed and complex issues of obligations to clients versus those to others pertain to lawyers. An extended discussion of these issues can serve as a model for other problems.

During the early 1980s, the American Bar Association debated the limits of lawyer–client confidentiality vis-à-vis third parties. The discussion was widely reported in the press, and many observers thought it was one of the profession's worst hours. The issue arose in considering the adoption of a new code of ethics—*The Model Rules*. The older *Code of Professional Responsibility* permitted lawyers to reveal information (1) when required by law or court order and (2) to prevent crimes by clients.[19]

The commission to write a new code first proposed that lawyers be *required* to disclose information (1) necessary to prevent the client committing an act that would result in death or serious bodily harm, (2) as required by law, and (3) to rectify false evidence or testimony. It also *permitted* the lawyer to disclose information (4) to prevent or rectify the consequences of a client's deliberately wrongful act except for past acts regarding which the lawyer represented the client.[20] These conditions were weakened in the draft submitted to the House of Delegates, which in turn further weakened them. The result is that under the *Model Rules* lawyers are *required* to disclose information to a tribunal (1) to prevent or correct a fraud on a tribunal and (2) to obey a law or court order.[21] They are also *permitted* to do so (3) to prevent a client's criminal act "likely to result in imminent death or substantial bodily harm."[22] Preventing or rectifying the consequences of deliberately wrongful acts dropped out as an exception to confidentiality. Preventing death no longer requires disclosure, but only permits it when the client's act would be criminal.

Interestingly, the final and weakened exceptions to confidentiality might not gain general acceptance. Each state must adopt the *Model Rules* for them to be effective. Some states have modified the rules to provide more exceptions. For example, Florida modified the rules to require disclosure to prevent a crime or to prevent a death or serious bodily injury.[23]

Civil Context. By the method suggested here, one must consider the values at stake for the client and for third parties. In civil cases, clients usually have two values at stake—the privacy involved in confidentiality and wealth (the damages to be received or paid). A reasonable ranking of third party values and interests is as follows:

1. Avoidance of death and serious bodily injury
2. Fraud on a tribunal
3. Fraud or legal wrong to another party
4. Obedience of laws and court orders

Fraud on a tribunal affects the administration of justice and also normally involves fraud or wrong on another party. Thus, fraud or legal wrong to another party can be limited to cases that do not involve a fraud on a tribunal. Obedience to laws and court orders is essential to legal order. Both fraud on a tribunal and obedience of laws and court orders affect the public at large.

One must then consider which set of values and interests—those of clients or third parties—one would normally judge to be more important. Moreover, when the third party is the public at large, one must weight the values by the number of people involved. Given these considerations, it is plausible that each of the previously listed third party interests outweighs those of clients. One might question whether fraud or legal wrong to another party does so because both will normally involve a loss of wealth and deceit or unfairness. These might not be greater than the loss of the client's wealth and privacy. Indeed, the interests of client and third party in wealth will normally balance each other, for what one gains the other loses.

One way to indicate the ethical weight of reaons for restricting confidentiality is to require or merely permit disclosure.[24] In civil cases, avoidance of death and serious bodily injury and fraud on a tribunal seem strong enough to justify requiring disclosure. The third and fourth values might merely support permitting disclosure. A permissive rule of disclosure for fraud or legal wrong to a third party permits a lawyer to balance the significance of the infringement of a client's privacy with the fraud or wrong to the third party. Sometimes a client might have little or no interest in privacy of the information except to avoid disclosure of the wrong. Also, the seriousness of the wrong to the third party can vary significantly. For obedience of laws and court orders, a possible reason for only permitting disclosure is that the courts and law have other methods, such as contempt of court, for enforcing failure to comply.[25]

Two points are worth noting. First, it does not appear to make any difference whether the disclosure is to prevent the harm in question or to rectify a past one. Of course, it is better to avoid the harm than to have it occur and correct it, but in both cases, the values involved are the same.[26] Second, the precise legal wrong committed by the client should not usually be relevant. For example, the *Model Rules* limits disclosures to prevent death or serious bodily injury to criminal acts. But surely that death or serious bodily injury would result from a noncriminal legal wrong is also sufficient reason for disclosure. However, few such cases are likely, for most civil wrongs that result in death or serious bodily injury are also criminal ones (for example, negligent homicide). One might not even require that the client's act be a legal wrong.[27] The value of life and bodily integrity plausibly outweigh the client's privacy. At least one might permit disclosure in such cases.

Criminal Context.   In criminal cases, instead of wealth, the client's freedom is at stake. Consequently, assuming freedom is more important than wealth, to justify disclosure, weightier values and interests of third parties will have to be involved in criminal than in civil contexts. There are, however, differences in the values of third parties at stake. First, no individual third parties are involved; the third party is always the public. One might object that the interests of victims or their relatives are involved, but their only justifiable interest is in seeing that justice is done. This interest is the same as the public interest.[28] Second, because the third party is the general public, fraud on third parties (part of third value on the previous list) collapses into fraud on the tribunal (the second value on the list). Wrongs become wrongs to the public, that is, crimes. Third, the public does have an interest in seeing the guilty punished and thus deterring crime. It also has an interest in not punishing the innocent, but frauds and wrongs will not further that aim.

Consequently, the values to be weighed are as follows:

Client	Third Party
1. privacy and freedom	1. death and bodily injury
	2. fraud
	3. criminal wrong
	4. obedience to law and court orders

Even though the client has more weighty values at stake in the criminal than in the civil context, it is plausible to hold that (1) prevention of death and serious bodily injury, (2) prevention of fraud, and (3) criminal wrong outweigh it. Moreover, many people would judge that (4) obedience to law and court orders also outweighs the client's values and interests. One might, however, have to disobey a law or order to test its legal validity.

Some people might immediately conclude that the criminal client's interests are always outweighed because, in their balancing, they would never be criminals. That is not the proper test. One must consider the probability of being a criminal. If 5 percent of the population is charged with crimes at one time or another, then one assigns a 5 percent chance to being a criminal. Not to do so is to ignore the values and interests of criminal clients, which is unfair.

Two qualifications to the exceptions to confidentiality are needed. First, confidentiality cannot admit of exceptions for past crimes for which the lawyer is representing the client. That would undercut the entire purpose of confidentiality and legal representation. If lawyers were required or permitted to disclose incriminating information clients revealed to them, reasonable clients would not reveal anything they would not reveal to the police. There would be little benefit from legal representation. Second, because even criminal wrongs can vary in significance, this exception should probably permit rather than require disclosure. The lawyer could then weigh in individual cases the seriousness of the crime and the seriousness of the effect on the client's privacy and freedom.

Three possible objections to this analysis can be considered for the crucial issue of client perjury during the criminal trial. The issue is what lawyers should do when they have good reasons to believe that their clients will take the witness stand and lie or subsequently discover that they did so. The first objection is that the previous analysis of clients' values at stake is inadequate. Clients' dignity is at stake. It is violated if they cannot confide all information to lawyers without incriminating themselves. However, one is not deprived of human dignity if one is not ethically permitted to lie in court. Human dignity as freedom of choice is left because clients can choose either to reveal information to lawyers or to lie on the witness stand.[29]

The second objection is that if lawyers are permitted or required to disclose client perjury, clients will not disclose information to lawyers. Thus, they will not be able to expose client wrongdoing; innocent clients might be deprived of effective assistance of counsel because they do not fully disclose information to their lawyers.[30] This rests on the empirical contentions that fewer wrongs will result if clients reveal incriminating information to lawyers who try to dissuade them from perjury and that clients will not reveal such information if it might be disclosed. Moreover, it is practically impossible to determine what percentage of clients do not disclose information to lawyers.

These claims are too strong. First, analogous evidence exists that when *Miranda* warnings of the right to counsel and that anything said could be used against one were given to criminal suspects, little difference in confessions resulted. Second, in other countries, such as Canada, lawyers must reveal such information, and criminals still receive effective assistance of counsel. Third, the exception is limited to future crimes or those, like perjury and bribing witnesses, committed during the legal proceedings. Thus, clients have no reason to withhold information unless it will indicate future crimes they will commit. Fourth, if guilty clients do receive less effective assistance of counsel because they wish to perjure themselves, that is their choice.

The third objection is that there is no acceptable method for lawyers to reveal client perjury.[31] Three alternatives to complete confidentiality are unacceptable. (1) The lawyer can withdraw from the case. To do so during trial, however, requires court permission and will probably indicate that the lawyer believes the client guilty. (2) The lawyer can confide in the judge and let the judge decide. However, this will probably bias the judge. Both this alternative and the previous one are likely to require a mistrial. (3) The lawyer might not examine the client on the testimony or simply ignore the perjurious testimony in the rest of the trial. However, that will probably indicate to the judge and jury that the testimony is false.

Mistrials should be avoided; otherwise defendants could continually avoid conviction by letting their lawyers know that they were committing perjury. However, the third alternative does not result in a mistrial. Nor is it clear what is wrong if the judge and jury conclude that the testimony is false. After all, by hypothesis, it probably is. Moreover, a fourth alternative exists. The lawyer could continue with the case in the normal fashion and reveal the information afterwards. If the client was convicted, the conviction would stand. If the client was found innocent, grounds would exist for a new trial. In either case, the client would also be open to prosecution for perjury.

It seems unwise to require any one of these alternatives. The precise method should probably be left to lawyers' judgments in particular situations.[32] Depending on the circumstances, any one of them might be best.

Two cases illustrate some of the difficulties that lawyers confront. Whiteside was charged with murdering a man.[33] Until just before trial, he told his lawyer Robinson that he had not seen a gun in the victim's hand, though he believed the victim had one. No gun had been found at the scene. Shortly before trial, Whiteside indicated that he would testify that he saw something metallic in the victim's hand. Robinson told Whiteside that if he so testified, it would be perjury; that he, Robinson, would have to advise the court; that he would probably be allowed to impeach the testimony; and that he would seek to withdraw. Whiteside did not commit perjury, but he attempted to overturn his conviction on grounds that he had been denied effective assistance of counsel. The Supreme Court held that he had not. Defendants do not have a right to testify falsely, and if they propose to do so, they risk withdrawal of counsel. The obligation of confidentiality does not extend to plans to engage in future crimes.

In another case, attorney Ellis Rubin asked to withdraw from representing a client charged with murder whom he believed was planning to commit perjury.[34] The judge ordered Rubin to continue to represent the defendant, and when Rubin refused, the judge sentenced him to thirty days in jail for contempt. The defendant, with another lawyer, was convicted in a subsequent trial. In part as a result of this case, the Florida Bar is considering an amendment to its code of ethics permitting lawyers to allow clients to take the stand but not question them and not use the testimony.[35]

Finally, there is an objection to the whole procedure of specifying limited exceptions to the obligation of confidentiality. The claim is that there are always other ethically justifiable exceptions not included, for example, to prevent another party's total financial ruin.[36] However, this approach leaves too much discretion to lawyers.[37] They would not know when they might be disciplined for unprofessional conduct because a disciplinary committee arrived at a different conclusion about the ethical justifiability of disclosure. It would also leave clients in great doubt about what would be confidential, and this would significantly deter them from disclosing information to lawyers.

Further Problems of Confidentiality

The detailed examination of lawyer–client confidentiality has implications for other problems in other professions. For example, one can readily conclude that other professionals should disclose information to prevent their clients committing crimes. The strongest claim to confidentiality regarding future crimes is that of lawyers where the crimes are involved in the representation, such as perjury. If an exception to confidentiality is justifiable there, it will be for other professsions. For example, suppose a social worker working with juvenile gangs witnesses a crime. From the therapeutic perspective, it is unclear whether it should be reported. Doing so is likely to undermine rapport with and trust of the juveniles. Yet failure to do so might undermine efforts to induce law-abiding conduct. However, once one puts the public interest in punishment of the guilty on the scales, the balance clearly tips to reporting it.

It does not necessarily follow that professionals should report all their clients' past crimes. A variable here is the seriousness of the crime. For example, the public interest, if any, in punishing people guilty of homosexual conduct is not likely to outweigh a client's value of privacy and the need for full communication to provide psychiatric help. Crimes of violence, such as murder, rape, and assault, are another matter. The public interest in punishing and deterring them is as great as for any crime. Consequently, professionals such as engineers, accountants, psychologists, and so on should be permitted to disclose past crimes but not required to do so, except perhaps for crimes of violence.

Similarly, when the law requires disclosure of information, then professionals should disclose it. Again, the exception to confidentiality can be justified the same as for lawyers. Of course, like lawyers, other professionals might refuse until there is a final determination that they are legally obligated to disclose. The crucial question is when the law should require disclosure. Two problems—abused children and AIDS patients—deserve consideration.

Child Abuse. Although all states require professionals to report suspected child abuse, some people have doubts about the wisdom of the policy. For the same reasons, professionals might not be complying fully with the laws. The arguments about reporting child abuse parallel one set about lawyers reporting client perjury. If lawyers will report proposed perjury, clients might withhold the information; the lawyers will not know that perjury is involved, so they cannot prevent or rectify it. If professionals report child abuse, then parents might not bring children for treatment. The children will not receive treatment, and future abuse cannot be prevented.

There are better reasons for thinking parents will not be deterred from seeking treatment for children than that criminal defendants will not be deterred from disclosing information to lawyers. First, most abusive parents do not want to hurt their children.[38] Consequently, at some point, they are likely to seek the child's treatment, whatever the limits of confidentiality. Second, abusive parents do not normally face as severe a threat to themselves as criminal defendants. The emphasis in many programs is to provide therapeutic help to the parents, not to impose criminal punishment. Of course, some situations can be so bad that criminal prosecution is appropriate. However, that is most likely when the child is dead. Before that occurs, there will probably have been an opportunity to report suspected abuse and to have removed the child from the situation. It is failure to have received previous help and intervention for the child that often permits further abuse and death.

The discussion so far suggests that the parents are the clients and the child the third party. However, if the child is brought for medical care, that is not the case. Instead, the child is the client, and the parents are the third party. In this perspective, obligations to the parents are nonmaleficence, truthfulness, and fairness. Reporting child abuse does not violate truthfulness. It does not violate fairness because the allegations will be investigated. Nor does it violate an obligation of nonmaleficence because any penalties the parents might receive would be duly imposed by law and thus not constitute wrongful harm.

Sometimes a parent might be the client. But a possible detrimental effect on a therapeutic relationship with the parent clearly cannot justify not reporting abuse. "A beaten child seems a worse case than a mother who clams up on an anxious therapist."[39] At worst, the parent's treatment will not progress, or another therapist will have to take over.

AIDS Carriers.   There are several purposes for legally requiring disclosure that a person has AIDS (acquired immune deficiency syndrome) or is a carrier of the virus that causes it. One reason is for epidemiological (statistical) research about its incidence, spread, and so on. The public interest is in further knowledge about the disease and possibly contributing factors. Because research can maintain subjects' anonymity, such reporting seems justifiable.

A second general reason is to warn persons who might have been in contact with the carrier. Two subdivisions are possible. (1) Because AIDS is primarily spread by sexual intercourse, common use of needles for injections, and blood transfusions, persons having had such relationships can be warned and advised to be tested. The benefits to those warned are either to avoid further contact or to determine whether they have acquired the virus. Carriers' identity cannot be kept anonymous in this situation. Previous attempts to trace sexually transmitted diseases were not very successful; too many people forwent treatment to avoid disclosure. More success is probably achieved by individual physicians informing those who are or have been in contact, preferably through the patients. Whether that is true for AIDS is unclear. If it is, then the interests of third parties are furthered by not disclosing.

(2) The purpose can be to warn all persons likely to come into some form of contact with AIDS carriers—fellow workers, parents of other schoolchildren, and so on. Here the interest of third parties do not seem strong. The risks to them from casual contact are quite small. For example, one estimate is that by 1990 over fifty thousand people in the United States will die annually from AIDS.[40] Although this is a large number, it must be put in perspective. It is about the same number as die from automobile accidents. The risks from casual contact with carriers might then be compared to the risks of pedestrians. Thus, the risk to people from casual contact is comparable to many other risks of daily life.

Moreover, the value of confidentiality is significant because carriers are subject to unreasonable discrimination and harassment. For example, in Arcadia, Florida, when three hemophiliac carriers entered school under court order, many parents kept their children home. In one of the most reprehensible acts possible, the family's home was burned by suspected arson. In another example, the Montgomery, Alabama, police department kept a list, supposedly compiled from voluntary statements, of AIDS carriers.[41] The mayor's justification for the list is that it is needed so police and fire fighters know when they might come into contact with a carrier. However, unless police and fire fighters have fantastic memories, they will be hard-pressed to remember the names and faces of all carriers.

A third reason is to isolate or quarantine the carriers. Given the small probability of spreading the disease by casual contact and the large number of carriers, no general quarantine could be justified.[42] However, a few extraordinary situations might justify quarantine or restraint. For example, in Sweden, one person who continued to share needles with others and to have sex without precautions was restrained.[43] Nonetheless, a general reporting of all carriers to avoid these few situations would not be acceptable. If one considers the values at stake for all the carriers and the small increase of risk to the public, one would favor confidentiality. This is not to say restraint might not be justifiable in special cases.

Loyalty and the Public Purse

One final conflict between obligations to third parties and to clients deserves brief consideration. The conflict arises when services to the client are being borne by the public at large. This occurs with patients being treated under Medicare or Medicaid or without insurance or ability to pay. It also occurs with lawyers in legal aid organizations. The issue is whether loyalty and benefiting the client outweigh any obligations to the public to control costs. No primary obligation to control third party costs was recognized in my previous discussion. If there is such an obligation, it must stem from the obligations of nonmaleficence or fairness. Increasing public expense is not a direct injury; at best, it is injury from inefficient use of public resources.

Fairness is more likely to apply, for the expense might impose an unfair burden on the public or part of it. First, fairness involves complying with the rules of third party payers. Because they are contributing the funds, they can direct how they shall be spent. There is, of course, an issue about the fairness of these rules, but that is not a direct issue for the professional–client relationship. However, it is difficult for a professional to be unfair by violating such a rule, for the third party payer, whether Medicare, Medicaid, or an insurance company, simply will not pay the bill. Second, within the rules, occasions might arise when costs can be saved without violating any obligation of loyalty to a patient. For example, if either an expensive or inexpensive antibiotic will cure an infection, then fairness to the third party payer involves using the less expensive one.[44]

Third, difficult situations arise when payment for the service will not be fully covered by insurance, public programs, or the patient. Two subdivisions of this situation are possible. One is when the patient is an outlier under a DRG payment type of system. That is, the cost of treatment will exceed the reimbursement. In this case, medically appropriate treatment should be provided, although cost can be an element in determining what treatment is appropriate (see Chapter 4). The DRG payment system is based on average costs and thus anticipates care for some patients exceeding the payment. If this might cut into hospital profits, that is the hospital's problem. Perhaps it should reorganize the service or not provide it. In any case, it is not directly an issue with a third party, but rather with an employer or organization having a relationship to the professional similar to that of an employer.

The second type of case arises when the procedure is not covered at all. A common instance is liver or heart transplant. If such a procedure is provided, then an issue of fairness does arise. In the first instance, the hospital absorbs the cost. However, that cost is then spread over the charges for all patients. Even if the hospital is a nonprofit one, it must still balance its income and expenses. It then passes this cost on to insurance companies and paying patients.

Third parties are thus paying for services for others. This cost is spread over everyone through higher insurance premiums. They were not asked about their willingness to do so, so the added cost is unfair. People who pay all or part of their medical costs are treated especially unfairly. Suppose insurance pays 80 percent of hospital costs. An operation, say, to remove a diseased kidney, might easily cost $30,000. Under such insurance, the patient pays $6,000. Suppose 10 percent of hospital bills are uncollected. For the hospital to break even, the bills for those who pay must be 11 percent higher than they would otherwise be. In short, the insured patient is $660 out of pocket to help pay for other patients. The unfairness is compounded if one realizes that the burden falls most heavily on those people who are sick. That is, the cost of the unpaid bills is disproportionately paid by those who are financially able and sick.

Unfairness to third parties results from treating persons when no one agreed to pay. Consequently, an obligation of fairness to third parties is clearly relevant in deciding to treat. Whether that outweighs the benefit to the client is another question. One must balance the benefit to the client against the unfairness of imposing costs on third parties. The balancing is not simply the cost of this particular treatment, but of treatment in all similar cases. If one used the former, the incremental cost to each individual third party would be minuscule. Even if one weights it by the number of people affected, one might easily decide for the client. However, the method for balancing is to establish a rule for a society in which one would live, so one must consider such treatment for all similar cases. Whether one would accept a norm providing treatment will vary, depending largely on the expected benefit to clients in such cases and the cost, because the greater the cost, the greater the unfairness. Nevertheless, the acceptable balance is a question appropriately considered by a professional. Of course, this issue can be avoided by adopting a system that provides medical (or legal) care for all (see Chapter 3).

Finally, this issue arises only for services that people have a right to independent of ability to pay, that is, medical, educational, and legal services. If services need be provided only when clients can pay, the obligation of loyalty does not extend to services for which they cannot pay.

SUMMARY

This chapter has concerned professionals' obligations to third parties, people other than their clients. These obligations are those of universal norms because professionals have no special relationship to third parties. The three fundamental obligations of professionals to third parties are truthfulness, nonmaleficence, and fairness. Candor, with its requirement of full disclosure, does not pertain because professionals do not have a special trust relationship to third parties.

Conflicts between role-related responsibilities to clients and universal obligations to third parties are at the heart of professional ethics. The proposed test for reconciling these conflicting responsibilities is to identify and weigh the values and interests of the client against those of third parties who will be affected, consider the general probability of being a client or affected third party, and remember that one is developing a rule to be applied to all similar cases. The result of such a procedure will frequently be a rule that reconciles the considerations in conflicting responsibilities. The procedure does not guarantee that all reasonable persons will arrive at the same conclusion; reasonable people may disagree due to subtle differences in weighing values, attitudes toward risk, or differences about factual matters. Nonetheless, great differences will be eliminated and a basis provided for reasonable discussion.

The test was applied to determine possible exceptions to lawyers' obligations of confidentiality to clients. In the civil context, it is suggested that confidential information should be disclosed to prevent death or serious bodily injury and to prevent or rectify a fraud on a tribunal, and it may be disclosed to prevent fraud or other legal wrong to other third parties and to obey the law or a court order. In the criminal context, confidential information should be disclosed to prevent a death or serious bodily injury and fraud on a tribunal; it may be disclosed to prevent other criminal acts or to obey a law or court order. Lawyers might plausibly be allowed discretion about the method of disclosing client perjury, but they should not be permitted discretion to disclose information whenever they think it justifiable.

The following suggestions were made for other problems of confidentiality. All professionals (except lawyers) may disclose confidential information to prevent illegal conduct and perhaps to rectify past conduct. It is appropriate for the law to require professionals to report suspected child abuse because avoiding injury to children is a greater value than preserving confidentiality of parents and not likely to deter parents from seeking treatment for their children. This holds whether the parents or the children are the clients.

The confidentiality of carriers of the AIDS virus might reasonably contain an exception for epidemiological research because anonymity can be preserved, and possibly for warning those who might have been directly exposed by sexual activity, sharing needles, or receiving blood from the carriers. It is not justifiable to warn those likely to come into casual contact with them because of the small chance of contracting the disease and the irrational discrimination and other conduct directed toward carriers. Nor is it likely to be justifiable to disclose their identity so as to isolate carriers.

Finally, professionals, particularly physicians, should consider the public cost involved in treating indigent clients because these costs are unfairly passed on to third parties without their direct or indirect agreement. Whether a treatment or procedure should be provided depends on a balancing of the likely benefits to the client and the unfair costs to the public from treating similar cases. This problem would not arise were there a system of providing health and legal services to all the poor.

NOTES*

1. *Tarasoff* v. *Regents of the University of California,* 17 Cal. 3d 425, 551 P. 2d 334, 131 Cal. Rptr. 14 (1976); see also *Hedlund* v. *Superior Court of Orange County,* 669 P. 2d 41 (Cal. 1983) (extending liability to child present when mother shot by patient); Carroll, Schneider, and Wesley, *Ethics in the Practice of Psychology,* pp. 34–37.

2. Engineers' Council, "Code of Ethics," Canon 1; National Society of Professional Engineers, "Code of Ethics," Canon 1.

3. Cahn, *Saints and Scamps,* p. 50.

4. A curious theory has developed in journalism, that of advocacy or adversary journalism. It seems to rest on the claim that a journalist will always be influenced by personal values, biases, and so on and thus cannot be completely fair and objective. Consequently, it is concluded that one should not try. The fallacy involved is obvious; that one cannot completely succeed does not mean that one ought not try.

5. ABA, *Code of Professional Responsibility,* DR 7-102(A)(1), DR 7-106(C)(2); ABA, *Model Rules,* Rules 3.1, 4.4.

6. ABA, *Model Rules,* Rule 3.4, is titled "Fairness to Opposing Party and Counsel," but it primarily prohibits illegal conduct.

7. ABA, *Code of Professional Responsibility,* DR 7-106(B)(1); ABA, *Model Rules,* Rule 3.3(a) and (b).

8. The strongest and most broad ranging attack is Simon, "The Ideology of Advocacy," pp. 29–114.

9. See Cheek, "Professional Responsibility," p. 620; ABA, *Code of Professional Responsibility,* comes close to making the distinction in EC 7-3; and it is explicit in the structure of ABA, *Model Rules.*

10. See David Luban, "The Adversary System Excuse," in *The Good Lawyer,* ed. Luban, pp. 113–17; Gewirth, "Professional Ethics," pp. 294–295.

11. Luban, "The Adversary System Excuse," pp. 93–111; Bayles, *Principles of Law,* pp. 33–39.

12. According to Geoffrey C. Hazard, Jr., the ABA *Code* holds that lawyers owe clients almost unqualified loyalty and owe others what is compatible with the obligation; see Hazard, *Ethics in the Practice of Law,* p. 8.

13. Quoted in Freedman, *Lawyers' Ethics,* p. 9.

14. See AMA, *Principles of Medical Ethics,* sec. 3; Lieberman, *Crisis at the Bar,* pp. 168–169.

15. Charles Fried, "The Lawyer as Friend: The Moral Foundations of the Lawyer–Client Relationship," in *1977 National Conference on Teaching Professional Responsibility,* ed. Goldberg, p. 153; see also Fried, *Right and Wrong,* pp. 191–193.

16. Fried, *Right and Wrong,* p. 183.

---

*See the bibliography at the back of the book for complete references.

17. Richard Wasserstrom, "Lawyers as Professionals: Some Moral Issues," in *1977 National Conference on Teaching Professional Responsibility,* ed. Goldberg, pp. 116–118. On the general problems for professionals' character from a divergence of universal and role-related norms, see the articles in *The Good Lawyer,* ed. Luban, part 4.

18. This test differs from Alan Goldman's proposed test of asking whether impartial contractors would agree to permitting lawyers to violate the moral rights of third parties so that they might do the same in one's behalf; see Goldman, *Moral Foundations,* p. 144. The proposed test is to help determine what rights should be recognized by appealing to underlying interests and values, whereas Goldman assumes certain rights. The issue is, however, what interests or rights of third parties should be recognized to override conflicting obligations to, or interests of, clients.

19. ABA, *Code of Professional Responsibility,* DR 4-101(2) and (3). Up to 1974, it also required disclosure of information to correct a fraud a client had perpetrated on another person or tribunal during a lawyer's representation. That was then amended to exclude privileged information, which was interpreted to include confidential information. See ABA, *Code of Professional Responsibility,* DR 7-102(B)(1); Moore, "Limits to Attorney–Client Confidentiality," p. 218, n. 192.

20. ABA, Commission on Evaluation of Professional Standards, *Model Rules of Professional Conduct,* Discussion Draft (Chicago: American Bar Association, 1980), Rules 1.7(b) and (c)(2) and (3), 3.1(b), and 4.2(b)(2).

21. ABA, *Model Rules,* Rules 3.3(a) and (b), and 3.4(c).

22. ABA, *Model Rules,* Rule 1.6(b)(1).

23. Florida Bar, *Florida Rules of Professional Conduct* (Tallahassee, Fl.: Continuing Legal Education Publications, 1987), Rule 4-1.6.

24. Freedman, "Lawyer–Client Confidences," p. 4.

25. Ibid., p. 6.

26. See also Moore, "Limits to Attorney–Client Confidentiality," pp. 234–242.

27. Ibid., pp. 231–233.

28. Vengeance is not an acceptable interest. See Bayles, *Principles of Law,* p. 286.

29. See Moore, "Limits to Attorney–Client Confidentiality," pp. 220–221; Alan Donagan, "Justifying Legal Practice in the Adversary System," in *The Good Lawyer,* ed. Luban, p. 144.

30. See Kipnis, *Legal Ethics,* pp. 76–77, arguing for unqualified or absolute confidentiality in criminal cases.

31. Freedman, *Lawyer's Ethics,* chap. 3; Kipnis, *Legal Ethics,* pp. 88–90.

32. See Note, "Professional Ethics of Criminal Defense Lawyers," pp. 548–551.

33. *Nix v. Whiteside,* 106 S. Ct. 988 (1986).

34. "Flashy Lawyer Calls Jail Term 'Humiliating,' " *Gainsville Sun,* 23 February 1987, p. 1B.

35. "Attorney Rubin Blasts Ethics-Code Proposal," *Tallahassee Democrat,* 5 September 1987, p. 4B.

36. Goldman, "Confidentiality, Rules, and Codes of Ethics," p. 9; see also Gerald J. Postema, "Moral Responsibility in Professional Ethics," in *Ethics and the Legal Profession,* ed. Davis and Elliston, pp. 171–172.

37. See Freedman, "Problem of Writing"; and Kipnis, *Legal Ethics,* p. 73.

38. Marilyn Heins, "The Necessity for Reporting Child Abuse," in *Difficult Decisions in Medical Ethics,* ed. Ganos et al., p. 57.

39. Ibid., p. 56.

40. "General Introduction," in *AIDS,* ed. Pierce and VanDeVeer, p. 1.

41. "AIDS List Provokes an Outcry," *Tallahassee Democrat,* 25 September 1987, p. 1A.

42. One to one and a half million carriers were in the United States by early 1987; "General Introduction (see n. 40 above), p. 2.

43. Carol A. Tauer, "Human Rights: An Intercontinental Perspective," in *AIDS,* ed. Pierce and VanDeVeer, p. 164. Two cases of restraining bleeding patients have occurred in England; ibid., p. 163.

44. Brazil, "Cost Effective Care," p. 7.

STUDY QUESTIONS AND PROBLEMS

1. Asher Bausch and his wife, Ashkenazic Jews, went to the local genetics unit to be tested for the chances of having a child with Tay Sachs disease. This recessive genetic disorder is untreatable and produces blindness, motor paralysis, and other symptoms leading to death, usually before the age of three. The tests showed that Asher was a carrier but his wife was not. Although he and his wife were not at risk of having a child with the defect, Asher's brothers had a 50 percent chance of being carriers, and if they married an Ashkenazic Jew, the chances were one in thirty that she would be a carrier, and so the odds were one in sixty that they would have an affected infant. When Dr. Cloe Dunlop explained these facts, Asher became upset. Dr. Dunlop asked Asher to send his brothers a letter the genetics unit had prepared suggesting that they be tested for the carrier status. Asher refused. He felt ashamed and could not bring himself to tell his brothers. Would it be ethical for Dr. Dunlop to write the brothers and recommend that they have genetic screening? Why or why not?

2. Edgar Farr is representing his client, who has been convicted on a criminal charge. They are now before the judge for sentencing. The judge asks the clerk if Farr's client has a criminal record, and the clerk says he does not. However, Edgar knows that his client does have a record. While he is trying to decide what to do, the judge says, "As this is your first offense, I shall give you a suspended sentence." What should Farr do? Why?

3. A clinical psychologist, Gerri Hudson, is treating Irwin Johnson, who was referred to her as being near a nervous breakdown. After a few sessions, Irwin

confesses to having murdered someone. Gerri does not think Irwin will murder again and thinks that she can assist him whether or not he turns himself in to the police, as he is thinking of doing. What should she ethically do? Why?

4. Engineer Katherine Lowell works for the Bright Lights Power Co. In examining the plant of a subscriber, Widgets, Inc., she discovers that Widgets can save considerable money by making a few inexpensive modifications at its plant. Should she inform Widgets or Bright Light of this fact? Why?

5. As President of Global, Inc., Malcolm Nevis has aggressively promoted the company. He has taken over various other companies and significantly increased Global's earnings. He has insisted that Global's accountants follow liberal methods so long as they conform to generally accepted accounting principles. Olive Patterson, Global's chief accountant, is rather worried about some of the methods Malcolm has insisted on. Global sold a subsidiary for $2,750,000, and Nevis wants to count $1,750,000 as profit for last year, although the subsidiary would not have contributed nearly that much to earnings for several years. He wants to include as earnings for last year oil and gas production payments for the next two years that were sold to another corporation. He also wants to include last year's earnings of three new subsidiaries purchased at the beginning of this year. Finally, President Nevis wants to capitalize over several years the administrative expenses of a subsidiary that would otherwise show a large loss. All of these items are within generally accepted accounting principles. If they are followed, however, will they provide a fair statement of Global's financial condition? Would they mislead potential investors? Is it ethical for the accountants to follow President Nevis's instructions? Why or why not? If not, what should Olive Patterson do? Why?

6. Attorney Quincy Reynolds is representing Trickle, Inc., in a contract negotiation with the Fillers Union. They are only a few cents apart on the wage increase. The union's chief negotiator, Susan Toms, phones Quincy and suggests that Trickle might release ten employees who do not belong to the union and who are not essential to Trickle's operations. The union will not support any grievance the employees may file, and Trickle will save more than enough money to meet the union's wage demands. What should Reynolds do? Must he convey the offer to Trickle's president? What should he recommend? Why?

7. Uriah Vishman was hired to audit two state institutions. He discovered serious irregularities and perhaps fraud. He reported his findings to his superior, but no action was taken. He then went to the district attorney, who was a close friend of the governor, who was running for reelection. The district attorney refused to take any action at this time, informally suggesting that he might do so after the election. Ethically, what should Uriah do? Should he make his findings public? Has he fulfilled his responsibilities by reporting to the appropriate authorities? Who are his actual employers?

8. Wilma Xuan is editor of the Clinton *Courier*. She receives a visit from Albert Bateman and a Mrs. Charles Douglas III. The day before, Mr. Bateman's wife had been arrested at a local department store for shoplifting $5.26 worth of goods. She had her four-year-old son with her. At her trial, she claimed she had

not taken the goods and that her son had probably put them in the shopping bag while she was looking at something else. However, a store detective testified that he had seen her take the items. As a warning to other shoplifters at Christmas time, the judge sentenced Mrs. Bateman to a week in jail instead of the usual $100 fine. Mrs. Douglas tells Wilma that Mrs. Bateman had been her maid for several years after immigrating to this country, was completely honest, and would not do such a thing. She is staying with Mr. Bateman to take care of the children while Mrs. Bateman is in jail. Mr. Bateman asks Wilma not to print any story about Mrs. Bateman's conviction or at least to delete her name. If her name appears, their two young children will be subjected to harassment by other children; Mrs. Bateman will not be able to face their neighbors, so they will have to sell their recently purchased home and move to another neighborhood. What should Wilma ethically do? If she withholds the name, will she be depriving the readers of information to which they have a right? Can justice operate in secret? Should the innocent children suffer for their mother's wrong?

9.   Reconsider problem 12 in Chapter 3. In light of obligations to third parties, do you wish to give a different answer? If so, why? If not, is the case for your position strengthened or weakened?

10. Professor Edsel Forel has just discovered that a student he had last semester has enrolled in a course of his colleague, Professor Genevra Hansen. Edsel particularly remembers this student, Israel Jernigan, because he turned in a paper that was plagiarized, the bulk of it having been copied from a book. Professor Forel failed Israel in the course and sent a notice to the academic honor committee. The committee keeps such records confidential unless a second incident occurs; in that case, further disciplinary actions may be instituted. Professor Forel discussed Israel's case only with the department chair when the incident occurred. Should Edsel warn Professor Hansen about Israel's past plagiarism so that she can be especially careful to see that it does not occur again? Is Israel now Professor Forel's client? Does that make any difference? Who would be affected if Israel plagiarized again and was not caught? What, if any, obligation does Professor Forel owe to them?

11. Reconsider problem 18 in Chapter 4. Suppose Mrs. Ventry has no health insurance, and her family cannot afford to pay for her treatment. Does this make any difference in your analysis of which patient should be treated? Is that always a sufficient reason to choose one patient over another? If so, why? If not, why not?

12. Dr. Kristen Liberis's patient Morton Nye is dying. He has a very rare, progressive neurological disorder. No experiments are presently under way anywhere in the world to find a cure for the disease. However, Dr. Liberis has an untested theory that suggests that lowering the body temperature under conditions of high pressure might cure the disease. This would involve putting Morton in ice packs for several weeks to lower his body temperature and running him through a hyperbaric chamber (as used for divers with the bends) a couple of times. Although the treatment is experimental, Medicaid would pay for it, or almost all of it. Assuming Mr. Nye consents, would it be ethical to

perform the treatment? Why or why not? Suppose Medicaid would not pay the expense, and Mr. Nye cannot afford to do so. Would that make any difference to the ethics of the treatment? Why or why not?

13. Oriana Proctor's engineering firm was consulted by Zap Construction Company, which is bidding on a state contract. The contract specifications call for removal of so many cubic yards of earth, but the president of Zap thought the amount excessive. Oriana went to the site and made her own survey and estimates. They indicate that much less earth than the specifications call for actually needs to be removed. With this knowledge, Zap will easily be able to underbid its competitors. Should Oriana inform state authorities of their mistake? Why or why not?

6 Obligations Between Professionals and Employers

Most professionals are and always have been employees. Those in the three largest professions—teachers, nurses, and engineers—are almost all employees.[1] During the last few decades, the percentage of employee members of traditionally self-employed professions has increased. For example, a greater percentage of lawyers has become employees of large law firms.[2] At the same time, the percentage of self-employed members of some traditionally employee professions, such as social work, has increased significantly.[3]

Many obligations between employers and employee professionals are the same as in any employer–employee relationship. This chapter emphasizes what is or might be thought to be distinctive when the employee is a professional. Employee professionals confront some ethical issues different from those confronted by self-employed professionals. They do not face issues of fee setting, advertising, and so on considered in Chapter 3. However, they have obligations to employers that need to be specified. These obligations to employers must then be reconciled with obligations to clients and third parties. Because employees and employers disagree on these and other matters, various issues arise concerning authority and conflict in organizations, such as whistle-blowing and strikes. Finally, employers might have distinctive obligations to employee professionals.

EMPLOYEE OBLIGATIONS

The employee–employer relationship is quite similar to the professional–client relationship. It is also a fiduciary one; the employee is expected to act for the best interests of the employer. In a nonfiduciary contractual relationship, the parties are not expected to act in behalf of the best interests of the other party, but only not to injure the other party by failing to fulfill contractual obligations. However, the employee–employer relationship partakes of many features of the agency model discussed in Chapter 4. Employers generally have more authority to direct employees' activities than clients usually have. This agency aspect is reflected in employees' obligations of obedience. Employees rarely act paternalistically toward their employers, although employers have been known to act paternalistically toward their employees.

Fiduciary Obligations

The legal obligations or duties of employees to employers are covered by the law of agency. Although classified somewhat differently, these obligations cover most of those included in the obligations of professionals to clients as discussed in Chapter 4. The chief exception is that of fairness. Because fairness primarily concerns how one client is treated in comparison to another, and employees usually have only one employer, such comparative concerns are irrelevant. Ethical obligations largely parallel the legal ones. They are required for a trustworthy employee.

Competence and Diligence.   These two obligations are often referred to as a legal duty of good care.[4] Professional employees warrant that they have the competence and skill of other members of their profession. In two respects, the employer–employee situation differs from the client–professional one. First, employers will have resumes of, and probably references for, employees. Particularly in professional organizations, employers should be better able than ordinary clients to judge the professional's competence. Still, professionals have an obligation to exercise that competence diligently.

Second, given that employers should know the limits of professionals' competence, they should not assign them tasks for which they lack competence. Yet it is not uncommon for them to do so. In one survey, 89 percent of law firm associates felt that they had been assigned tasks for which they lacked sufficient expertise, and 83 percent felt that they had been assigned tasks without sufficient time to do them properly.[5] If professionals are assigned tasks beyond their competence or without time to perform them adequately, then they should so inform their employers. Many employees are reluctant to do so, for fear that it might jeopardize their jobs. If they do raise the issue, their responsibility becomes uncertain if the employer replies, "Do the best you can."

Honesty and Candor.   Employees are obligated to be honest with their employers. This obligation includes not stealing from them. Some common forms of dishonesty often not recognized as such by employees are making personal long distance phone calls and conducting personal affairs while at work. The latter is complicated by the fact that professionals often do not punch a time clock and are likely to devote many hours at home to business. Moreover, the distinction between personal and employer business can be unclear. For example, although most college teachers are expected to publish, they are usually entitled to any royalties from their writing. Is their writing a book part of their employment or separate, personal business? If it is the former, then using college computers, paper, and other supplies is not dishonest. If it is the latter, then it is a form of theft.

The obligation of candor pertains to all information that affects an employer's interests.[6] Failures in fulfilling this responsibility are most likely when having to provide bad news. If employees uncover information beneficial to an employer, they are likely to report it to obtain credit and look good. But if the information is bad, especially if it involves a mistake by the employee, he or she does not want to report it. Nonetheless, candor requires that one do so. Thus, if engineers find that a part or design is ineffective, they should report this to their employer. Similarly, nurses should report all information relevant to a patient's care.

Discretion.   Just as professionals are obligated to maintain the confidentiality of client communications both while and after persons are clients, so professional employees are obligated to keep employer information confidential while and after being an employee. Employers have the same interests as clients in keeping information confidential. Public knowledge of employer activities can adversely affect employers' financial and other interests, such as reputation. In business, *trade secrets* are crucial information to be kept confidential. These are particular designs or processes that employers attempt to keep secret and that often provide them a competitive edge. Lawyers and accountants working in corporations often have access to information about impending business moves that obviously should be kept confidential.

Many professionals are employed by governments. Although in the United States there is a commitment to the public's right to know and "government in the sunshine," some governmental business needs to be kept confidential at least for a time. Premature leakage of some information can harm public interest or provide some persons an unfair advantage over others. Potential prosecutions for crime or antitrust violations should not be prematurely leaked. A few years ago in Canada there was a controversy about premature leaks of governmental budgets. When the minister releases the budget there, new taxes and other changes can have significant financial impact. Unlike the United States, where proposed budgets are not adopted until after lengthy debate and changes, in Canada, the changes are practically certain and swift. Thus, advance information concerning a budget can provide significant advantages in financial markets and other activities.

Despite the potential for abuse, executive privilege for information and discussions in formulating policy and plans should be confidential. The reasons are similar to those for professional–client confidentiality, namely, without it, advisors and others will not speak freely, and decisions will not be based on full information and consideration of all pros and cons. This concern applies at all levels within government.

Loyalty.   Employees have an obligation of loyalty to employers. Difficulties with this obligation usually concern its scope. Employers are inclined to take loyalty to mean not saying or doing anything that reflects adversely on them. For example, I was once criticized by a dean for having made a disparaging remark about the university at a small faculty meeting. A Ford Motor Company employee was once fired for purchasing a car made by a different manufacturer.[7] These interpretations of loyalty surely go too far. Loyalty does not require faithfulness to employers no matter what. Both within and outside of one's employment, freedom, especially of expression, carries weight.

As with loyalty to clients, the central concern with professionals' loyalty to employers is preservation of their independence and objectivity of judgment. Conflicts of interest can remove that independence. Significant financial investment in competing firms or suppliers would likely affect employees' independence of judgment and loyalty to the employers' best interests. Normally, not investing in such companies will not seriously limit employees' investment opportunities. However, some conglomerate corporations deal with so many other companies that this might become a serious limitation. For example, an engineer working for IBM or Digital Equipment might practically be banned from investing in the computer industry, for most firms are suppliers of, or competitors with, those giant firms.

Kickbacks, bribes, and significant gratuities are not only dishonest, but affect independence of judgment. Many firms indicate that employees are not to accept gifts of more than nominal value from other businesspersons with whom they deal, such as suppliers. Often "nominal value" is specified in dollar amounts; the underlying moral principle is that it not be enough to affect an ordinary person's independence of judgment on behalf of the employer. Some professional codes of ethics contain explicit bans on accepting gratuities.[8]

Perhaps one of the most important issues for professional employees is *moonlighting*. This refers to holding a second job, either for another employer or as self-employed. Engineers might undertake work evenings on special projects for organizations; legal associates might take on a few clients personally; salaried university physicians often expect to enhance their income from private patients; other professors often make money from writing and lecturing; and social workers are now often engaging in part-time private practice.

Moonlighting does not usually involve activities directly contrary to employer interests, for example, working for a competitor. Rather, the concern is the extent to which an employee forgoes employer interests in favor of his or her own. For example, a computer engineer who has an innovative idea might not use it for the employer but set up a private company to market a product incorporating the idea. Most companies have a written policy or agreement that employees give them rights to all inventions they develop in return for a share in the profits. Often an employee's share of the profits is quite small, so an employer might well make a huge profit from an idea and the inventive employee benefit very little.[9] Were these agreements more equitable, employees might be more encouraged to work on ideas and share them.

Employers' concerns about moonlighting go beyond loyalty to include diligence and honesty. Employees might spend time at work on their secondary jobs rather than on employer's work. Further, they might use an employer's facilities and equipment for their secondary work. For example, employed social workers with a part-time private practice might find renting an office for their part-time work prohibitively expensive. Thus, they might use their agency offices after hours or keep their private files in the office along with agency files. Various solutions to such problems are possible, such as paying rent to the employer, seeing clients in their homes, and letting clients keep records.[10]

A general ethical solution for all the various issues of moonlighting is employer consent. If employers are informed and consent to the practice, then all obligations to them are fulfilled or waived. However, if an employer refuses to consent, it does not follow that moonlighting is unethical. Provided an employee still exercises independent judgment in an employer's best interests, works diligently, and does not use employer facilities or supplies, the secondary work is no more objectionable than an employee spending Saturdays remodeling his or her house. Nevertheless, employers are more likely to tolerate the latter than the former. Hence, prudence rather than ethics might dictate not moonlighting if an employer unjustifiably refuses consent.

Obligation of Obedience

The obligation of obedience has two parts: (1) to act as one's employer directs and (2) to act only as one's employer directs. For example, if a nurse is told to give a medication to a patient, the nurse should do so; contrarily, if a medication is not ordered, then a nurse should not give it. Nonetheless, matters are often not so simple. First, it might be unclear what one has been directed to do or not to do. Employers' directions might be quite general, ambiguous, or not completely intelligible. If so, employees should use reasonable judgment or follow customary practice. Second, acting only as one's employer directs can be especially unclear. Employers simply cannot list all the things employees should not do. Moreover, employees who act successfully without explicit direction are often praised and promoted for their initiative. Both of these considerations are especially important for professional employees. Unlike assembly line workers, their tasks are not and cannot be minutely specified as to the most efficient movements to make. They must be left some room for professional judgment, although they need not have the work autonomy of self-employed professionals.

The obligation to obey is limited to legally and ethically permissible conduct. The values and interests of potential victims outweigh those of employers, which is why the conduct is illegal or unethical. Just as people have no good reason to permit professionals to act illegally or unethically in behalf of clients, they have no good reason to allow them to do so in behalf of employers. However, employers and employees can disagree over whether directives involve illegal or unethical conduct.

Because ethics and law are not coincident, an employee can get trapped in a no win situation. Suppose an act is legal but unethical, and an employer orders an employee to do it. Because the conduct is legal, the employee has a legal obligation to do it. But because the conduct is unethical, the employee has no ethical obligation to obey and an ethical obligation not to so act. If the employee fulfills the legal obligation, he or she acts unethically. If the employee acts ethically, he or she violates the legal obligation to obey, and the employer has legal grounds for firing him or her. Law and ethics have never coincided and should not do so; so as long as employers order legal but unethical conduct, employees will face this unpleasant choice. Ethical conduct can require personal sacrifices.

The obligation to obey can significantly limit a professional's work autonomy. A requirement of clients' informed consent does not prevent professionals analyzing problems as they think best. Instead, it gives clients a veto power on carrying out recommendations. Employers' authority to direct work can extend into professional practice or work methods, although not to the extent possible for some nonprofessional employees. For example, a hospital might require certain routine tests on all new patients, whether or not a physician thinks they are needed or worthwhile. A teacher can be required to cover certain material in a course, perhaps even in a specified way, whether or not the teacher thinks it useful material or the most effective way of covering it.

Although such control goes to the very heart of professional autonomy and judgment, it is not necessarily unethical. Sometimes detailed direction is appropriate because professionals are still learning, such as medical interns and residents or law firm associates. When the directions are not part of a learning experience, professionals might complain that they are not being treated as professionals, but it is not unethical to ignore their professional status. If compliance with orders would amount to incompetent professional practice for a client, then there is an ethical objection. But the objection is based on violating an obligation to clients, not one to respect the work autonomy of professionals. Depriving professionals of work autonomy is perhaps unwise or downright stupid, but that does not make it unethical.

Finally, the obligation to obey combines with other factors to enable employed professionals to rationalize their not being responsible or accountable for untoward results of their activities.[11] Because employers or superiors direct one's activity, one can claim that they, and not oneself, are responsible. With the division of labor and professionals often working on only a small aspect of a problem, responsibility and accountability are diffused. One also becomes acculturated to types of practice, such as lawyers using discovery for purposes of delay or physicians withholding information. Indeed, joining an organization as a junior professional who has much to learn, one can view such conduct as learning how the real world works.

EMPLOYERS VERSUS OTHERS

Professionals' obligations to employers might conflict with those to clients and third parties. Consequently, besides balancing conflicting obligations to clients and third parties, employed professionals might also have to balance obligations to employers with those to clients and third parties. However, the contention of this section is that no theoretical *ethical* (or legal) conflicts arise. Conflicts can arise between a legal duty to obey an employer and ethical obligations to clients or third parties, but an ethical obligation to obey an employer cannot conflict with ethical obligations to clients or third parties. Nonetheless, this conclusion provides little practical help because conflicts between employees and employers can arise due to differences about what ethical (legal) obligations are owed to clients or third parties. Moreover, employers do sometimes order employees to engage in unethical or illegal conduct.

Clients

To consider possible conflicts between obligations to employers and clients, it is useful to distinguish between professional and nonprofessional organizations. Law firms, health maintenance organizations, accounting firms, and engineering consulting firms are professional organizations. Nonprofessional organizations include most business corporations (such as Ford Motor Company and Sears Roebuck).

As with any nonmathematical distinction, borderline cases exist. For example, colleges and newspapers are close to the borders between professional and nonprofessional organizations. Colleges and universities were historically deemed to be governed by their faculty and would thus clearly be professional organizations. Today's colleges and universities are not in fact governed by their faculties. However, their purposes are primarily teaching (service to clients), research, and public service (service to third parties). Newspapers, despite journalists' adherence to the credo of providing information to the public, are more likely run primarily to make a profit. As one moves from newspapers and news magazines to less news oriented publications, the profit motive comes to dominate more. Note that television networks usually try to keep the news division separate from the entertainment division; the news division is not expected to be a profit center (at the national level), but the entertainment division is.

In doubtful cases, two factors are useful in classifying an organization as a professional or nonprofessional one. The first is whether it is headed or chiefly directed by a member of the profession in question. The second is whether its purpose is primarily to make money or to provide professional services. Of course, professional organizations are not unconcerned with making a profit, and professional organizations might be headed or chiefly administered by a nonprofessional. Some large law firms hire business administrators.[12] So these are not litmus tests. However, as the subsequent discussion should make clear, a bright line is not needed.

Consider the situation of a professional working for a professional organization. The professional is a subagent of the organization, so clients are clients of both the organization and the professional. Consequently, the organization has the same responsibilities to clients as any professional. In fulfilling obligations to clients, professionals are also fulfilling employers' obligations to clients. Put another way, if an employer orders an employee to act in a way that violates the professional's obligation to a client, the conduct also violates the employer's obligation to the client and thus is unethical for the employer. Because the obligation of obedience to employers does not extend to unethical directives, the employee has no ethical obligation to obey.[13] Consequently, an employee cannot have an ethical obligation to obey an employer directive that would conflict with an ethical obligation to a client.

Two points must be noted about this argument. First, it does not follow that an employee's conduct might not be contrary to the employer's best interests. Just as an individual's self-interest can conflict with ethical obligations, an employing organization's interests can conflict with its ethical obligations. However, an employee's obligation of obedience is to promote the employer's best interests within the bounds of law and ethics. Second, an employee and employer can disagree about what the obligations to a client are. This problem is discussed in the next section.

Suppose the employer is not a professional organization. Two possibilities arise. First, the other party is in a professional–client relationship to the employee. If this is so, then the organization must have contracted to provide professional services to the client. In doing so, the organization agreed to comply with the ethical requirements of professional service and thus assumed the obligations professionals have. Consequently, the situation is the same as the previous one.

Second, the other party is not a client of the organization, that is, the organization did not agree to provide professional services. But because the employee's relationship to the other party is mediated through the employer's, the other party is not the employee's client. For example, an engineer working as a sales representative for an equipment manufacturer does not have a professional–client relationship with purchasers. Consequently, the employee cannot have professional obligations to a client that conflict with obligations to an employer. Instead, the situation must be a possible conflict of obligations between those to third parties and to employers.

Third Parties

As for clients, the key point is that employees and employers have the same obligations to third parties. Because obligations to third parties stem from universal norms or their specification, they apply to everyone or everyone in a type of situation. Thus, they apply equally to professional and nonprofessional organizations, rendering that distinction irrelevant here. Because employers and employees have the same obligations to third parties, the argument is the same as for clients. Employee conduct fulfilling obligations to third parties also fulfills those of employers. If employers direct employees to act in ways that would violate obligations to third parties, the directives are unethical, and employees have no obligation to obey. Consequently, an employee's ethical obligation to obey an employer cannot conflict with an ethical obligation to third parties.

Obligations to third parties can exist when an employee and employer have ethical obligations to a client. Obligations to third parties might be affected by obligations to clients (see Chapter 5). Nevertheless, the obligations of employers and employees will be the same because any balancing of such obligations would be the same for all similar situations. Consequently, an ethical obligation to obey, or any other obligation to an employer, still cannot conflict with obligations to third parties or clients.

Other Employees

Sometimes employed professionals provide services to other employees or persons associated with an organization. Writers on medical ethics have been especially troubled by such situations, giving them the title of "double agent" problems. For example, suppose a school psychiatrist diagnoses a medical student as having latent schizophrenia.[14] Is the psychiatrist's obligation primarily to the student or to the medical school? If the former, then an obligation of confidentiality prohibits placing the information in a school file, where it can be used to deny readmission should the student drop out for a semester and reapply. If it is to the school, then the information should plausibly be placed in a file for use in readmission. Another typical situation involves a company physician who diagnoses an employee as having a work-related illness.[15] Is the physician's primary loyalty to the employee-patient or to the company-employer?

Three different models are possible for such situations. First, an employer might have professional–client obligations to an employee. An employer or school might have contracted with employees or students to provide professional services. This would clearly be the case were the provision of company medical care part of a union contract, and it is plausible when students pay a fee for health services. In this model, the previous analysis of obligations to clients applies. In short, employers or schools have the same obligations to employees or students as physicians do to patients. Consequently, an employer ought not use information gained from employees to its advantage and employees' disadvantage without clients' consent.[16] Thus, no conflict can arise between obligations to employees and to employers.

Second, sometimes the model of a lawyer's stock opinion letter or an accountant's public audit applies.[17] As noted in Chapter 4, these situations are perhaps best handled by switching roles—the employing corporation becomes a third party, and the public becomes the client. Similarly, sometimes employees agree to medical examinations for the benefit of employers or others. Thus, with a health examination prior to employment or for insurance purposes, a patient becomes a third party, and an employer or insurance company becomes a client. That is, prospective employers and insurance companies are owed all or most of the obligations owed to clients.

Three points must be noted. First, a corporation that hires a lawyer for a stock opinion letter or an accountant for an audit receives that information. Similarly, a patient examined for employment or insurance purposes is entitled to the results. The information is about that person, and although confidentiality is waived, candor is not. Second, confidentiality is waived only as far as necessary for the benefit of an employer or third party. Matters discovered that are not relevant to their purposes should not be disclosed. Third, prospective employees or insurance applicants must be fully apprised of the situation; otherwise they cannot give their informed consent to examinations.

The third model is that of a lawyer who has two or more clients with conflicting interests. In such situations, a lawyer can serve both if he or she has a reasonable belief that the conflict will not adversely affect the service rendered, and the clients consent after full disclosure.[18] This model might be appropriate for a physician hired by a defendant in a personal injury lawsuit to examine the plaintiff's injuries.

This model also seems appropriate for the relationship between a student of psychoanalysis undergoing analysis as part of his or her education.[19] Because it is part of the educational process, relevant information about a student's abilities and problems belongs in the record. (This leaves open whether an analyst's findings are educationally relevant.) Insofar as psychoanalysis is a noneducational service to the student, the situation resembles ordinary provision of professional services. Consequently, the situation is best considered as a conflict of obligations to two different clients (school and student) or the student in two different client relationships (professor–student and analyst–patient). In other student training programs, students are not also clients, and only the usual professor–student relationship applies.

AUTHORITY AND CONFLICT

The theoretical coincidence of professional and employer ethical obligations to clients and third parties does not clarify what those obligations are. Moreover, employers and employees do not always conform to what they believe or know to be their ethical (or legal) obligations. Thus, significant conflicts arise between professional employees and employers and between different employees.

Bureaucracy Versus Professionalism

A pervasive conflict concerns the nature of bureaucratic organization and decision making in contrast to professional organization and decision making.[20] Employers, especially nonprofessional organizations, incline to the bureaucratic mode of operation; professionals incline to the professional mode. To the extent the two modes diverge, tension will be inherent in an organization with professional employees. The following sets out ideal types of bureaucratic and professional modes of operation. Rarely, if ever, are the ideals found in practice. Organizations with professional employees make accommodations between the two models.

Five features can be used to describe each mode of operation. First is the goal of the process. Second is the value sought to be achieved by the process. Third is the subject matter of decision. Fourth is the type of standard used in decision making. Fifth and last is the amount of discretion allowed a decision maker.

In the bureaucratic model, the goal is to implement a purpose or policy set by others, such as top management or a legislature. The underlying values are certainty and regularity of classification. If every case or situation can be properly classified, then certainty and regularity will result. For example, a student knows that a specific number of credit hours is necessary for graduation. All students who graduate have at least that number of credit hours; otherwise, a bureaucratic decision maker will not certify them for graduation. The subject matter of decision is factual classification. One needs to find the facts for an appropriate classification. For example, a customs officer tries to find out what goods were bought abroad and their dollar value. If it is less than some specified amount, then no duty is owed. If it is over that amount, then taxes are owed at some fixed rate. The standards applied are those of the organization whose goals are being implemented. To provide certainty and regularity, standards must be precise and cover all cases. Consequently, little or no room is left for a decision maker's discretion.

Professionals, especially those with individual clients, operate with a different model. Their goal is to improve a client's health, legal, or other status. The value being pursued is the client's welfare. The subject matter of judgment is the client's needs, desires, abilities, or skills and what will satisfy or improve them. Physicians and teachers, for example, are concerned with the physical or mental abilities and skills of patients and students. The standards for decision making are set by professional peers. Unlike the standards for bureaucratic decision makers, the standards are not established by a superior in a hierarchy. A professor's standard for sufficient knowledge to pass a course in professional ethics is that used by other teachers of professional ethics, not something established by a university president or vice president. Finally, because professional standards leave scope for professional judgment, a decision maker has significant discretion.

The potential conflict of these two approaches is exemplified by the following example. A physician works for a county health agency charged with providing medical services to indigent children. A mother brings a seriously ill child into the clinic. The professional goal is the child's welfare, the child is diagnosed as seriously ill, so appropriate medical treatment should be given. The bureaucratic goal is to provide medical care for indigent children in the county. The clinic is funded by county taxes. Inquiry reveals that the mother and child actually live in the next county. This factual classification places the child in the category not to receive services because providing them does not promote organizational goals. The factual criteria leave no room for discretion. Consequently, the physician is caught between two models of decision making. From the professional perspective, political boundaries are irrelevant to the appropriateness of care. From the bureaucratic perspective, political boundaries are central to organizational goals.

These conflicts can easily be multiplied for any profession. An organization wants an engineer to use a certain component, but the engineer believes another would work better. Legal aid will provide one service but not another, but a client could easily benefit from both. Schoolteachers are required to cover certain material in a curriculum at a specific time, but they believe it better omitted or introduced at another time. Social work agencies have specified procedures that are inappropriate or counterproductive for particular clients. Nurses are required to follow certain procedures, such as giving pain medication at fixed intervals rather than when needed, but alternatives would be better for patients or more efficient.

Authority Relationships

Professional employees can be in a variety of authority relationships with other employees. The standard bureaucratic organizational line of authority is the familiar hierarchy so popular on organization charts. Each level on the chart has authority over those levels below it. Moreover, in the typical industrial hierarchy, the supervisor can exercise complete control over the work of persons below. This is not to say that good managers do so, but it is always possible in principle for a supervisor to countermand any decision made by a person under the supervisor's authority. Hierarchies of professionals usually differ from industrial bureaucratic ones.[21] Because professional practice involves the use of judgment, more leeway is left for discretion by subordinates, although, as noted earlier, usually not as much as by self-employed professionals.

Many professionals are more familiar and comfortable with co-equal authority. Two varieties of co-equal authority exist. In the collegial version, each person has equal authority over the same matter. This version is normally followed in academic departments and committee meetings. It does not imply that the professionals are equally knowledgeable over the whole area. Specialists' expertise is usually recognized. For example, if a philosophy department is discussing a logic requirement for students, the judgments of those faculty members with special expertise in logic might be accorded special weight by individual members. But when it comes to voting on a proposal, each person's vote counts equally. Law students frequently learn to interact with one another on this basis when they form study groups. Each student specializes in a particular course; then the students share their information and discuss the subjects. This training might be useful in later life because many large law firms operate on a collegial model among partners.[22]

The second variety of co-equal authority involves a strict separation of areas of authority. It is a common relationship between professionals of different types. Lawyers and accountants distinguish what belongs to each domain. Historians, chemists, and biologists have separate domains. This sort of co-equal authority results in part from the division of labor and specialized knowledge.

A final possible authority relationship can be called *overlapping hierarchies*. It is a combination of the hierarchical and co-equal separate spheres relationships. Perhaps its best exemplar is the relationship between physicians and nurses on a hospital floor. The physicians have a hierarchy from attending physician to medical student. Nurses have a separate hierarchy from supervisor to nursing assistant. Physicians also have some authority over nurses, at least those at the lower end of the nursing hierarchy. If conflicts are generated, say, between a resident and a nurse, they might have to be resolved by their superiors negotiating as between equals from two separate hierarchies. A similar situation and practice exist for corporate counsel.[23] When junior counsel cannot convince business counterparts not to act in some way, they refer them to their supervisors.

Employed professionals can come into conflict with supervisors in their hierarchy, with other professionals at their level in their hierarchy, or with persons in other hierarchies (for example, engineers in design and production). Within organizations, the latter two types of conflicts (between equals in the same or different hierarchies) are usually resolved by a decision of someone higher in the hierarchy. If the losing party still disagrees, the conflict is turned into one between a subordinate and superordinate in a hierarchy. Consequently, the rest of this discussion focuses on that type of conflict.

One other factor must be introduced. A professional's supervisor might or might not be a member of the same profession. An attempt is usually made to keep a professional's supervisor a member of that profession. The American Bar Association goes further than any other profession by forbidding the practice of law in a professional organization for profit if nonlawyers have a financial stake, are corporate officers, or can direct or control professional judgment.[24] One should note the careful limitations—to professional organizations for profit. Supervisors need not be lawyers in nonprofessional or nonprofit organizations. These broad exceptions include corporate counsel and government lawyers. Although immediate supervisors for most professionals can be members of that profession, except in professional organizations, one cannot require that persons at the top of the hierarchy be members of that profession. Otherwise, nurses could require that hospital boards be composed only of nurses, physicians that boards be only physicians, and pharmacists that boards be only pharmacists.

Subjects of Conflicts

The subject matter of disagreement between professional employees and superordinates can be divided into two broad categories.[25] The technical or factual category concerns matters of professional judgment. Included here are the likely effectiveness of a particular treatment on a patient, the proper wording of a contract clause, or whether an engineering design will carry a specified load. Although called technical and factual, some value concerns can well be embedded in the judgments. For example, the adequacy of the wording of a contract clause depends on its purpose. The second category can be called moral. These are largely disputes about professional ethics. For example, is it ethical or unethical not to resuscitate a patient? Or are the risks of an engineering design too great for it to be used?

Technical.   In practice, superordinates expect and usually receive deference to their judgments whether the disagreement is about a technical or moral matter. Such expectations and practices are not fully justifiable. With technical disagreements, one should distinguish between situations in which the superordinate does and does not have expertise on the subject of disagreement. Superordinates need not be professionals in the same field as subordinates, only have expertise in it. Thus, a physician can have expertise concerning many nursing activities, and pharmacists can have the same expertise as physicians concerning the effects of drugs.

If a superordinate does not have expertise on a technical subject of disagreement, one might think that the subordinate should never defer. The subordinate can claim to have greater knowledge and be more likely to be correct. If following the superordinate's judgment will merely result in a failure to benefit as much as might otherwise be the case, then deference does not seem objectionable, although a professional should make his or her views known. One might contend that subordinates should never defer if they reasonably believe harm will result. However, one should distinguish situations on the basis of who might be harmed. If harm would come to clients or third parties, then subordinates should not defer. If, however, the harm is to the employer organization, and the subordinate has fully expressed his or her view and the reasons for it, then deference is permissible. Because the superordinate is acting in behalf of the organization, the situation is analogous to a fully informed client accepting a risk of harm.

If a difference of opinion concerns a technical matter, and the superordinate has expertise in the field, then deference to the superordinate's judgment is usually reasonable. It does not follow that one should always follow the judgments of a superordinate with expertise. Superordinates make mistakes, just as subordinates do, though fewer of them, one hopes. A subordinate might be quite certain that this was occurring, and if the error would cause serious harm to clients or third parties, then it would be wrong to defer. In emergency situations, the grounds for deference and compliance with orders one believes technically incorrect are even stronger than for nonemergency situations, because doing something is often better than doing nothing, and, on average, superordinates are more likely to be correct. Yet even then, in rare situations, subordinates can be practically certain they are correct, and refusal to obey can be permissible or obligatory.[26]

Moral.   If the disagreement concerns a moral issue, then plausibly the superordinate has no more expertise than the subordinate. With technical disputes, deference is ethically wrong only when injury might occur to others. But if a dispute is ethical, then presumably the subordinate believes an act or omission is wrong, and the superordinate believes it is permissible or obligatory. (It would be silly for a subordinate to dispute an act or omission he or she thinks is permissible.) For example, if a superordinate directs a subordinate to lie to a client, the subordinate can reasonably believe that doing so is wrong. He or she need not normally analyze whether the lie would injure the client or others; it is plausibly wrong even if it does not. Because superordinates do not have authority to engage in or direct unethical conduct, that being outside their sphere of authority, deference is not required.

The discussion so far has implicitly distinguished degrees of conviction that one is correct. In discussing deference to superordinates without technical expertise, the criterion for not deferring was reasonable belief that injury to clients or third parties might result. For not deferring to superordinates with expertise, the criterion was practical certainty. A further complication must be added. One can have strong convictions about ethical and even technical matters yet recognize that other people have equally strong but opposite convictions. In short, there are arguable or debatable matters. This point does not affect disagreement with superordinates who lack technical expertise, but it does with superordinates who have expertise or when the disagreement is ethical.

The American Bar Association makes allowance for such situations. A subordinate lawyer may defer to or comply with a superordinate's "reasonable resolution of an arguable question of professional ethics."[27] From the perspective of professional discipline, this is a reasonable rule. Otherwise, a subordinate is placed in an untenable position. If a subordinate did not defer or comply and a superordinate were correct, then the subordinate would have violated a duty of obedience and could be fired. If a subordinate did defer or comply and a superordinate were mistaken, then the subordinate could be disciplined.

Conscientious Refusal.   This does not solve a subordinate's problem of conscience. Even on arguable issues, people can have firm convictions. For example, lawyers can be utterly opposed to allowing criminal defendants to commit perjury, although it is arguable that lawyers should permit them to take the stand, question them normally, and argue their testimony. Acting contrary to firm moral convictions weakens people's integrity and self-esteem. Employers are generally better off with employees who have strong moral integrity. Consequently, in arguable cases, employers should recognize a right of conscientious refusal. Thus, for example, nurses should be permitted to refuse to assist in abortions or *in vitro* fertilization if they are ethically opposed. Of course, employees should make their views known in advance so employers can obtain substitutes.

Nonetheless, limits exist to employees' rights of conscientious refusal. Suppose a nurse is morally-religiously opposed to blood transfusions and claims a right of conscientious refusal to assist in them. May a hospital fire the nurse for failure to obey? The answer is plausibly "yes" if the nurse's job regularly involves giving blood because then the nurse's moral beliefs interfere with performance of the job. If the nurse worked in a unit that did not regularly give blood, then the answer seems "no." Two points make such a case puzzling. If a nurse's position regularly involves giving blood, one wonders why the nurse applied for or took the job. Nurses opposed to abortions do not apply to abortion clinics for jobs. Also, the nurse probably should have disclosed his or her opposition to giving blood when applying for the job. Normally, one need not disclose one's moral or religious convictions in applying for a position, but if one has minority views that might significantly affect one's performance of the tasks involved, then one should plausibly do so.

Organizational Disobedience

Conscientious refusal provides for the conscience and moral integrity of professional employees, but it rarely does anything for clients or third parties. A law associate who conscientiously refuses to work for a weapons manufacturer does nothing to help those killed by the weapons if someone else does the work. Consequently, professional and other employees sometimes consider organizational disobedience to try to prevent harm or wrong. *Organizational disobedience* refers to conduct violating an organization's policies or procedures to prevent or correct a harm or wrong.[28] It is not confined to disagreements with superordinates, for it can also apply when an employee is aware of harmful or wrongful actions of others in the organization.

Internal Disobedience.   Organizations have lines of authority and responsibility. Internal disobedience occurs when, to try to prevent harm or wrong, an employee violates these internal procedures. Typically, subordinates go over the head of immediate supervisors. Organizations generally do not like people going outside of channels, and immediate supervisors especially dislike it because it often reflects adversely on them.

Nonetheless, internal disobedience seems justifiable whenever deference to a superordinate's judgment is not required. The primary purposes of lines of authority are efficiency and quality. If a subordinate reasonably believes a technical error is being made, then the quality of work is in question. Hence, it cannot be assumed that the organizational channels are fulfilling that purpose. "Quality" can be construed more broadly to include avoidance of ethical wrongdoing. If employers have obligations to clients and third parties that would not be fulfilled, the ethical quality of the work is in question. When an employer's concern with efficiency is balanced against harm or wrong to clients or third parties, reasonable people who might be in any of the positions would sacrifice efficiency. Often, the employer would benefit. For example, in 1987, Chrysler Motor Company was accused of having previously illegally disconnected odometers of new cars that employees had driven home. The company suffered from the notoriety of its alleged illegal conduct and would have been better off had someone violated channels of authority to report the conduct when it occurred.

Nevertheless, employees are often in a difficult position. Because of the hostility to going outside of channels, if they do so, even if they are correct, they might receive bad evaluations if not dismissal. Employers can easily change their organization to avoid this difficulty. They can have committees or ombudspersons to whom such concerns can be taken.[29] If these are recognized procedures for reporting disagreements or ethical concerns, then no internal organizational disobedience occurs. Because these are recognized processes, hostility against employees who use them will probably decrease.

Whistle-blowing.   Reporting harmful technical errors or unethical conduct outside the organization, external disobedience, is commonly called *whistle-blowing*. Whistle-blowing threatens not only efficiency but also often confidentiality. Although some people believe it violates a duty of loyalty, the duty of loyalty does not extend to unethical conduct. Employers' reputations are also at stake, but they do not have a claim to an undeserved good reputation. So if whistle-blowing employees are correct, employers are not injured (wrongly harmed).

Whistle-blowing is an employed professional's problem similar to that of violating client confidentiality. As discussed in the first section, except for a stronger obligation of obedience and none of fairness, employees have the same obligations to employers that professionals have to clients. Consequently, much the same reasoning applies. The test is what balance of responsibilities reasonable persons who might be in the position of any party would accept for a society in which they expected to live. Moreover, just as one distinguishes between when a professional may and should disclose client confidences, one can distinguish between when a professional may and should blow the whistle.[30]

The following conditions are a plausible set for permissible whistle-blowing. (1) Employees are not ethically required to defer to superordinate judgments. As previously discussed, this requires either a reasonable belief or practical certainty that conduct is harmful or wrongful. (2) Internal organizational disobedience has normally been used first. Not only should employees raise issues with supervisors, they should pursue them within the organization before going outside it. A superordinate does not necessarily speak for an entire organization, and internal disobedience does not threaten confidentiality, only efficiency. (3) The harm or wrong that has been or will be done is significant. Because professional employees have not been hired to represent employers against criminal charges for past conduct, whether harm or wrong is future or past should make no difference. However, it must be significant enough to outweigh the values at stake for the organization. For example, often it is illegal to fail to file various types of paperwork with the government, but the absence of such reports at best makes more work for the government. A failure to file such forms hardly justifies whistle-blowing.

These conditions do not suffice to require employees to blow the whistle. One cannot ignore the possible personal sacrifice and other obligations of employees. All, or at least almost all, moral obligations have an implicit proviso for exceptional hardship to actors. Thus, people are not morally obligated to incur grave risks to rescue others in distress. Moreover, employees often have other obligations, such as to support their families, fulfillment of which might be jeopardized by whistle-blowing. Whistle-blowers do not always fare well after their act.[31] These obligations must be placed on the side of not blowing the whistle.

Professional employees plausibly have an obligation to blow the whistle if two further conditions are met. (1) Blowing the whistle is likely to prevent death, serious bodily injury, or a serious crime. Serious crimes include all crimes of violence and those causing significant financial losses such as due to stock fraud. Whistle-blowing is obligatory only for future harms and wrongs, although it is also permissible for past ones. (2) Employees can present or lead others to clear and convincing evidence that they are correct.[32] This condition differs from that for not deferring to superordinates by requiring that the evidence be available to others. One can have a reasonable belief or near certainty based on evidence that one cannot present to others. For example, one has seen documents that have since been destroyed.

With these two further conditions, reasonable people would accept a principle or rule requiring whistle-blowing. One can probably prevent serious injury. Others can be convinced either to help or that one has done so. Usually, the probability of preventing serious injury depends on one's ability to convince others that it is threatened and that steps need to be taken to prevent it. The harm or wrong to be avoided is more significant than any violations of efficiency or confidentiality of the employer. In effect, this obligation is a specification of that to rescue others. Consequently, it still has an exception for serious danger to oneself.

One might be inclined to add a further condition, namely, that whistle-blowers make their identity public. That condition does not seem necessary. A whistle-blower in accord with the above criteria is not doing wrong in blowing the whistle, although he or she often has participated in the wrong being reported. Maintaining anonymity might decrease the possibility of retaliation on the person and thus decrease personal risks. One might argue that disclosure of identity is necessary so that one can check the whistle-blower's motives; some people make allegations for personal aggrandizement, advancement, or spite. However, if a person presents or directs others to clear and convincing evidence of potential danger or wrongdoing, the person's motives are irrelevant to preventing the injury. For example, during the Watergate scandal, an informant known only as "deep throat" gave investigative reporters Robert Woodward and Carl Bernstein invaluable tips. Deep throat's identity has never been revealed, but that does not diminish the appropriateness of his or her actions.

Many people have suggested legal protections for whistle-blowers' jobs, and some have been enacted.[33] The purpose of these laws is to prevent retaliation (usually firing) and to encourage people to come forward. Although their purposes are laudatory, their utility is questionable. The adoption of such a law for federal employees has not significantly increased their whistle-blowing. Complaints are often against superiors, who are not dismissed and can retaliate in various subtle ways (as in employee evaluations). To avoid such retaliation, either the superiors must be fired or transferred or the whistle-blower must be transferred to another unit. Even if the persons against whom complaints are lodged are co-workers and not superordinates, cooperation, amiability, and other intangible work factors will be disrupted. Finally, it is simply a psychological strain to continue to work daily with people whom one considers lacking in ethical integrity or professional competence.

A preferable solution would be a willingness of other employers to hire such persons. Many other employers fear to hire whistle-blowers on the ground that they are disloyal. If their motives are suspect, then good reasons might exist not to hire them. But if a whistle-blower acted from ethical concern, another employer would gain an employee of high ethical integrity or professional competence. It is reasonable to seek rather than shun such employees.

Finally, professional employees might be worse off regarding whistle-blowing than many nonprofessionals. If a unionized employee charges a company with wrongdoing and an attempt is made to retaliate, usually the union will immediately step in with a grievance and probably a lawyer. The case might eventually lead to binding arbitration. Professional societies have not historically taken strong action to protect professional employees. The American Association of University Professors has tried to defend professors' academic freedom by censuring and boycotting offending institutions. That procedure rarely works effectively, especially against prominent institutions or when jobs are scarce. Engineering societies have not traditionally done much to protect whistle-blowers, although that might be changing. During the early 1970s, some societies took an active role regarding three engineers who blew the whistle about the Bay Area Rapid Transit system in Northern California. Nevertheless, the power of independent professional organizations to intervene and protect professional employees is limited. Thus, some professionals believe unionization is a better alternative.

Unionization and Strikes

The extent of unionization among professionals varies widely. Most elementary and secondary schoolteachers are represented by unions. College and university teachers are less likely to be so, and even where unions exist, often less than half the faculty belongs. Somewhat surprisingly, engineers have generally resisted unionization. One might have expected that working in industries with widespread unionization of other workers, engineers would have become strongly unionized. However, they seem to identify more with management than with workers. Unionization is more widespread in some industries than in others. Finally, at the other end of the spectrum, very few lawyers and physicians are unionized. Union membership of lawyers is almost completely within legal services organizations, which are routinely unionized, and amounts to only about 1 percent of salaried lawyers.[34]

Professionalism and Unions.   Many professionals believe that union membership is incompatible with professionalism. One argument is that union membership conflicts with one's obligation of loyalty to an employer. Although loyalty means acting for the best interests of the employer, it primarily refers to the performance of job tasks.[35] It does not mean that when employees' desires for salary conflict with employers' for profits, employees should work for low wages. Analogously, one could then argue that professionals' loyalty to clients conflicts with charging them big fees for services, for surely it is in clients' best interests to have services provided at low cost or free.

A second argument is that unions lower professionals' status and lead to their being treated like nonprofessional workers. It is tempting to conclude that this concern is simply a preference for prestige rather than money, but that would be unfair. Unionization is sometimes thought to be an impetus to bureaucraticization.[36] As noted previously, a tension exists between bureaucratic and professional modes of operation. Perhaps because of their industrial background, unions are inclined to press for standardized job descriptions and classifications, promotion on the basis of seniority, and standardized salary increases. Many professionals prefer considerable discretion and variation in their work assignments and to distinguish among themselves by competence. They believe that, unlike that of assemblyline workers, the work product of one competent professional is not the same as that of another. Degrees of ability and skill exist and should be recognized, in part by differential monetary rewards.

Proponents of unions counter by claiming that those very features that many professionals desire—varied work assignments, differential rewards, and so on—have been used unfairly by management. Those professionals whom management dislikes or deems troublesome, say, for raising ethical issues, are penalized. Standardized job descriptions and uniform salary increases are protections against such abuses. Unions also provide support for employees who resist unethical directives and speak out against questionable employer actions.

Not surprisingly, unions seem to do best among professional employees who are not treated well by management. Where management pays good salaries, rewards special effort and ability, and provides due process, unions are not likely to thrive. When these conditions do not exist, employees, whether professionals or not, are likely to look to unions to improve working conditions. Unionization is not inherently incompatible with professionalism; whether it is desirable depends on the particular situation.

Strikes.   One argument against unions is that sooner or later they are likely to lead to strikes. Because professionals provide important services to society, strikes by them violate obligations to clients or third parties—the public. Consequently, some professional codes have explicitly or implicitly prohibited strike action.[37] Logically, of course, unionization need not lead to strikes. Many union agreements contain no-strike provisions. In practice, the claim is more plausible. Teachers, doctors, and nurses have all gone on strike or taken collective action, but such activity also occurs without unions.

One should distinguish the reasons for professional strikes or other job actions. The traditional industrial strike is for gains for employees—higher pay, better fringe benefits, shorter hours. Some professional demands are for benefits for clients or the public as well as themselves. Teachers sometimes ask for smaller classes, more special education, and so on. Nurses and doctors sometimes demand more staff, better equipment, and so forth. The United Auto Workers, perhaps one of the more progressive unions, never claims that its strikes are for the public benefit, except insofar as better salaries and job security of auto workers is good for the economy.

To the extent that strikes or job actions are for conditions benefiting clients or the public, potential gains must be balanced against potential harms. Here it is useful to distinguish between compensable and noncompensable harms. Compensable harms can be made up in kind. For example, settlements of protracted schoolteachers' strikes often specify longer school days or school years to make up for lost classwork. Noncompensable harms cannot be made up in kind. If patients die because nurses or doctors are on strike, they cannot be brought back to life after the strike is over. Money is not compensation in kind except for financial losses.

If compensable harm caused to clients or the public by strikes or job action is in fact made up, then the harm does not constitute a reason against the strike. In effect, harm does not occur. Striking nurses or physicians normally leave enough persons on duty to provide basic care and emergency services, thus avoiding noncompensable harms. Consequently, obligations to clients and third parties do not provide reasons against the strikes, and professional employee self-interest is adequate to justify them.

It does not follow that strikes causing noncompensable harm or in which compensation is not in fact given are unjustified. It is tempting but probably incorrect to claim that strikes causing noncompensable harm are justifiable if, and only if, potential benefits to clients and the public outweigh potential noncompensable harms to them. In dire circumstances, perhaps even professional self-interest can justify strikes at least risking noncompensable harm.

The 1983 physicians' strike in Israel provides a plausible example.[38] Most Israeli physicians are paid a salary (directly or indirectly) by the government. In the spring of 1983, their salaries were well below the average in society; to make as much as a nurse, doctors had to work six to eight night shifts a month in addition to regular forty-five hour workweeks. The physicians began a general strike but left one-third of the usual staff in public hospitals and instituted an alternative fee-for-service system of medical care. Subsequently, the strike became tougher. For a period, only 10 percent of the staff was on duty, and finally physicians staged a widespread hunger strike.

One can argue that such difficult working conditions significantly affected physicians' ability to provide competent services to patients; thus, the strike's potential benefits to patients outweighed its potential risks. Alternatively, one can argue that the low physician salaries were blatant exploitation of the physicians by the government with the acquiescence of the public. If the employer and public persist in such exploitation, then they must run the risk of noncompensable harms. The government and public are ethically responsible for the noncompensable harm, for had they acted ethically, it would not have occurred.

The Israeli physician strike can be contrasted with a 1986 strike by physicians in Ontario, Canada, to protest government action preventing their billing in excess of the government reimbursement rates.[39] Unlike physicians in Israel, those in Ontario are paid by the provincial government on a fee-for-service basis. Fees are set by negotiation between the medical association and the government. However, prior to a new provincial law, physicians were permitted to charge patients in excess of the government-paid fee, so-called "extra billing." The average income of Ontario physicians is among the highest in Canada. The extra billing could not plausibly be claimed to be a benefit to the public, nor were the physicians being exploited. Consequently, the risks of noncompensable harm could not be justified.

EMPLOYER OBLIGATIONS

Employer obligations to professional employees can stem from universal norms. They can also stem from the role of employers. Most of these role-related obligations pertain whether or not an employee is a professional, but a few may be special to professional employees. Finally, employer obligations can stem from particular contracts. Because these contractual obligations depend on the agreement of individual professionals and their employers, they are not discussed.

Universal

In as much as universal norms apply to everyone, they also apply to employers. To try to specify all of them would amount to specifying an acceptable ethical code. However, it is worth noting that employers have the same obligations to employees that clients have to professionals, namely, to keep commitments, to be truthful, and not to ask them to act unethically. Enough has already been said about the limits of an obligation to obey unethical directives. I need only note here that it is wrong to ask or order someone to act unethically.

The keeping of commitments pertains not simply to legal commitments but to moral ones as well. Employers often make prospective employees promises that are not included in a legal contract. Suppose a university hires a new professor promising her the opportunity to teach a specific course as well as a substantial salary increase in the second year to match what she would have received at her previous university. Although not legally bound, the dean or department chair has a moral obligation to provide the opportunity to offer the course and the pay raise. Of course, as with any promises, some conditions justify not keeping them. For example, if insufficient funds are available for the salary increase or the legislature imposes a limit on salary increases, then the promised increase need not be given in the second year. But it should be given when possible.

Employers should be truthful in all communications to employees. If they do not want to be truthful, they need not say anything. Employers need not fully disclose information about a project on which a professional employee is working. With the division of labor and the need or desire to keep trade and other secrets, an employer might disclose to an employee only what is necessary for the employee's job. Just as clients need not disclose information necessary for a professional to perform a task as well as possible, employers need not do so either. It might be unwise not to do so, but that is a risk employers are entitled to take.

There is an exception. If there is a client, then an employer has an ethical obligation to disclose to a professional employee all information that the client disclosed relevant to the employee's task. Professional employees have an obligation to provide competent professional service to clients, and without relevant information, they cannot do so. Clients, of course, may take the risk of less adequate service due to failure to disclose, but employers are not entitled to make that judgment for them.

Role Related

All employer role-related obligations to employees generally also apply to professional employees. A detailed discussion of them is more appropriate for a book on business ethics and so is not presented here. However, three possible special role-related obligations to professional employees are briefly examined.

First, employers might have special obligations of due process to professional employees. One can plausibly argue that employers have some due process obligations to all employees.[40] These obligations plausibly include an opportunity to present information before promotion and salary increase decisions are made and before being disciplined, demoted, or dismissed for cause. Due process obligations might be more stringent when professional employees are disciplined, demoted, or dismissed for violating professional obligations rather than employer rules. The reason is that the employer is the final legislator and interpreter of its rules (unless, say, a union contract calls for arbitration). However, the employer does not establish, nor is it the proper interpreter of, professional rules of conduct. Instead, interpretation is more appropriately left to official organizations. If an employee has a good faith claim that he or she did not violate a professional norm, then at least an informal hearing by an impartial third party is due. In any case, employers should report such violations to professional norm enforcing organizations.

One might question whether an employer is entitled to penalize a professional employee for violating professional obligations as opposed to obligations to the employer. However, the previous argument that obligations to employers and to clients or third parties cannot conflict implies that violation of a professional obligation is a violation of an obligation to an employer. Recall that an employer has the same obligations to clients and third parties as does a professional employee. Consequently, if a professional employee as an employer's agent violates an obligation to clients or third parties, so does the employer. Consequently, if a professional employee violates a professional obligation, he or she thus violates an obligation to act competently in the employer's interest, namely, the employer's interest in fulfilling its obligations.

The result is that many professional obligations are incorporated into the professional employee–employer relationship.[41] The earlier argument was that employers are not entitled to direct employees to violate professional obligations. The argument here is that employees have an obligation to employers not to violate professional obligations. However, the argument has concerned only obligations to clients and third parties. It does not necessarily follow that other professional obligations, such as to provide free services to the poor, are included.

A second obligation of employers to professional employees might be one of confidentiality. Generally, all employers have an obligation of confidentiality of personnel records. The interesting twist with professional employees is that they might also be clients. For example, hospital nurses might be treated by the hospital on an inpatient or outpatient basis. Some of their nursing friends are hospital employees and might have access to their records. Of course, any of them involved in the nurse's care should have access to relevant information. However, others also often have access to patient records. Thus, the hospital might have a special obligation to restrict access to these records. This concern is perhaps especially strong if an employee receives psychiatric or social work services.

Finally, employers might have a special role-related obligation to professional employees to assist in their professional education and development. The "Guidelines to Professional Employment for Engineers and Scientists," which has been endorsed by numerous professional societies, states that employers have a responsibility "to provide a supportive attitude and environment."[42] Among other things, it states that employers should rotate work assignments to broaden an engineer's experience and support continuing education by various means. Large law firms rotate assignments of new associates to provide for their development.[43] Medical interns and residents are rotated through different services as part of their training. Hospitals also routinely provide in-service education programs. Colleges provide faculty travel funds to attend meetings and sabbaticals for study.

Perhaps the best argument for such an obligation rests on employers' obligations to provide competent professional service. Knowledge is increasing rapidly in all professional fields. Unless professionals have an opportunity at least to keep abreast of these developments, they cannot provide competent professional service and thus neither can employers. However, one might still contend that employees are obligated to be competent, so the primary burden is on them. Employers are obligated only to ensure the continuing competence of their professional employees or to dismiss them. It does not follow that employers must provide or help provide professional development. Of course, it is generally in employers' interests to have employees maintain and improve their skills rather than to dismiss them. The real issue is the extent to which employers rather than employees should pay by released time and reimbursement for travel costs and registration fees for employees' continuing education.

SUMMARY

Employed professionals have obligations to employers. Many of these obligations are similar to those to clients—competence, diligence, honesty, candor, discretion, and loyalty. They raise issues similar to those with respect to clients, such as kickbacks, conflicts of interest, and confidentiality of trade secrets. However, the obligation to obey employers is stronger than an obligation to clients. It includes acting as, and only as, authorized. Professional employees do not have an ethical (legal) obligation to obey unethical (illegal) employer directives. However, the obligation to obey can limit professional work autonomy.

I argued that ethical obligations to employers, particularly that to obey, do not theoretically conflict with ethical obligations to clients or third parties. If a professional employee has a client, the employer—either as a professional organization or a nonprofessional organization agreeing to provide professional services—has the same obligations to the client as the professional. Any employer directive that would require violating these obligations to clients is unethical, so there is no ethical obligation to obey it. Similarly, because obligations to third parties are universal, they also apply to employers. Again, directives involving a violation of those obligations are unethical, so there is no ethical obligation to obey them. However, because ethics and law are not coincident, professional employees can have legal obligations to obey employers' unethical directives.

Authority relations in organizations are important for various conflicts employee professionals confront. First, bureaucratic organization and decision-making procedures are often in tension with professional decision-making procedures. Bureaucracies tend toward uniform, fact-based, nondiscretionary decisions furthering institutional goals. Professional decision making favors judgment based on professional standards furthering client goals.

Various authority relationships are possible. Bureaucratic relationships tend toward the traditional hierarchical form. Many professional relationships involve co-equal authority over either the same subject or separate spheres. One can also have overlapping hierarchical authority structures. An important consideration is whether superordinates are members of the same profession as subordinates or otherwise have expertise in the field.

Superordinates and subordinates can disagree over technical or moral matters. If a superordinate does not have expertise over the subject, then a subordinate need not defer to the superordinate's judgment if the subordinate reasonably believes doing so would harm clients or third parties. If a superordinate has expertise over a technical subject, then a subordinate should defer to the superordinate unless practically certain the superordinate is incorrect and that doing so would harm clients or third parties. If the subject matter is moral, then a subordinate who reasonably believes a superordinate's judgment is ethically wrong is not ethically required to defer to it. A subordinate may do so if the superordinate has a reasonable position on a debatable matter of professional ethics. Employers should recognize professional employees' rights of conscientious refusal to participate in activities that violate their firm moral convictions.

When a professional employee ethically need not defer to a superordinate, internal organizational disobedience is justifiable. This involves violating the organization's lines of authority to bring the matter to the attention of a higher authority in the organization. Employers are well advised to institute committees or ombudspersons to obviate the need for internal disobedience.

Whistle-blowing, taking the matter outside the organization, is permissible if (1) a subordinate is not ethically required to defer to a superordinate, (2) internal disobedience has been tried, and (3) the harm or wrong is significant. An obligation to blow the whistle exists if, further, (4) it is likely to prevent death, serious bodily injury, or a serious crime and (5) one can present or lead others to clear and convincing evidence. The utility of legal job protections for whistle-blowers is questionable. Perhaps more useful protection can result from anonymity and other employers' willingness to hire whistle-blowers with good motives.

Although many professionals oppose unionization, it is not unethical. Whether it is desirable depends on particular situations. Strikes that do not threaten noncompensable harms are permissible to further professional employees' self-interests. Generally, if noncompensable harms to clients or third parties are possible, strikes can be justified only if potential benefits for clients and third parties outweigh the risks to them. However, in rare situations when clients and employers have severely exploited professionals, strikes might be justifiable solely for employees' self-interests.

Employers' obligations to professional employees are universal, role related, and contractual. The universal obligations include those clients have to professionals—to keep commitments, to be truthful, and not to ask them to act unethically. The role-related obligations include fairness (especially due process), confidentiality, and perhaps support for continuing professional education and development. Employer–professional employee contracts incorporate professional obligations to clients and third parties.

NOTES*

1. About 90 percent of engineers are salaried employees in large organizations; Martin and Schinzinger, *Ethics in Engineering,* p. 64.

2. The percentage of lawyers employed as private practitioners in firms increased significantly from 1960 to 1980, but the percentage employed in government and private industry remained constant at 10 percent each. Curran, *Lawyer Statistical Report,* pp. 12, 13.

3. See Chapter 1, note 23.

4. Gross, "Ethical Problems," pp. 262–263; C. G. Luckhardt, "Duties of Agent to Principal," in *Business Ethics,* ed. Snoeyenbos, Almeder, and Humber, pp. 116–117.

5. Gross, "Ethical Problems," p. 302, n. 185, pp. 314 and 315.

6. Luckhardt, "Duties of Agent," p. 117.

*See the bibliography at the back of the book for complete references.

7. Martin and Schinzinger, *Ethics in Engineering,* p. 213. The union won reinstatement for the employee.

8. Engineers' Council, "Suggested Guidelines," 4, e.

9. Martin and Schinzinger, *Ethics in Engineering,* p. 195.

10. Kelley and Alexander, "Part-Time Private Practice," pp. 255–256.

11. See generally, Martin and Schinzinger, *Ethics in Engineering,* pp. 68–69; Rhode, "Ethical Perspectives," p. 637.

12. Spangler, *Lawyers for Hire,* p. 30.

13. See also John Ladd, "Some Reflections on Authority and the Nurse," in *Nursing,* ed. Spicker and Gadow, p. 165.

14. Veatch, *Case Studies,* pp. 76–77.

15. Ibid., p. 82.

16. See ABA, *Model Rules,* Rule 1.8(b); AMA, "Current Opinions," 5.09.

17. ABA, *Model Rules,* Rule 2.3; AMA, "Current Opinions," 5.09, states that "no physician–patient relationship exists" in such situations.

18. ABA, *Model Rules,* Rule 1.7(a).

19. See Levy, *Social Work Ethics,* pp. 189–193.

20. See also Jerry L. Mashaw, *Bureaucratic Justice: Managing Social Security Disability Claims* (New Haven, Conn.: Yale University Press, 1983), pp. 23–34.

21. Freidson, *Professional Powers,* chap. 7.

22. Spangler, *Lawyers for Hire,* pp. 32–33.

23. See ibid., p. 94.

24. ABA, *Model Rules,* Rule 5.4(d); ABA, *Code of Professional Responsibility,* DR 5-107(C).

25. Cf. Natalie Abrams, "Moral Responsibility in Nursing," in *Nursing,* ed. Spicker and Gadow, pp. 150–151. See also Bosk, *Forgive and Remember,* chap. 2. The distinction between technical and normative errors that Bosk found in the training of surgeons does not quite correspond to that in the text. Bosk includes as normative errors inability to work with nurses or to secure the cooperation of patients and their families. These need not be moral failures or disagreements.

26. See Benjamin and Curtis, *Ethics in Nursing,* p. 91, for an example.

27. ABA, *Model Rules,* Rule 5.2(b).

28. Schaub and Pavlovic, *Engineering Professionalism and Ethics,* p. 339.

29. Martin and Schinzinger, *Ethics in Engineering,* p. 208.

30. See Abrams, "Moral Responsibility," p. 156; De George, "Ethical Responsibilities," p. 6.

31. See Glazer, "Ten Whistleblowers," and "Whistle-Blowers Face Retaliation, but Have Few Regrets," *Gainesville Sun,* 22 February 1987, p. 7E.

32. Cp. De George, "Ethical Responsiblities," p. 6, "evidence that would convince a reasonable, impartial observer."

33. See Martin and Schinzinger, *Ethics in Engineering,* pp. 206–207; Patricia Werhane, "Individual Rights in Business," in *Just Business,* ed. Regan, p. 119.

34. Spangler, *Lawyers for Hire,* p. 172.

35. Martin and Schinzinger, *Ethics in Engineering,* p. 184.

36. Spangler, *Lawyers for Hire,* p. 159.

37. National Society, "Code of Ethics," Professional Obligation 1(e). ABA, *Code of Professional Responsibility,* EC 5-13 (as interpreted by Informal Opinion 1325); see Semad, "Unionization of Law Offices," p. 1317. Although not explicitly supporting strikes, the ANA *Code Nurses* (9.2) supports collective action and collective bargaining.

38. Grosskopf, Buckman, and Garty, "Ethical Dilemmas."

39. For an account of the actions of Ontario physicians, see Meslin, "The Moral Costs."

40. See, for example, Werhane, "Individual Rights in Business" (see n.33 above), pp. 107–114. Her argument, however, seems to confuse a right to due process in being fired with a substantive right to be dismissed only for cause.

41. See "Engineering Ethics: The Amicus Curiae Brief of the Institute of Electrical and Electronics Engineers in the BART Case," in *Engineering Professionalism and Ethics,* ed. Schaub and Pavlovic, pp. 381–387, arguing that engineers' professional code requirements to protect the public safety are incorporated into all engineers' contracts of employment.

42. In American Society of Civil Engineers, *ASCE Guide to Employment Conditions,* p. 4.

43. Spangler, *Lawyers for Hire,* p. 36.

STUDY QUESTIONS AND PROBLEMS

1. Reconsider problem 5 in Chapter 5 in light of obligations to employers. Do you want to change your opinion? Why or why not?

2. Lawyer Astrid Bourgeois is an associate with a large corporate law firm. For the last two months, she has been working evenings pro bono on a sex discrimination case. She has been representing hourly workers in a suit filed against Your Slave Corporation, which provides maid and janitorial services. One day Conroy Deak, the managing partner of the law firm, calls her into his office. He complains that she has been moonlighting and using the firm law library and her office for the job.

   Astrid replies that she has not done it during the day when she is working for the firm, but evenings on her own time. Moreover, her use of the firm library and her office during the evening does not cost the firm anything. She checked to see that Your Slave was not a client of the firm, so no conflict of interest is involved. Finally, she argues, the firm has an obligation to make services available by supporting pro bono services to the poor.

   Conroy, however, is not persuaded. He contends that all the associates frequently work evenings on client cases. The time she spends on the Your Slave case could have been spent in billable hours for the firm's clients. Thus, the firm is in fact supporting her services. Moreover, he argues, the obligation to assist in making services available applies only to individual lawyers, not firms. Although the firm does provide some pro bono services, the decision to do so is one for the management committee. Because Astrid never asked permission to work on the case, he must request that she withdraw from it.

Evaluate the ethics of Astrid's and Conroy's conduct and the soundness of their arguments. Did Astrid violate an obligation of loyalty or of honesty to her employer? One of candor? Does the firm have an ethical obligation to provide pro bono services? Is Conroy justified in asking Astrid to withdraw from the case? Does she have an obligation to obey?

3. Nurse Erna Faison works in a psychiatric hospital. Her patient, Gaston Hargrett III, has been troublesome, frequently becoming upset and shouting at nurses and other patients. The staff physician has ordered that Gaston be given a mood altering drug. Nurse Faison does not think this is in Hargrett's best interests. He has never harmed anyone, and he primarily needs to confront his psychological problems and work them out. What should Erna do?

4. Computer specialist Ianthe Jaggers has been employed by Multi Industries for five years. She has completely designed and supervised the installation of Multi's computer system. She is the only one who fully knows the system—both hardware and software. Believing that she can make considerably more money as an independent consultant, she resigns her position. Ianthe then contacts Multi Industries and offers to advise on their computer system for a fee 50 percent higher than her previous salary. Is her conduct ethical? Why or why not?

5. Accountant Kit Ladd processes buyer travel expense reimbursement forms for Zay Mart stores, a national retailer. Three buyers in the clothing division seem to have excessive claims for entertainment and meals. Indeed, cross-checks with other buyers in the same and other units indicate that the three buyers' claims run 15 to 20 percent higher than those for other buyers traveling to the same cities. What should Kit do? Why?

Suppose Kit reports the discrepancies to his supervisor, Marigold Nickleson. Further suppose her response is that the supervisor in the clothing division has approved the reimbursements and that accounting's business is merely to process the reimbursements. What should Kit then do? Why?

6. Law associate Ortiz Pasco is assigned to produce with twenty-four hours a memorandum on whether the client's new process for producing genetically engineered organisms violates a competitor's patent on a similar organism. However, Ortiz has never studied patent law or worked in the field, and the time is inadequate for him to research the background. What should he do?

Suppose Ortiz tells his supervising partner that he lacks the competence and time to do the task. Further suppose the partner indicates that she realizes that, but no other associate is available, and she must give the client some preliminary indication of its position tomorrow. "There will always be time later to do it more thoroughly," she says. What should Ortiz then do? Why?

7. Physician Quan Roche writes a prescription for a drug for a hospital patient. Simeon Tidwell, a pharmacist in the hospital pharmacy, notes that the amount is twice the normal dosage. Although the drug is not likely to be lethal at that level, it will probably cause nausea, vomiting, and significant water retention. What should Simeon do?

   Suppose Simeon checks the prescription with Dr. Roche, and she states that she would not have ordered it if she had not meant it. Then what should Simeon do? Why?

8. Accountant Uranus Vertuno works for a large accounting firm that provides audits to major corporations. She has recently been moved from a branch office to the New York office. She is the first black female to reach this high a position in the firm. Her first assignment is to work on the international books of a corporation doing business in South Africa. However, Uranus is morally opposed to apartheid and believes in disinvesting in firms doing business in South Africa. What should she do? Why?

   Suppose she explains her situation to her superior, Wystan Xnix. He in turn states that much of their business is with corporations doing business in South Africa. Her first loyalty should be to the accounting firm, and it does not do business in South Africa. If Uranus continues to refuse to work on the audit or those of other companies doing business in South Africa, would the firm be justified in firing her or demoting and moving her to a regional branch primarily working for small companies and wealthy individuals? Why or why not?

9. Yellowbird Zurko is a social worker in a large city agency. She is appalled by the careless manner in which files are kept, often lying open on unattended desks. Consequently, to try to help protect the confidentiality of her clients, she begins to make fewer and less detailed entries in her files. In his annual evaluation of performance, her supervisor, Alonso Ballar, notes the dearth of information in her files. He tells Ms. Zurko that she is not doing an adequate job in keeping her files and that if she does not improve, he will have to dismiss her. Ethically evaluate the actions of Yellowbird and Alonso. Provide reasons for your opinions.

10. Professor Consuela D'Agnillo has had several athletes in her classes. Although most of them have done reasonably well, a few have flunked most of the exams but managed to pass by turning in good term papers. One day in looking up a past roll in the department files to remove an incomplete for a student, she finds that one of the grades she had given an athlete had been changed from a D– to a D+.

   She storms into the department chair's office with the file and tells him about it. Chair Erastus Fallon responds that he changed the grade. He had had a phone call from an assitant coach about the grade. He reviewed the student's work, and to him it seemed deserving of the higher grade. Besides, he said, you know you are one of the most severe graders in the department. It is not fair that this student receive the lower grade from you and become ineligible for the team when he would have received the higher grade in any other section of the course.

   Professor D'Agnillo is outraged. She immediately returns to her office and telephones a friend of hers who writes a sports column for the local newspaper. She tells him the story, and the next day it appears in the local paper.

   Was the chair's conduct ethical? Why or why not? Was Professor D'Agnillo's conduct ethical? Why or why not?

11.   Dr. Ginny Hearn does a routine physical exam on a patient for an application for a life insurance policy. The patient is a forty-five-year-old single professional woman. Ginny discovers that the woman has an inoperable malignant tumor. Chemotherapy might delay her death a few months, but no more. Ginny decides not to tell the patient, who at present is feeling fine. She discusses this decision with the staff, some of whom feel the patient should be told. Nonetheless, Dr. Hearn orders that the patient not be told of her condition. Nurse Ingram Joiner disobeys the order and informs the patient that she has cancer. Was Ingram's conduct unethical? Why or why not?

12.   Engineer Kay Lasko and lawyer Montague Nestor both work for Corrosive Chemicals. Both Kay and Montague have bought several hundred shares of Corrosive Chemicals under the company stock option plan. On the advice of her stock broker, Kay has bought one hundred shares of National Distillers, a prominent chemical company but primarily in different chemicals from Corrosive. Montague owns a substantial number of shares in a mutual fund specializing in the chemical industry. Is the stock ownership of either of them unethical? Why or why not?

13.   Teacher Olympia Peebles writes a letter to the editor of the local newspaper and signs it "Olympia Peebles, Civics Teacher, Local High School." Is it unethical for her to use the school identification? Does it make any difference whether it is a letter highly critical of the mayor, a letter criticizing the local school board, or a letter praising local citizens for supporting the school? Give reasons for your answers.

14.   Consider whether it would be ethical for the following groups to go on strike or honor picket lines in the given circumstances.
   a.   Lawyers in the local legal services–funded organization go on strike over working conditions and wages. They are paid about half the salary of similarly experienced attorneys in large regional law firms in the city, and although their contracts specify caseloads of no more than fifty cases, they actually average seventy-seven each.
   b.   Mine engineers refuse to cross the picket lines of mine workers on strike. Would it make any difference whether the mine workers were striking solely for wages or if they also had plausible demands for safer working conditions? Does the obligation of engineers for the safety, health, and welfare of the public make any difference?
   c.   The United Faculty of Underfunded University go on strike. The American Association of University Professors salary analysis indicates that at all ranks, they are in the poorest paid category for comparable universities. Would it make any difference whether Underfunded University was a private or public university (assuming there was no law against a strike at a

public university)? Would it make any difference whether the strike started at the beginning of the fall term, the beginning of the spring term, or one month before the end of the spring term? Why or why not?

d.   All news reporters for the Knight-Ridder newspapers go on strike for higher wages and better working conditions.

7 Obligations to the Profession

In the social structure of American society, professionals are at the top—in prestige, wealth, and power within their own communities and the country as a whole. This leading role is due partly to their being among the best educated people in society, which prepares them for leadership outside their profession. Because they make many decisions that significantly affect others, they share responsibility for the realization of values in society.

Most ethical codes recognize a responsibility for the public good.[1] This responsibility belongs to a profession as a whole. In their respective areas, the professions contain almost all the available expertise and have a near monopoly over implementation of social policies. Other people can design and administer health, legal, or construction programs, but professionals provide their day-to-day implementation. For example, legislatures, health system agencies, district councils, and hospital boards—consisting of many or mostly lay members—set many health care policies. Nevertheless, the practical administration of many of these policies is done by members of the health care professions. Many administrators in the medical side of the Department of Health and Human Services are physicians. At the most concrete level, decisions by physicians to order this or that diagnostic procedure or to institute one treatment regimen or another determines whether many policies are effectively implemented. In the legal profession, policy implementation is controlled by judges, prosecutors, and private attorneys. Construction engineers implement consultants' designs, and engineers take a large part in the development and enforcement of safety and pollution control policies. The policies of lay school boards must be implemented by professional school administrators and teachers, and the same applies to social workers in social welfare agencies. Given their special knowledge and actual services, professions to a large extent unavoidably bear the responsibility for implementing policies for the public good.

Responsibility for public good has three main facets. First are activities of social leadership, such as service with charitable organizations, government commissions, and so on. This participation is due more to professionals' positions in the social structure than to their special knowledge. Such responsibility also devolves on business people and others occupying prominent positions or having the time to contribute, such as knowledgeable homemakers.

A second facet of responsibility for public good is the improvement of professional knowledge, tools, and skills. New medical knowledge, legal and accounting tools, and teaching and social work skills can be used to promote the public good. For physicians, academics, and engineers, improvement of service primarily concerns research; for lawyers, social workers, and accountants, it chiefly concerns reform. However, all professions have responsibility for both research and reform; only the relative emphasis differs.

A third facet of this responsibility is to preserve and enhance the role of the profession itself. Professionals maintain that the continued high status and respect of their profession is for the ultimate benefit of society. Ethical questions arise when professionals use their talents to aid special interests that conflict with or are contrary to public interest.

The last two facets of responsibility for the public good support obligations of individual professionals to their professions and are the subject of this chapter. These responsibilities are those of a profession as a whole and are not reducible to precisely similar obligations of individual professionals. No one individual professional can be responsible for research and reform, for example; both must be products of the whole profession. Moreover, the freedom of individual professionals would be unnecessarily limited if each were required to participate in, say, research. Such a requirement is unnecessary, though, because all appropriate research could be conducted by some members of a profession.

Nonetheless, individual professionals have obligations to assist the professions in improving skills and in maintaining a position that enables them to fulfill their social role. Although the ultimate beneficiary is the general public, for individual professionals, the obligation is immediately to the profession. Unfortunately, individuals sometimes forget that their ultimate justification must be the good of society, just as Richard Nixon's advisors forgot that an obligation to assist a president must rest ultimately on the public benefit. Professionals are sometimes blindly devoted to the profession regardless of the effect on social values.

RESEARCH AND REFORM

Responsibility for research in their respective fields devolves on professionals as the only people qualified to perform it. Only they have the necessary knowledge. Nonprofessionals can pursue reform, but only with significant assistance from professionals. To undertake reform of automobile insurance or safety law, for example, requires information about the possible alternatives and their likely consequences. Lawyers, actuaries, and engineers must provide such information because the public and legislators lack expertise in these areas.

Other important reasons exist for professionals to carry a significant part of the burden of reform. Knowing social defects in their fields, they are better prepared than nonprofessionals to pursue reform. In their work, they frequently discover matters needing reform and for which no organized reform group exists. If reform and enhancement of social values are to occur, they must advance reform at least enough to interest a significant group of nonprofessionals in pursuing it.

Implementing the results of research and reform studies is an issue for society in general. The function of professionals in reform is similar to their function with respect to clients. Professionals diagnose the problems, suggest alternative approaches, predict likely consequences, make recommendations, and implement programs. The decision to adopt a program, however, is a value judgment for which professionals have no more training and expertise than particular clients or the public. Thus, these decisions are for the public either at large or through democratically elected representatives.

Two general issues concern research and reform by professionals. The first is who does or should carry them out. Not everyone is equally competent at, or interested in, these activities. For the most part, the decision to engage in them should be left to the individual professionals. Nevertheless, professionals who do not actively engage in either have an obligation to promote and support such activity by other members of their profession. In their daily work, they can keep their eyes open for areas in which research or reform is needed and call attention to the needs they perceive.

The second issue is the obligations relevant to research and reform. The primary responsibilities of professionals engaged in research and reform are candor and independence. These are essentially the same as the responsibilities professionals have to their clients, and they rest on similar considerations, namely, the users' needs for complete and unbiased information. Few people would dispute that researchers must be candid and independent in their judgments. The purpose of research is to discover the truth. A lack of candor or independence thwarts this purpose. Some people deny that candor and independence pertain to reform activity. Although these factors are mitigated in the context of reform activity in the United States, they are still relevant. The following discussion considers these obligations and others with respect to research and reform.

Research

Funding.   Several centuries ago most research was privately funded. Either the researcher or private benefactors supported it. Today few private individuals can afford to fund research. Most research funds come from society, the government being the major source of research funds.[2] Because the results of research add to society's store of knowledge, that is probably as it should be. Private foundations are another important source of funding for professional research. In part, governments indirectly support these foundations by their tax exempt status. A third major source of funding is private corporations. They do not usually support so-called basic research, but only that with potential for relatively immediate benefits to them. The proportion of funding from these sources varies greatly among the professions. For example, engineers receive much, and lawyers little, of their research funding from private corporations.

The sources of funding and self-interested motives raise significant issues for researchers. The funding of research by private corporations or interest groups raises a question about researchers' independence of judgment. When corporations fund research, they are usually interested in certain results. For example, drug companies want their drugs proven safe and effective. Because the researchers depend on corporation grants for their funding, they might be biased in favor of them. Tests have been designed and results presented so as to appear to support conclusions more strongly than they do. Social opinion survey research is especially prone to bias in the way questions are formulated.

Funding sources, however, are not the only factors that can lead researchers to lose their objectivity and independence of judgment. Researchers are often motivated by fame and fortune for themselves. Indeed, some of the most egregious instances of faked data and biased research have resulted not from bias due to funding sources but researchers' personal desires for prestige and recognition.

In scientific and nonscientific research, candor serves two important functions. First, it makes methods and results available so others can check them. Others can examine the methodology to determine its soundness and thus the reliability of the results. Second, others can use the results to make further advances and thus promote the public good.

Funding sources and the desires for fame and fortune can adversely affect researchers' candor. The purpose of research is often to develop new knowledge that can be exploited for commercial advantage. To reap full commercial advantage, however, discoveries will often need to be kept as trade secrets. Consequently, researchers will not fully disclose and publish their findings. Even when not so funded, some academic researchers are now keeping their discoveries confidential and forming their own companies to make a profit.

One should here distinguish between trade secrets and patents. As noted in the previous chapter, trade secrets are information that a company tries to keep confidential; it can be commercially exploited because no one else has it. Patents are government protected rights to the use of new processes or products. Although anyone wanting to use the patented process or make such a product must obtain the permission of the patent holder, the process or product design is a matter of public knowledge available from the patent office. Thus, both trade secrets and patents can enable the holder to make profits, but patents do not prevent others using the discoveries to make further discoveries and inventions.

A second reason for keeping discoveries secret is national security. As noted, much research is funded by the government, and a significant portion of government funded research is for defense purposes. If national defense is in the public interest, then keeping the results of such research secret is in the public interest. However, one might still object to particular defense research programs as not in the public interest, either because of the inherent nature of the weapons (biological warfare) or the unlikelihood of their being successful (the Strategic Defense Initiative or "Star Wars").

During the last decade, private corporations and universities have formed cooperative ventures for research, and a significant part of defense research is being done at universities. Universities have traditionally been centers for the discovery and dissemination of knowledge. Consequently, keeping discoveries secret for commercial or defense purposes is often thought incompatible with universities' purposes and academics' professional obligations.[3] Moreover, even if discoveries are made public, say, by universities or academics obtaining patents, some people question whether they should be permitted to profit from publicly funded research.[4] These issues cannot be pursued further here.

Human Subjects.   Because medical and social sciences are directly concerned with human beings, they often use human subjects in experiments. Ethical issues of human experimentation are far too complex to discuss adequately here. Congress established the National Commission for the Protection of Human Subjects of Biomedical and Behavioral Research, which spent several years exploring different aspects of the topic.[5]

Informed consent is the most fundamental requirement in research with human subjects.[6] Obtaining this consent is part of a responsibility of nonmaleficence. Without the subjects' consent, any harm that befalls them is injury. As noted in Chapter 4, the elements of informed consent are (1) a capacity to understand and choose; (2) an explanation of the experiment, its alternatives, and the risks and potential benefits of each option; and (3) free and voluntary consent. A responsibility of candor is central to the second element. Unless a researcher is candid with subjects, their consent will be uninformed, and the experiment constitutes injury to them.

The underlying ethical value is protection of people from injury by others. A physical or psychological harm does not constitute a wrongful injury if a person freely and knowingly participates in an activity with a risk of harm—for example, plays softball in the neighborhood and breaks a leg. Because the choice is the individual's, he or she is responsible for the risk and harm. For this principle to apply, the elements of informed consent must be met. Some people, for example retarded, very young, or senile persons, lack the capacity to understand the activity or risks involved in an experiment. A problem that arises and cannot be discussed here is the extent to which others should be permitted to consent for a person unable to do so. Should they be permitted to consent to a person's participation in research from which that person will not benefit, or is that unjustly using the person as a means to the ends of others?[7]

Requiring that a person have the capacity to understand and choose is pointless if the person is not given all relevant information for deciding. Crucial information includes what will be done to the person (e.g., blood will be taken on three occasions in a total amount of 30 ml), the risks of the procedure (a drug has side effects such as loss of hair and dizziness), and its potential benefits (a drug might be more effective in curing a disease). Frequent problems that arise with this element are a failure to provide the information in nontechnical jargon a layperson can understand (for example, using "apnea" instead of "temporary stopping of breathing"); a failure to explain the alternatives available, including no treatment; and difficulty in deciding what counts as a relevant risk (for example, a bruise from the drawing of blood).

Complications concerning informed consent arise when an experiment is double-blind (neither the subject nor the experimenter knows which drug a person receives) or involves a placebo (an inert drug) or deception. In a double-blind format, subjects can be told that they will receive either of two specific drugs. When placebos are used alternatively with an active drug, subjects can be told that what they receive could be an inert substance. Experiments involving deception are much more difficult. A classic example was one in which subjects were told to administer electric shocks to another person whom they could not see but could hear.[8] Actually, the other person did not receive any shocks but merely screamed at the appropriate times. The point was to see whether people would obey authority to give shocks at lethal doses. Immediately after the experiment, the subjects were informed of the deception, but was this sufficient for informed consent? If not, should such experiments be forbidden?

Finally, even if everything is explained and subjects understand, they must still voluntarily decide to participate. If, for example, subjects think they will not receive medical care if they refuse, then they do not freely decide to participate. Some of the more difficult problems with this requirement concern whether prisoners can ever freely volunteer, whether students in a course may be required to participate in research by the instructor (in the past, a common requirement in many psychology courses), and whether high payment for participation is permissible.[9]

Volumes have been written on these topics, and it is not possible to begin to review all the arguments and problems. The National Commission's published reports and appendixes provide a good starting place for those who are interested in the problems. Nonetheless, even though difficult questions remain, the principle of informed consent to participate in human experimentation is now established in professional ethics. Many other issues about research still exist, however, and the relevant responsibilities have not been widely recognized or discussed.

Significance.   The value of research is particularly relevant to its ethics. Insofar as society supports research, a responsibility exists not to waste resources. Even when the research is privately funded, society is the indirect funder. Companies obtain their research funds from the prices they charge for their products. Ultimately, the consuming public or public at large pays for research. More importantly, if human subjects are involved, to risk their well-being when no significant results are obtainable exhibits a callous disregard of the welfare of others; they are put at risk for no possible significant gain. The Department of Health and Human Services regulations governing the ethics of research on human subjects requires research to be significant. Institutional review boards are to determine that "risks to subjects are reasonable in relation to anticipated benefits, if any, to subjects, and the importance of the knowledge that may reasonably be expected to result."[10]

An example illustrates a reseacher's responsibility to engage in only significant research. One common type of research is testing drug products that will compete with those of other companies. For example, company A markets a good selling eyewash, and company B wishes to compete with it. The eyewashes of both companies have essentially the same chemical ingredients. Should a researcher conduct tests of B's new eyewash? Although it is harmless to the subjects, no social benefit will be derived from it except perhaps slightly lower prices through competition. Trained researchers and healthy subjects will spend time and effort that could be better spent in other activities. What makes the problem more difficult is that government regulations require B's product to be tested even if it is essentially the same as A's.

One might question whether ethical considerations ever justify preventing a researcher and a fully informed, consenting subject from engaging in a research project. Consider the situation in problem 12 in Chapter 5. A researcher has an untested theory for treating a fatally ill patient who consents to the treatment. The theory is speculative but plausible. Even if the treatment works and an effective treatment of this very rare disease were found, the understanding of its causes and prevention would not be significantly advanced. Moreover, the treatment could make the disease worse. Should such research be undertaken?

Some people argue that if the experimental subject gives an informed consent, then no one has a right to interfere with the freedom of the researcher and subject. Without the experiment, the subject will certainly die; if it is successful, other lives can be saved. This argument, however, ignores the funding of research. Because society is being asked to underwrite the costs of the experiment, it may refuse to support it. The probability of the treatment being successful cannot even be estimated, so it might not be worth the cost, at least until animal experiments have confirmed the theory. Moreover, if an application were made to a funding agency to support the experiment, it might well decide that other research showed promise of greater benefits for the money spent. Not being able to fund all research proposals, it should fund them in order of their expectable benefit.

This discussion of the value of research has glided over the main, underlying consideration—the value of knowledge. The professions, especially academics, have tradtionally argued that knowledge or the truth should be pursued wherever it leads. Only recently have people seriously considered that perhaps the truth should not be sought in some areas. Some research poses grave risks to society. The defense of research of all kinds has rested on three contentions. (1) Knowledge itself is valuable, so a prima facie justification for research always exists. (2) Discovering truth can be distinguished from the uses to which it is put. (3) Researchers cannot know the uses to which their results will be put.

Although each of these considerations is important, even together they are not sufficient to justify absolute freedom of inquiry. The intrinsic value of knowledge is quite limited. It can be considered the satisfaction of curiosity, the desire for knowledge for its own sake. People who are curious simply want to know something; they do not have any plan for using the knowledge. There are many things, such as the color of pen I am using, about which no one is curious; so much possible knowledge has no intrinsic value. Most of the knowledge people prize, such as the structural properties of a new alloy, is valued for its consequences—the ability to use it in construction. Although such knowledge is frequently gained because a researcher was simply curious, if the knowledge had no instrumental value, the only loss from not doing the research would be frustrating the researcher's curiosity. If the knowledge were to be put to harmful uses, the harm caused might be much greater than the good caused in fulfilling a researcher's curiosity.

Knowledge is distinct from the uses to which it is put, but some knowledge is more appropriate for certain uses. Basic research is sometimes distinguished from applied research. Basic research is primarily concerned with theory construction for the advancement of understanding. Applied research is directed toward uses, although it can have a significant theoretical component. The knowledge of most professions is not a mere knowing that; it is also a knowing how, and knowing how is related to uses. A lawyer's knowledge of how to draft contracts and conveyances to prevent racial groups purchasing property in a housing development is more apt to further than to end discrimination. A physician's knowledge of undetectable poisons is more apt for use in committing than preventing murder. A nuclear engineer's knowledge of explosive mechanisms is more apt for war than peace. Only "pure" scientists and some academics are concerned with merely knowing that something is the case.

Finally, although researchers sometimes do not know the ultimate uses to which their results will be put, that is not always or even usually the case. For example, those scientists who work on the development of bacteria and chemicals for warfare know the intended use of their results. And even when researchers do not know to what use their results will be put, they usually know its potential uses. Consequently, they cannot completely escape responsibility for them because they both know of and have some control over these results.

A striking example of these types of concerns was the debate during the 1970s over recombinant DNA research.[11] Recombinant DNA is the technique of manipulating the genes of organisms to produce new ones. This research raises significant questions. First, such research might be dangerous. New strains of viruses or bacteria might be created that are both harmful to humans and resistant to human defense mechanisms or chemical means of destroying them. So one question is the safety of this research for the workers and the general public. Second, such research has potential for both beneficial and harmful uses. One might develop genetics to prevent or rectify diseases. One might also, perhaps, develop methods for killing people, producing monsters, and so on. So a second question concerns the uses to which the results of such research will be put. Third, both of these concerns raise questions about legal reform to control such research.

This complex and fascinating topic cannot be considered in detail. The issue here is the responsibility of the professionals involved. Much to their credit, some scientists recognized the issues and raised them in the scientific community. A voluntary moratorium on such research was instituted until further study of the problems could be conducted and guidelines developed. Regardless of the merits of the different sides of the debate, the raising of the issues and their consideration are examples of professional responsibility with respect to the value of research and the uses to which it can be put. Of course, researchers must still ask these questions about particular research projects.

This discussion shows that researchers are responsibile for the value of their research. They are aware of its potential value and voluntarily decide to undertake it. This responsibility also includes the uses to which the research is or might be put. The extent of responsibility for uses is the extent to which they can be foreseen, because researchers cannot be justly held responsible for what they cannot know. For example, researchers might discover something that thirty years or so later, much to their surprise, is used to create something harmful, such as an agent to defoliate plants in warfare. The fact that research can have harmful uses does not imply that it should not be undertaken. Nevertheless, the possibility of harmful uses must be taken into account. The greater the potential harm of the research, the greater the possible benefits should be and the stronger the safeguards to ensure that it is not used in harmful ways.

Reform

The ethical responsibilities and duties of professionals for reform are best developed with the respect to lawyers because they are most concerned with social reform through the law. Other professions are also responsible for legal reform in their areas of activity; physicians are as responsible as lawyers for health and sanitation codes. Moreover, reform need not result in legal requirements but can result in rules voluntarily implemented by people in the field, such as changes in childbirth procedures to provide a more homelike and psychologically rewarding experience. The responsibility for reform is consequent on professionals' expertise and, in some cases, monopoly.

The two primary methods of bringing about reform are participation in lobbying and public interest groups. Whether or not these activities help fulfill a profession's responsibility for reform depends on whether one's participation is interested or disinterested. To be disinterested is not to be uninterested. No reformer is uninterested. Being disinterested means that no one group or set of interests is given special weight in determining the best course of conduct. Professionals and professional societies often lobby for their own interests, for example, medical associations lobbying for reform of medical malpractice law. However, professionals might join a public interest group such as the Sierra Club and lobby on environmental issues because they believe the positions advocated are in everyone's best interests. The essential determinant is probably whether the professionals or their profession stand to benefit more than the average person from the proposed changes. If so, then their disinterestedness is suspect, and they should be treated like any other interest group.

The position of lawyers is fundamentally different from that of most other professions. When they serve as lobbyists or representatives of public interest groups, the interest group is a client. Consequently, they have an obligation to promote that group's interest over that of others provided they do not violate obligations to third parties. The same applies to any professional hired to support a lobby or public interest group, such as an engineer or scientist hired by an environmental group to analyze pollution. In short, they are professionally obligated to take an interested rather than disinterested position. Nevertheless, any obligations that apply to lawyers will also apply to those who are not lawyers representing the groups.

A leading text on legal ethics states that the general obligation of the lawyer as lobbyist is honesty to both legislator and client.[12] If honesty includes candor, then that is at least a significant responsibility of the lobbyist. The conditions of lobbying differ from those of advocacy. In court advocacy, the other side will usually have an attorney to present the facts most favorable to its position. In lobbying, there are frequently informal meetings in which only one side is present. When the other side is not represented, if a lobbyist does not present the situation candidly, the legislation will probably be based on incomplete and misleading information. Moreover, in advocacy, the law is already established and provides a framework within which a lawyer may argue.[13] In lobbying, the question is what that framework should be, and no substantive principles limit the injustice that can result from securing passage of an evil law. The responsibility of candor becomes more important because a lobbyist does not have the independence of a researcher, does not operate in an adversarial context, and is not limited by a framework of substantive law.

Lobbyists, like researchers, are responsible for the ultimate results of their activities. Although legislators make the final decision concerning the advantages and disadvantages of legislation, an uncandid lobbyist is apt to bias the information on which legislators' judgments rest. If a lobbyist delays the imposition of safety rules that would prevent accidents, then the lobbyist is partly responsible for accidents. If lobbyists provide accurate and unbiased information, then they have done as much as can be expected and have fulfilled their responsibility. If the legislators still delay imposing safety rules, then they have made the decision and are alone responsible. Of course, they might have made a correct decision because the ultimate disadvantages of the legislation might have been too great for the good it would have done.[14]

Some lawyers believe that by representing public interest groups or practicing in so-called public interest firms they fulfill their responsibility for reform. If they happen to believe in the causes they represent, they could be doing so. However, in one sense, they are representing special interests.[15] For example, when the Corps of Engineers wanted to construct a dam on the Red River in Kentucky, lawyers representing environmentalists opposed its construction. Such representation was not of the public at large because a number of Kentuckians favored construction of the dam to prevent flooding. As any good lawyers would, the environmentalists' lawyers argued that alternative ways of preventing the flooding existed. In this sense, they took into account the interests of those who favored the dam. However, the lawyers for construction of the dam argued similarly that its environmental impact would not be serious and so took into account the interests of those opposed to the dam. These sorts of considerations occur in any lawsuit of that nature and do not mean that either side represents the public interest.

Representing so-called public interests is not representing all the interests of people in society. As the dam example illustrates, both sides took account of the interests of people on the other side, but neither could claim necessarily to have the correct view of the public interest. That is a decision to be made by a judge, public agency, or legislature after hearing both sides. Of course, these latter are not necessarily correct about the public interest either, but their role is to try to arrive at such a decision rather than to make the best case possible for one course of action. Public interest law is advocacy of a selected set of interests, even if these interests are shared by very many people and have not been adequately represented in the past.

Public interest lawyers do, nevertheless, help fulfill the responsibility of the legal profession for law reform. They represent interests that have previously been un- or underrepresented in many legal decisions. A half a century ago, Karl Llewellyn warned that the legal profession had developed so that its best talents were exerted primarily in behalf of the business and financial side of the law, to the neglect of other aspects.[16] The same note was sounded by Jerome E. Carlin in his study of the ethics of lawyers.[17]

The problem is even deeper, however, than these authors indicate. In some areas, interests or people are not organized. For example, victims of negligent accidents and purchasers of property are not and are not likely to become organized as environmental and antinuclear energy groups are. Few lawyers can take a distinterested position on such topics. Informal estimates are that over 60 percent of the bar would have their income substantially affected by abolition of the fault system for personal injury.[18] Yet, only lawyers are likely to be in a position to develop new systems. Similar considerations apply to engineers and teachers, for example, concerning aerospace engineers and space policy or teachers and educational policy.

Consequently, reform in these areas depends on professionals who can take a disinterested view of the problem. This requires that their incomes not depend on the current practice or a particular policy. Many of these professionals, such as lawyers specializing in corporate taxation, are not especially qualified to analyze these problems. About the only professionals left to engage in such reform are academics. The government should probably fund their research to support legal reform in these areas. In Canada, the Science Council and various law reform commissions have been established to do research and recommend policies and law reform. In the United States, similar organizations have not generally been officially created, although the National Academy of Sciences does some of this work in science. Academic professionals have to assume a special responsibility to consider and support reform that can be detrimental to the income of other members of their profession simply because they are often the only people in a position to do so. If they do not, the profession cannot fulfill its responsibility for reform.

RESPECT FOR THE PROFESSION

Professionals usually consider it important for the public to hold both their profession and its individual members in high esteem. Probably no profession takes this consideration as seriously as the law, and everyone rises as robe-clad judges enter the courtroom.[19] Yet, some of the important authors on legal ethics dismiss public opinion of a lawyer as unimportant. George Sharswood wrote, "Nothing is more certain than that the practitioner will find, in the long run, the good opinion of his professional brethren of more importance than that of what is commonly called the public."[20] A contemporary text continues the theme: "The lawyer, as any professional man, is seldom concerned with the layman's view of his conduct. But he is very much concerned with how his fellow lawyers view his actions."[21] The accepted opinion is that although it is important for the public to have a good opinion of the profession as a whole, public opinion of a particular professional, especially a lawyer, is of little importance. Nonetheless, many professionals are upset when some of their members incur the public's wrath because they claim it reflects adversely on the profession as a whole.

The first questions, then, are whether, and if so why, professionals should be concerned with the public opinion of their profession. Professionals exercise considerable authority in their respective spheres of activity. The exercise of authority requires willing compliance by those subject to it. If those subject to authority do not respect and trust the authorities, the system will break down. Given the importance of the subjects with which professionals are concerned—health care, legal justice, accurate financial reporting, education, safe buildings and equipment—the proper performance of their activities is important for the public good. Consequently, the public respect and confidence necessary for the professional role are also important.

Just as one must distinguish between particular professionals being trusted by their clients and their being worthy of such trust, so must one distinguish between a profession having public respect and confidence and its being worthy of them. A profession could receive undeserved respect and confidence. Indeed, professions have often tried to conceal activities by their members when such activities show that respect and confidence are not deserved. Some citizens believe that professionals will not inform authorities of the negligence or misconduct of other professionals because it would be detrimental to their mutual "club" and well-being. This claim is supported by some studies.[22] The responsibility to maintain the public's respect for, and confidence in, a profession is to promote not the wealth and prestige of its members, but the well-being of society.

Professionals can confuse their self-interest in the maintenance of respect for, and confidence in, the profession with the ethical reasons for it. Deserved respect rests on fulfilling the obligations of the profession as a whole, especially those of candor and fairness. Three specific duties usually recognized in professional codes pertain to these obligations. First, professionals should exhibit respect for one another. Only if they respect one another can they expect the public to do so. Exhibiting respect for another professional does not require withholding respectful criticism. In particular, professionals have a duty to testify in courts and other forums about the competence and morality of other professionals.[23] Second, professionals have a duty to provide any information they have concerning the competence and character of applicants for admission to their profession. When on committees or boards considering applicants, they have a responsibility to apply the standards rigorously but fairly. Third, professionals have a duty to bear their fair share of the work in fulfilling the profession's social role. The obligations of the profession as a whole can be fulfilled only by the individual members, and each member owes it as a duty of fairness to the others to do a fair share in fulfilling these obligations.

Although the foregoing matters are rather straightforward, a more complicated issue is also involved with respect for the profession, namely, the identification of a profession, or important members of it, with special interests. As argued in Chapter 1, the privileges accorded a profession as a whole are for the benefit of all citizens, not for the special interest of a few. At different times, almost all the professions have been identified, at least in the minds of a significant segment of the public, with special interests. This identification has often resulted from a failure to make services equally available, but it also stems from other sources. In recent years, for example, physicians have been thought to be closely tied to drug companies and to prescribe brand name medicines when drugs of generic description would do as well and cost patients less. On the whole, however, physicians have been less identified with special interests than other professionals. Civil engineers have been identified with construction interests, disregarding their projects' environmental impact; and accountants are sometimes identified with large corporations and tax evasion. Social workers are occasionally identified with the poor and welfare cheaters.

This sort of identification with special interests arises most for the legal profession. A physician who treats a corporate executive for an illness does not become identified with the executive's business activities. Lawyers, accountants, and engineers, however, serve corporate executives in the conduct of their business, and they are readily thought to be personally committed to the views of such clients and employers. The rub of the problem comes when one considers that every person, no matter how hated in society, is entitled to legal counsel. Even the disliked financier is entitled to legal representation. As discussed in Chapter 3, people are not entitled to be provided most other nonmedical, noneducational professional services, although they should be equally available. Moreover, although professionals sometimes do and should refuse to assist clients or employers in pursuing unethical courses of conduct, they should give them benefit of the doubt. If lawyers refused to serve clients whenever they disapproved of them or their activities, many of those most in need of legal counsel would be deprived of it and the value of equality of opportunity subverted.

The debate over the identification of lawyers with their clients has gone on for well over a century.[24] It was raised with respect to the confirmation of Supreme Court Chief Justice Charles Evans Hughes, who was thought to have served primarily a limited group of special-interest clients. The problem has probably become more acute during the twentieth century because of the unofficial specialization of legal practice. Lawyers concentrating on corporate taxation, corporation law, criminal defense, and so on are almost certain to have a clientele drawn from special interests. The same consideration applies to engineers in such fields as nuclear and petroleum engineering. By specializing, a person appears to identify with special interests.

Two distinctions help clarify the issue. The first is between representing a particular client and the pattern of clients represented. The legal profession's obligation to provide services to all citizens requires that even the most obnoxious and ruthless persons be represented. Consequently, one cannot attribute to a lawyer the character or interests of a particular client. This consideration applies with less force to a consulting engineer because engineering services need only be equally available, not provided. However, the pattern of clients an attorney chooses to represent indicates his or her character. Lawyers who always represent social radicals, large corporations, or particular industries are responsible for the goals and policies they thereby further. Because American lawyers, unlike English barristers, may refuse to serve clients who ask for their services, they can exercise control over the interests they represent. Similarly, consulting engineers who always work for companies exhibiting the strongest disregard for the environment or public safety may be identified with them.

Although professionals are appropriately identified with the interest of the predominant pattern of their clients, it does not follow that they are not conscientious. If they believe that these interests are generally valuable and support the welfare of society, then their activity does not necessarily indicate a reprehensible character.[25] However, they must stand by and not deny responsibility for the character of the interests they represent. Perhaps the exception here is criminal defense attorneys. Unlike attorneys in most civil fields, they do not have an opportunity to take cases of plaintiff and defense. Although they are often the first to be attacked by unenlightened members of the public, they perform an invaluable task in upholding social values. Some law firms specialize in plaintiff or defense work to avoid a conflict of interest in representing opposing sides of issues, but by so doing, they sacrifice a reputation for independence of judgment and become identified with special interests.[26]

For employed professionals, similar considerations apply. They should not be identified with all the particular policies and actions of their employer. However, they are appropriately identified with the organization's predominant policies. What makes the problem more difficult for such professionals is that refusal to work for the company can mean a total loss of income (one's job); for self-employed professionals, it merely means a partial loss of income—that from a particular case or project or perhaps from a few of them. Thus, personal considerations become much more significant, especially if other employment is not easy to obtain. This consideration does not alter the principle involved. It does make it more important to assure oneself of the ethics of an organization before starting work and implies that the unethical conduct must be more serious before one ought to quit for ethical reasons.

The second distinction is between the interests served and the way in which they are served. Lawyers can represent, say, the coal industry so as to aid its proper consideration within the legal system. They can also represent it in a manner that totally disregards other interests and values in society. One can expend all energy and every legal technicality to avoid regulation of strip mining, or one can represent strip mining companies so as to secure a reasonable consideration of their interests in balance with interests in a clean and unspoiled environment. Even lawyers representing the government can do so in a way that reflects discredit on them.[27] The same points apply to employed professionals, say, working for a coal company.

SUMMARY

This chapter has considered some of the obligations individual professionals have to their professions. These obligations rest on the responsibilities of a profession as a whole to further social values. The responsibilities of a profession as a whole are not reducible to similar obligations of individual professionals, but individual professionals do have an obligation to assist in fulfilling them. The emphasis has been on obligations of research, reform, and maintaining respect for the profession, although these do not exhaust the list of such obligations. For example, there are obligations to provide candid and independent judgment in evaluating articles submitted to professional journals, and there are perhaps obligations with respect to professional schools. However, those considered here are the most basic.

The primary responsibilities in research and reform are candor and independence. Researchers must be unbiased and fully disclose their findings. Sources of funding and desires for fame and fortune can adversely affect researchers' independence of judgment and candor. Maintaining the secrecy of discoveries in national defense research is not contrary to the public interest, provided the research is justifiable. Researchers are responsible for the value and possible use of their research. Useless research should not be undertaken. To the extent one can foresee the possible uses of research, this must be considered and the likely good consequences balanced against the likely bad ones. In conducting research, a researcher has a duty to secure the informed consent of human subjects. For informed consent, the subject must be competent to understand and choose; must be informed of the nature of the experiment, of the alternatives to participation, and of the risks and benefits of each; and must freely and voluntarily consent.

In reform, the obligation of candor requires that relevant information be fully disclosed, whether advantageous or not. Similarly, independence is required to help ensure that the efforts are for the public good. To fulfill the obligation of reform, lobbying and public interest activities must be based on a disinterested point of view. Professionals hired to work for lobbying or public interest groups do not have a disinterested point of view because they have a responsibility to further their clients' interests. In some areas, academic professionals have a special responsibility for reform because they are the only experts who do not have a financial stake in opposing some possible reforms.

Respect for the profession must be deserved. Respect is important so that professions can properly perform their functions and contribute to the public good. To ensure that respect is deserved, professionals have duties to provide evidence to proper authorities concerning the conduct of other practicing professionals and the character of applicants for admission and to bear their fair share of the work in fulfilling the obligations of the profession as a whole. They are also responsible for the interests and conduct of the predominant pattern of their clients and of the general conduct of their employers and the way they serve them.

NOTES*

1. ABA, *Code of Professional Responsibility,* Preamble; ABA, *Model Rules,* Preamble; AMA, *Principles of Medical Ethics,* sec. 7; Engineers' Council, "Code of Ethics," Canon 1; National Society of Professional Engineers, "Code of Ethics," Preamble; NASW, "Code of Ethics," Principle VI (P).

2. In Canada, for example, 35 percent of research and development is funded by industry, and most of the rest (at least half of the total funds) comes from governments. Ministry of State, Science and Technology, Canada, "A Rationale for Federal Funding of University Research," Background Paper No. 8, November 1979, p. 1.

3. See, for example, Hill, "The University and Industrial Research," and Miller, "Biotechnology and University Ethics."

4. See Lomasky, "Public Money," and Goldworth, "Moral Limit."

5. U.S. National Commission for the Protection of Human Subjects of Bio-medical and Behavioral Research, *The Belmont Report,* and the various other reports issued by the commission.

6. 45 CFR Part 46, sec. 46.116 (revised as of 10-1-85); AMA, "Current Opinions," 2.07.

7. See 45 CFR Part 46, Subpart D (revised as of 10-1-85), for Department of Health and Human Services special requirements for research involving children.

8. See Stanley Milgram, *Obedience to Authority* (New York: Harper & Row, 1974).

9. See 45 CFR Part 46, Subpart C (revised as of 10-1-85), for Department of Health and Human Services special requirements for research involving prisoners.

10. 45 CFR 46, sec. 46.111(2) (revised as of 10-1-85).

11. For a brief history and commentary on the public's role, see Callahan, "Recombinant DNA," pp. 20–22.

12. Patterson and Cheatham, *Profession of Law,* p. 154. See also Michael

---

*See the bibliography at the end of the book for complete references.

Pertschuk, "The Lawyer-Lobbyist," in *Verdicts on Lawyers,* ed. Nader and Green, p. 206.

13. Lieberman, *Crisis at the Bar,* pp. 173–174.

14. Ibid., pp. 174–175.

15. See Hegland, "Beyond Enthusiasm and Commitment," p. 809.

16. Llewellyn, "The Bar Specializes," p. 179.

17. Carlin, *Lawyer's Ethics,* p. 178.

18. Patterson and Cheatham, *Profession of Law,* p. 348.

19. The Michigan Supreme Court found it important to adopt a rule requiring judges to wear robes after a judge in Detroit had not been doing so. Judge Justine C. Ravitz, "Reflections of a Radical Judge: Beyond the Courtroom," in *Verdicts on Lawyers,* ed. Nader and Green, p. 256 n.

20. Sharswood, *Essay on Professional Ethics,* p. 75.

21. Patterson and Cheatham, *Profession of Law,* p. 180.

22. See, for example, ABA, Special Committee, *Problems and Recommendations,* p. 219.

23. ABA, *Code of Professional Responsibility,* DR 1-103(B); ABA, *Model Rules,* Rule 8.3; AMA, *Principles of Medical Ethics,* sec. 2; ANA, *Code for Nurses,* sec. 3; Engineers' Council, "Suggested Guidelines," 1, d.

24. See the correspondence of David Dudley Field, a prominent lawyer who handled cases for many nineteenth-century "robber barons," and his son, with Samuel Bowles, a prominent newspaper publisher, in *Problems in Professional Responsibility,* ed. Kaufman, pp. 424–444.

25. Spangler, *Lawyers for Hire,* p. 47, notes that "by joining the [big corporate] law firm, both partners and associates signal their willingness to serve the interests of big business."

26. Hazard, *Ethics in the Practice of Law,* p. 91.

27. See Alan B. Morrison, "Defending the Government; How Vigorous Is Too Vigorous?" in *Verdicts on Lawyers,* ed. Nader and Green, pp. 242–246.

STUDY QUESTIONS AND PROBLEMS

1. Professor Avery Bottoms is a plant geneticist at prestigious, private Yalard University. He receives a grant from the state deparment of agriculture to do research on corn, a major crop in the state. Although the purpose of the research project is to develop a higher yielding hybrid, Professor Bottoms discovers a way to get corn to fix nitrogen in the soil like legumes. With this new seed, farmers will not have to fertilize with nitrogen. Professor Bottoms keeps his discovery confidential, and he and Yalard form a private corporation to produce and sell the new seed.

   Is Professor Bottoms's conduct ethical? Why or why not? Would it make any difference if he patented the new seed? If Yalard were a public university? If he worked for a private seed company? Why or why not?

2. Dr. Charlene Dawson and her associates are aware of problems that may arise in securing informed consent in random clinical trials with placebos. If research subjects are told that they might receive an inert pill that will not help their condition, it can influence both their psychological reaction and reporting of effects. Consequently, they devise a study to test the effects of informing patients that they may receive placebos. In one center, subjects will be told that they have a 25 percent chance of receiving a placebo, that the researchers cannot explain whether they will or not because they will not know, and that this is the only way to determine whether the drug really has a beneficial effect. At another center, the same trial will be run, but neither the subjects nor the researchers will be told that a placebo is being used on some patients. They will simply be told that there is some chance the new drug might not be effective in their case. Is the information provided sufficient to ensure the *informed* consent of the subjects? If this project cannot be carried out, can one ever know the significance, if any, of informing patients that they may receive a placebo? If one does not know whether to discount that information, how reliable will future random double-blind clinical trials be? In the end, is this experiment ethically permissible? Why or why not?

3. Ephraim Franks, a psychologist, is asked by Xandu, Inc., to devise a test for its employees to determine their sympathy for union organizers. The test is to look like one for job competency. Is it ethical for Ephraim to accept this job? Why or why not?

4. Gloria Henderson, a professor of pharmacy at State University, has been asked by Yahoo Pharmaceuticals to test a new parenteral (injectable) formulation of their antibiotic drug. The drug has already been approved for use in oral form, which is more quickly absorbed into the blood system and therefore better than a similar antibiotic manufactured by a rival firm. Both drugs are equally effective over the same range of organisms, and the rival firm's drug is already approved for parenteral use. Yahoo's drug is not better in the injectable formulation because both it and the rival's are absorbed at the same rate. Gloria has doubts about the usefulness of performing the research. Why expose patients to some risk and waste valuable research time when the drug will not add anything to medicine's arsenal against diseases? At best, it will help Yahoo's profits. However, Yahoo's chief of research argues that many physicians currently use the rival's drug when patients must receive it parenterally and then switch to Yahoo's when the patient is capable of taking an oral dosage. If their product is approved in parenteral form, patients will not have to switch drugs. Moreover, competition between the two drugs might lead to a lower price and so benefit the public. Is it ethical for Gloria to do the trial testing? Why or why not?

5. For several years, Isaac Jacobs has represented a number of welfare recipients. He has become very concerned about some injustices that he sees they are subject to. One day a representative of the Justice for Welfare Recipients organization approaches him. They would like to hire him to represent test cases for welfare reform. They would bring him clients and pay for their representation, but he must press only the issues they want raised. As the representative explains, if he

raises various issues that are relevant to the particular client, then the courts will avoid the central issue they want decided. Although some particular clients are likely to suffer, in the long run, more welfare recipients will benefit, and will do so sooner, by this tactic. If Isaac agrees, he will do more for welfare recipients than he can by the way he has been practicing. Would it be ethical for Isaac to agree to take such cases? Why or why not?

6. The directors of a state engineering society want to form a political action committee. The committee will accept contributions from its members of up to $5,000. They will use it to support particular candidates who are sympathetic to reform legislation regulating the profession and standards in the industry in which they are involved. Is it ethical for the society to engage in this activity? Why or why not? If so, would members have an ethical obligation to contribute to it as a way of furthering reform? Why or why not?

7. Kathy Lunt works as an engineer for a large manufacturing corporation. She has been engaged in a study of the pollution emissions at the corporation's plants. She has discovered that the plants' new process greatly reduces discharges of the major pollutants but that a different chemical is given off in small quantities. This chemical has not been proven harmful, but in one study of an area downwind from where the chemical was introduced into the air for a prolonged period, there was a significant increase in temporary respiratory illnesses. Her supervisor has asked her to testify on the company's behalf before the environmental regulatory agency as to the reduced pollution by the new process. When Kathy presents her discovery of the new chemical, her supervisor tells her not to mention it. If the members of the agency ask her about it, then she is to give them a truthful answer, but he is sure they will not ask because no one has raised the issue. Is it ethical for Kathy not to volunteer the information to the agency? Why or why not?

8. Marmaduke Nimmons III, an attorney, has brought suit against Zeckman Industries on behalf of black and Spanish-speaking persons, challenging its employment practices as discriminatory. On the first day of the trial, he attempts to introduce evidence that the test given applicants is failed more often by minority candidates than whites. This evidence has been received in other trials and has shifted the burden of proof to those using the tests to show that they are relevant to the job. However, the judge rules the evidence inadmissible. The next day, Marmaduke is interviewed on a local television show and remarks that the judge is unaware of recent legal trends and that it is unfortunate they will have to go through an appeal to get his rulings reversed. A few days later, columnist Oona Parmenter, who is also an attorney, writes that the judge is quite ignorant of the law and that his racism shows throughout the trial. His conduct is, she writes, a disgrace to the bar and bench. Were the comments of attorneys Nimmons and Parmenter ethically permissible? Why or why not? Does the fact that Oona is also a journalist make a difference? If she were not a lawyer, would that make any difference to the ethics of her comment? Why or why not? If any of the comments were improper, what, if anything, should be done about them?

9. Quincy Rennick is a famous criminal defense attorney known for defending some shady persons. When he defended a notorious reputed crime boss on charges of filing a fraudulent tax return, he pulled one of his best "tricks." The unsuspecting prosecutor let him get a jury three-fourths of which were blacks. On the day the case went to the jury, he invited the star black player from the city's baseball team to come in and meet his client. With the jury in the courtroom, the ballplayer stopped by the defense table, shook hands with the defendant, and loudly remarked that he hoped his good friend would beat the bum rap. After two hours of deliberation, the jury returned a verdict of acquittal. Were Quincy's tactics ethical? Why or why not?

10. Stacy Trent, an elementary schoolteacher, and her husband belong to a private club called the Dionysians. At a private party, an undercover news reporter, Usher Vrains, observed her committing serveral acts of oral copulation, which he wrote about in the paper the next day. The response, of course, was public shock and outrage. Has Stacy violated a responsibility to maintain respect for the teaching profession? Why or why not? Has Usher violated a responsibility to maintain respect for the profession of journalism? Why or why not?

8 Ensuring Compliance

Having considered the obligations of professionals, we face questions concerning how one ensures compliance with them. How does one prevent misconduct—violation of professional norms—from occurring? If misconduct occurs, what responses are appropriate? Most discussions focus on sanctions (ranging from blame to loss of license to practice) for misconduct, assuming that adequate sanctions deter misconduct by others. That assumption is doubtful, at least at present levels of sanctioning. Avoiding original misconduct is preferable, and other policies might help prevent it.

The traditional methods for controlling the conduct of professionals have been selective admission and discipline of members. These are considered in the first section. Historically, the professions have been self-regulating. The second section analyzes the appropriateness of self-regulation and alternatives to it. The concluding section discusses motivations for compliance with professional norms.

CONTROLS

The control professions exercise over the conduct of their members varies among the professions. The legal profession probably has the most control; with some modifications, the ABA codes are adopted by courts or legislatures and thus have the force of law. The ultimate sanction for violation of the disciplinary rules is disbarment. Within the other professions, enforcement is not as strong. Professional societies can only remove persons from membership for misconduct. Hospital boards can remove physicians' hospital privileges, but loss of privileges at one hospital does not automatically involve loss of privileges at another hospital. State authorities can suspend or revoke a professional's license to practice.

Admission

Admission to a profession often involves a long process of undergraduate education, admission to and graduation from a professional school, and then one or more examinations for a license. For professions such as nursing, teaching, and engineering, training occurs at the undergraduate level. Nonetheless, today one must often apply for admission to the programs after one or two years of undergraduate study. The difficulty of admission to various professional programs varies with demand. For example, in the late 1970s, when demand for teachers was low, some colleges of education became more selective. With an expected national shortage of teachers during the 1990s, standards might well fall.

Admission to professional education is usually based on academic performance—grade point and score on a standardized test. When demand for slots in professional programs is high, students are under great pressure to make high grades. Academic excellence is probably correlated with competence in a profession, but it is unlikely to be correlated with ethical performance.

An unofficial criterion for admission to professional education is money. Even undergraduate professional programs often have heavy course requirements, so students cannot realistically expect to complete them in four years. Moreover, one's job prospects are also correlated to the program's prestige, and many of the more prestigious programs are in private universities with high tuitions. Consequently, most professionals come from middle-class backgrounds.

Discrimination.   Admission to the professions should respect equality of opportunity. The history of the professions in the twentieth century has not reflected favorably on their preserving or promoting equality of opportunity in admission. Between World Wars I and II, the legal profession rather widely discriminated against ethnic minorities, especially Jewish and Catholic persons of recent immigrant origin from Southern or Eastern Europe.[1] Among the methods used were increasing educational standards for bar admission, integration of the bar (making everyone belong to the state bar association), and, in Pennsylvania, a system whereby all new attorneys had to secure another attorney to allow them to serve a six-month clerkship. The reasons for these changes were not simply to discriminate; they also had the worthy aim of increasing professional competence for the sake of clients and the public. The medical profession greatly strengthened medical education just prior to World War I, resulting in a significant improvement in the quality of medical care. However, another immediate effect was to close six of the eight black medical schools in the country.[2]

One might respond that this type of discrimination rapidly ceased after World War II. However, it is widely recognized that discrimination against women and blacks continued until at least the 1970s. For example, in 1972, women generally comprised a small percentage of the professions (see Table 8.1). Although some improvement had occurred by 1984, the respective percentages were still not large. Of course, these gains are in the entire membership in the professions, and there already were many practicing male professionals. Therefore, great gains in the percentage of women admitted into a profession will not immediately result in as large a percentage increase in their membership of the profession as a whole. This consideration is not significantly relevant for blacks. The percentages of black dentists, engineers, nurses, and physicians actually declined between 1972 and 1984!

Table 8.1   Women and minorities in the professions

Profession	Percentage of Membership			
	1972		1984	
	Female	Black	Female	Black
Accountants	21.7	4.3	40.9	5.5
Dentists	1.9	5.6	6.2	0.9
Engineers	0.8	3.4	6.2	2.6
Lawyers	3.8	1.9	16.2	2.6
Nurses	97.6	8.2	96.0	7.6
Physicians	10.1	8.2	16.0	5.0

SOURCE: Statistical Abstract of the United States, 100th ed. (Washington, D.C.: U.S. Department of Commerce, Bureau of the Census, 1979), p. 416 (No. 687), and 106th ed (Washington, D.C.: U.S. Department of Commerce, Bureau of the Census, 1985), p. 400 (No. 680).

Efforts to increase female and black enrollments in professional schools have resulted in widespread ethical and legal discussion of the merits of affirmative action admission programs. Too much has been written on this complex issue to even summarize the arguments here. The issue concerns the proper interpretation and implementation of equality of opportunity in society. Those favoring affirmative action argue that to compensate for past discrimination and provide equality of opportunity, special efforts must be made to enroll women, blacks, and other disadvantaged minorities. Those opposed to affirmative action argue that white males lack equality of opportunity if they are denied admission in favor of academically less well qualified female or black applicants.

After years of controversy, the Supreme Court of the United States partially settled the constitutionality of affirmative action programs by its decision in the *Bakke* case.[3] The medical school of the University of California at Davis had two admission programs, one for regular applicants and one for members of minorities, to which sixteen of the one hundred slots for new students were allocated. Allan Bakke twice applied for admission under the general admission program and was rejected, although applicants in the special program with Medical College Admissions Test scores significantly lower than his were admitted. He filed suit alleging that he was discriminated against. In a complex decision, the court held that a special (quota) admissions program is unconstitutional but that race may be taken into consideration in the admissions process. The division in society over this issue can be seen by the split in the court in its opinion. Justice Powell wrote the opinion. He was joined by four justices in holding that the special (quota) admissions program is illegal, but these four justices disagreed with the holding that race could be taken into account. Four different justices joined Justice Powell in holding that race could be considered in admissions, but they would also have permitted the special (quota) admissions program.

Moral Character. After having been admitted to and graduated from professional school, in some professions, one must still become licensed to practice. A significant issue concerns the requirements for licensing and admission to the profession. Should an applicant's moral character be a standard for admission? If so, what aspects of moral character should be considered?

One argument for restricting admission requirements to competence rests on the presumption of innocence. Applicants for admission should receive due process—that is, an appropriate hearing and the opportunities to present evidence in their behalf, to hear and counter evidence against them, and to appeal. This much is not disputed. The significant question is should applicants be presumed to be likely to act in an ethical fashion, as average citizens are presumed not to have broken the law, or should they be required to present evidence of good moral character. In many professions, applicants will not have had an extended period of practice on which their ethical conduct can be judged. (This claim does not hold for those professions, such as engineering, which require a period of practice before licensing.) Unless there is evidence of unethical conduct, applicants should be presumed to be likely to act in an ethical fashion.

The argument to the contrary is that admission to a profession is not a right but a privilege. Without previous practice by applicants, they may be required to provide evidence that they will act in an ethical fashion. The point of licensing is to protect the public and future clients from unethical and incompetent professionals. Therefore, not requiring evidence of good moral character for admission would thwart the purpose of licensing. Consequently, not only must applicants have good moral character and so be likely to act in an ethical way, but they also may be required to shoulder the burden of proof of their moral character, as of their competence.

Several other arguments can be made against licensing boards evaluating applicants' moral character for admission.[4] A central one is the inability of boards reliably to predict persons' subsequent conduct. It is notoriously difficult for even psychiatrists to predict a person's future behavior after a thorough examination. Licensing boards are usually composed of members of the profession, not psychiatrists and social scientists. Moreover, they do not have access to much information. To a large extent, they rely on self-reports and recommendations secured by applicants. In short, this initial screening for moral character is not likely to prove effective.

Even if one requires good moral character, one must determine what that ambiguous phrase means. Without clarification, the phrase permits much discrimination on the basis of personal prejudices. Obviously, any qualification for admission to a profession should be related to the abilities required to perform the tasks of that profession ethically. Indeed, this is constitutionally required.[5] The central character traits required for the ethical performance of a profession are those that correspond to the responsibilities identified in the previous chapters—a concern to serve, an interest in reform or research (or more generally, to assist the profession in fulfilling its responsibilities), nonmaleficence, fairness, honesty, candor, diligence, loyalty, discretion, and competence. Character traits are relatively enduring dispositions to act in certain ways, so presumably a person who has good ones on admission will likely continue to act appropriately.

Nevertheless, disputes exist concerning the relevance of certain traits. For example, at first glance, homosexuality seems not to be relevant to professional practice, at least as compared to a tendency to forcible sexual conduct. After all, heterosexuals also have sexual inclinations toward some of their clients. Nonetheless, one might argue that a person who engages in homosexual conduct where it is illegal has a disposition to violate a criminal statute and thus lacks an appropriate character for being a lawyer.[6] Yet, the concern should be with character traits that affect a professional's relations with clients or third parties, for licensing exists to protect them. There is no reason to believe that a homosexual is more likely than a heterosexual to show an unethical disregard for clients or third parties. Thus, even if a homosexual applicant might frequently violate a criminal statute, that is not in itself sufficient to refuse admission, even to the legal profession.

Discipline

Even if persons have the requisite character traits for admission, they might not continue to possess them. This raises the issues of enforcement of professional norms, especially by sanctioning professionals for violation of them. The client is often the person who suffers most from professional misconduct. The "natural" penalty for professional incompetence falls on the client rather than the professional. Incompetent lawyers lose cases; incompetent physicians or nurses misdiagnose or mistreat diseases and injuries; incompetent engineers build structures that collapse; incompetent teachers leave students ignorant or misinformed; and incompetent accountants mess up books. Their clients bear the consequences! Of course, many failures do not indicate incompetence. Someone must lose a lawsuit, and medical and engineering knowledge is not sufficient to guarantee a cure or an indestructible building.

Due to rapidly changing laws and knowledge, competence is probably the most easily lost trait of new professionals. Despite this, most professions do not have strong checks on the continuing competence of their members. Physicians are usually required to participate in some continuing education, and lawyers are developing more continuing education than previously. But periodic examinations, say, every three or five years, to ensure continuing competence are not usually required. Considerable controversy has arisen when states have instituted tests of minimal competence of already certified teachers. The mistaken assumption persists that competence is an enduring character trait.

Many types of sanctions are socially imposed on professionals. Courts can impose at least eight different types of sanctions for lawyer misconduct.[7] The following is a more general list:

1. Other professionals or nonprofessionals blame a professional for misconduct. In society at large, blame is the chief sanction for unethical conduct.

2. Social or professional ostracism and boycott can occur. Clients might refuse to consult unethical professionals, other professionals might not refer clients to them, and organizations might refuse to hire them.

3. Professional societies or licensing bodies can give private or public reprimands to offending professionals.

4. Professionals can be excluded from membership in a professional society.

5. Professionals can be sued for malpractice. Although most malpractice indicates

momentary carelessness rather than misconduct, some malpractice does involve misconduct.

6.   A professional's license to practice can be suspended or revoked.

Suspension and revocation differ significantly, but both deny permission to practice for a period of time. Where specialization exists, certification in a specialty can be withdrawn without depriving a professional of a right to practice. Revocation of certification will not even deny the right to practice a specialty if general practitioners are also permitted to perform the work, such as general surgery. For example, a local society of periodontal dentists removed the certification of one dentist. Much to its members' chagrin, the dentist simply broadened his practice to do more than periodontal work and had an even more thriving business than before.

SELF-REGULATION

The professions have historically evaluated the ethical conduct of their members and applied the third, fourth, and sixth sanctions in the preceding list. Nonprofessionals are minimally involved. The licensing of professionals other than lawyers often ultimately stems from a nonprofessional public authority; yet review and determination of misconduct are almost always performed by other professionals.

A fundamental issue is whether this self-regulation by professionals is justified. Professional licensing and regulation exist for the benefit of clients and society, not the interests of professionals. To evaluate professional self-regulation, one should consider its advantages and disadvantages. This provides a prima facie case for or against self-regulation. One should also compare self-regulation with alternatives. This step is important because professional self-regulation might be like democracy—a bad form of regulation but better than all the rest. Moreover, self-regulation of professions cannot be intelligently assessed as a whole. One must consider what aspects of what type of regulation of what subjects. Consequently, some distinctions need to be made before considering the merits of self-regulation and alternatives to it.

Distinctions

One should not confuse professional self-regulation with the autonomy of professionals in their work. The former concerns allowing members of the profession to establish and enforce the norms of professional conduct; the latter concerns freedom from external influence in professional work complying with those norms. It is one thing for the bar to set standards of competence and conduct for lawyers and another for lawyers to settle claims against insured clients without influence from insurance companies. The former is the subject of self-regulation.

One can distinguish between formal and informal regulation. Formal regulation generally occurs through written rules, special procedures, and so forth. Much professional conduct is also guided or regulated by informal norms of the professional culture. There are accepted and unaccepted ways of conducting oneself toward clients, various members of one's profession, and others. Perhaps the most ritualized forms are those for lawyers appearing in court.

One must keep regulation of admission to professions distinct from that of the conduct of recognized professionals. Within regulation of professional conduct, one can distinguish three aspects—setting norms, applying norms, and reporting suspected violations of norms. Norm setting is simply the formulation and adoption of norms for professional conduct. Norms are applied whenever professionals use them to guide their conduct. Here, however, the focus is on the use of norms by others to determine whether a professional's conduct conforms to them or not. This activity depends on the third aspect, the reporting of suspected norm violations. Professions cannot watch and check all conduct of all professionals. Like the criminal law, formal regulation depends on the reporting of suspected violations.

Finally, one can roughly distinguish between economic, ethical, and technical professional norms.[8] The basis for this distinction is the norms' actual function. Some norms chiefly concern the economics of a profession, for example, most norms about fees, solicitation, advertising, and so forth, which in Chapter 3 were discussed under the heading "Economic Norms." Many of these norms were adopted on the basis of ethical arguments, but their objective function is usually to control the economics of a profession. A second group of norms chiefly concerns ethics, for example, the norms requiring informed consent to medical procedures, confidentiality of client information, and the truthfulness of communications. A third group of norms concerns professional competence in the performance of tasks. These are the technical norms of a profession. Examples are the requirements that lawyers research land titles back fifty years, that physicians prescribe medications in therapeutic doses, and that engineers use different coefficients in calculating the rate of water runoff of various surfaces. Some norms, of course, involve mixtures of these functions or are on the borders of two of them. For example, the norm that employed engineers not accept gratuities from suppliers' representatives is both economic and ethical.

The net result of all these distinctions is that formal regulation concerns eleven topics. Admission can check both ethical dispositions and technical competence. It does not make sense to regulate for economic factors at admission, although some consideration is included in the ethical test—being of good moral character usually includes not being prone to use disapproved methods of attracting work. For the rest, there are issues of norm setting, applying, and violation reporting for economic, ethical, and technical norms.

Advantages and Disadvantages

Setting and Applying.   The setting and applying of norms is best considered by subject matter because the same arguments apply to both. The general issue with norm setting and applying concerns who should make decisions. Because clients or the public bear most of the consequences of improper professional conduct, they have a claim to set and apply norms. Professionals' claim must rest on their expertise, but that is quite limited for economic and ethical norms because those are not their area of expertise. More specific objections exist to allowing professionals to set and apply economic and ethical norms.

Allowing professionals to set the economic norms for their professions is like hiring the cookie monster to guard Girl Scout cookies; the temptation to take a little bite here and another there is too great. The empirical evidence on this point is quite telling. As discussed in Chapter 3, minimum fee schedules, limitations on advertising, and so forth, which are clearly anticompetitive restrictions, have been found in many professions. A profession is a subgroup of a population whose members have certain common interests. These common interests can be divided into three sets: (1) self-interests in promoting the economic well-being, prestige, and power of the profession; (2) technical interests in the development of professional knowledge and technique; and (3) other directed interests in the primary value served by the profession.[9] Public and professional interests are congruent only if other directed interests always override self-interests and technical interests. In short, an obvious conflict of interest exists, and economic norms are not designed by professionals in the interest of clients or the public.

Moreover, self-regulation often results in one part of a profession discriminating against another. Jerome Carlin's classic study of the New York City Bar concluded that many economic norms worked to the disadvantage of certain classes of lawyers—those in solo practice dealing with problems of the average citizen.[10] In Alabama, the legislature delegated control of optometry to a board composed of members of the optometrists' association.[11] Only independent optometrists could be members of the association. The board sought to sanction employee optometrists as engaged in unprofessional conduct. In this case, one can see the self-regulation only as a power play by one part of the profession to which the Alabama legislature acquiesced. Thus, the inherent conflict of interest in professionals setting and applying economic norms militates against professional self-regulation. The results are unfair to clients and often to other members of the profession.

One might think that professionals would be significantly better at setting and applying ethical norms because no inherent conflict of interest exists. Yet a significant bias is likely. Establishing and applying ethical norms often involve balancing the value of effects on one group of persons against those on another. Professionals are educated, if not indoctrinated, to hold certain other directed values as fundamental, if not absolute. Physicians take health, or in a perverted view, biological life itself, as perhaps the most fundamental value. Lawyers are taught to protect their clients' economic and liberty interests above all else. One analysis of the American Bar Association's *Code of Professional Conduct* found that it places the interests of attorneys first, those of clients second, and those of the public last.[12] The American Bar Association *Model Rules of Professional Conduct* rectify some of these biases. But as discussed in Chapter 5, the tension came out in the debate over rules of confidentiality, to the benefit of clients over the public.

These biases are not limited to professions that serve individual clients. They occur in professions, such as teaching and engineering, that generally serve the broader public. Although most engineering codes of ethics take the responsibility to the public for safety as primary, they significantly emphasize duties to employers.[13] Nor can one reasonably conclude that universities and colleges are primarily structured to serve the interests of students first. For example, faculty desires often take precedence over student interests in determining which upper level courses will be offered. General education requirements reflect the outcome of power struggles between departments for students more than any defensible conception of the needs of a well-educated person.

The problem of bias in setting and applying ethical norms is more subtle than that of economic conflict of interest, but it is nonetheless real. If members of a social subgroup are permitted to set the ethical standards for their conduct that significantly affects others, then they will place the values and interests of themselves and those on whom they depend (clients and employers) above those of others. People naturally develop closer ties and a greater concern for those with whom they associate and on whom they depend. Consequently, the case for professionals setting and applying ethical norms is little better than that for setting economic norms.

Professionals' best claim to norm setting and applying pertains to norms of technical competence. Their expertise strongly supports professionals making these decisions. Persons possessing the special knowledge of a profession are best qualified properly to determine what level of competence is needed to practice it. Moreover, they are the only ones qualified to test for such knowledge. Consequently, even though clients and the public bear the consequences of incompetent professional practice, they really cannot set and apply technical norms. Professionals, then, can justify largely unfettered self-regulation in setting and applying norms of competence and evaluating the competence of applicants for admission to the profession.

Violation Reporting.   One cannot generally rely on professionals for reports of norm violations.[14] Almost every profession has an ethical rule requiring professionals to report norm violations, and in each profession, this is probably the most violated of all norms. A recent newspaper study of medical malpractice in Florida found that medical societies rarely report physicians to the state licensing officials.[15] In six years, of 6,378 reports, only 106 came from medical societies. With about 22,000 practitioners in the state, that is a reporting rate of less than 0.5 percent over six years or less than one per thousand physicians a year. Indeed, because some of the reports might have been of the same physician, the rate is probably less than that. It is incredible that among each one thousand physicians only one norm violation known to other physicians occurs each year.

The likelihood of reports of norm violations varies with the subject matter of norms. The self-interest that creates conflicts of interest for professionals setting and applying economic norms makes them especially diligent at reporting violations of some of them. If a professional's violation of an economic norm (such as solicitation) is likely to disadvantage other professionals, they are likely to report it. In law, it is not unusual for one party to raise a conflict of interest issue to get opposing counsel removed and thus disadvantage the other party.

Professionals reporting violations of economic norms does not usually include violations taking advantage of clients. For this problem, clients are undoubtedly the best watchdogs, provided they have easy access to a simple process for fairly resolving the complaint. For example, in Canada, lawyers' clients who believe they have been charged excessively can complain to a taxing master, who informally hears the complaint and makes appropriate adjustments. A friend of mine had a bill reduced over 25 percent by this process. This procedure is still flawed, however, because a member of the profession applies the norm and therefore is still likely to have subtle biases in favor of lawyers. In contrast, in the United States, complaints about excessive fees are likely to be dismissed as not within the purview of a regulatory organization.[16] Thus, professionals are likely to be efficient reporters of economic norm violations, but clients are also needed to report their violations.

One cannot reasonably rely solely on professionals and clients to report violations of ethical norms, for many ethical violations involve the connivance of professionals with clients or employers. For example, patients are not going to report physicians who improperly prescribe narcotics to support their habits. Nor are students likely to report professors they persuade or bribe into awarding higher grades than deserved. A student in an ethics course told me it would be okay to give her a higher grade than I thought she deserved because no one else in the class would know about it. The confidentiality of professional–client relationships also makes it more difficult to detect unethical conduct. Essentially the same problem arises for professionals employed by firms or dependent on a corporate client for much of their work; it is not to either's advantage to report misconduct outside the organization or corporation. Consequently, reports of ethical norm violations must come from professionals, clients, employers, and the general public.

Finally, although professionals' expertise makes them best qualified to report professional incompetence, they are reluctant to do so. How many college or university faculty has one heard of being reported as incompetent, let alone dismissed for incompetence?[17] One reason for this reluctance is the comradery of persons who work together. Another is the fear of reprisals, such as a defamation suit for false reporting. It is thus important to have statutes protecting persons from good faith reports of improper professional conduct.[18]

Clients can be an important source for complaints of incompetence. Some people claim that clients are not qualified to judge the quality of professional work, but that is an exaggeration. Clients are perfectly capable of determining incompetence when it involves such actions as an accountant omitting an expense item amounting to 3 percent of the budget, a lawyer failing to date a will or including the cost of a lot in the contract price for the construction of a house on the purchaser's lot, a physician prescribing a drug to which he knew the patient was allergic on the ground that he gave only a little bit, and an architect designing a house with the stairs to the second floor going out the front door.[19] The public can also sometimes detect and report incompetence of professionals whose work is primarily directed toward them.

To sum up, self-regulation is best supported for setting and applying technical norms of competence for admission and professional conduct. Professionals are also probably as capable as others of evaluating ethical character for admission to a profession. The disadvantages of conflicts of interest and likely bias count strongly against self-regulation in establishing and applying economic and ethical norms. Both professionals and clients are important sources for reports of all types of norm violations, and the public is a crucial source for reports of ethical norm violations. These results are summarized in Table 8.2.

Alternatives to Self-Regulation

As mentioned previously, even if there are good reasons against self-regulation of various topics, one must consider whether alternatives are any better. Three plausible alternatives exist. One is the use of administrative agencies. A second is

Table 8.2   The Best Persons to Regulate Professionals

	Economic	Ethical	Technical
Admission	DNA	P+O	P
Norm setting	O (~P)	O (~P)	P
Norm applying	O (~P)	O (~P)	P
Violation reporting	P+C	P+C+O	P+C

Abbreviations: P = professionals; ~P = not professionals; C = clients; O = others, i.e., public; DNA = does not apply

malpractice litigation. A third alternative is the use of what might be called civilian boards, that is, regulatory boards much like currently existing ones but composed chiefly of laypersons.

Administrative Agencies.   The use of administrative agencies differs little from what presently exists in many professions. Usually, professional regulatory boards are technically under administrative agencies. They report to agencies that make the final decision, but agencies rarely reject recommendations of professional boards. The idea in this alternative is largely to abolish professional boards and have straightforward administrative agency oversight. To some extent, the Federal Trade Commission provides this for economic norms; it can and has acted against professions for unfair practices. However, it does not set norms; it merely prohibits some. Moreover, because of jurisdictional limits on the FTC, state level agencies would be needed to set and apply norms dealing with intrastate matters.

Problems exist with regulatory administrative agencies. They are sometimes captured by the regulated. When staffing such agencies, the first thought is to obtain experts, and these turn out to be persons working in the regulated field. In short, such agencies are apt to be staffed primarily by members of the professions. To the extent they are career members of the agency, the economic conflict of interest is removed, but the professional bias would probably remain.[20] Moreover, government agencies are not always the most efficient organizations. They have often been hesitant to act, and the process involved is often slow.[21] Consequently, this approach does not offer much improvement over professional self-regulation.

Malpractice Suits.   The second approach is simply greater reliance on malpractice or other lawsuits. To win a malpractice action, one must show that a professional was negligent, that is, violated a standard of care common for members of that profession. Many violations of professional ethics do not constitute negligence. However, the liability rules for malpractice and professional contracts could be expanded to include more ethical and economic considerations, for example, making it easy for clients to sue to recover excessive fees.

Nonetheless, litigation is not an adequate substitute for regulation of professions.

Instead, it occurs and increases when regulation fails. The best method of reducing malpractice suits is not to limit professionals' liability or the amounts injured clients can recover, but effectively to regulate the professions to eliminate the malpractice.[22] This is brought out by a newspaper study of medical malpractice in Florida. It found that four of the nine most sued physicians in Florida have been investigated for such mistakes as operating on the wrong knee, selling illegal drugs, and making mistakes in routine surgery.[23]

Moreover, the nature of malpractice and other tort litigation makes it a poor method for improving practice. Its primary aim is compensation, not prevention. It supposedly prevents improper conduct by the fear of malpractice suits, but it is not very effective. Physicians admittedly practice improperly—perform unnecessary tests—to avoid any possibility of malpractice. Moreover, for all their complaints, most professionals are protected from the major burden of a malpractice award by insurance, the costs of which are passed on to clients.[24] Thus, increased malpractice does not offer an improvement over self-regulation.

Civilian Boards.   Finally, civilian boards would not differ much in structure from the current method of professional regulation. The primary change would be to substitute nonprofessionals for the professionals on the regulatory boards and hearing panels. In some states and professions, laypersons are on the boards, but they are minorities.[25] The minority membership and frequent dominance of national model codes developed without any lay participation weaken the impact of such practices. Were laypersons a majority on the boards setting and applying economic and ethical norms, one might find a significant difference in the content of norms. One could also bifurcate decision making by having a subcommittee of mostly professionals set standards for competence and administer competence tests for admission. Thus, laypersons would predominate in the areas where professionals are apt to have conflicts of interest or professional bias, but professionals would still have primary control of matters of technical competence. Civilian boards thus appropriately divide decision making in accordance with the qualifications of persons for it.

However, the introduction of civilian boards would not necessarily increase the rate at which violations are reported. Some increase in reporting by clients and the public might occur if they saw that prompt and sympathetic attention was given to complaints, followed by swift and significant action when warranted. Providing well-advertised and local or toll-free telephone numbers to report professional misconduct might also increase reporting of violations. Nonetheless, the primary need for increased reporting is for professionals to fulfill the responsibility they all recognize, namely, to report improper professional conduct. For that to occur, both attitudes toward reporting violations and the structure of the workplace will have to change. After all, avoiding professional misconduct is a benefit for the profession and those affected by it.

Consequently, the case against self-regulation is not overwhelming. A moderately strong case can be made for a preponderance of laypersons being involved in the regulatory process. Nonetheless, many practical problems would be involved, such as compensation for serving. Other methods for ensuring compliance focus on changing professionals' motivations to comply rather than on who does the regulating.

MOTIVATIONS

Philosophers have been accused of assuming that the main motivation of professional behavior is compliance with a code of ethics.[26] Clearly, if any philosophers have done so, they are mistaken. If professionals engage in unethical conduct, it is not likely to be because of slavish adherence to a mistaken code that prescribes unethical conduct. Codes do not prescribe much conduct that is arguably unethical.

Professionals engage in unethical conduct for much the same reasons other people do. One primary motive is financial gain. Consciously or unconsciously, this can account for much unethical conduct—engineers accepting bribes and kickbacks, physicians providing unuseful services, and lawyers' settling contingent fee cases contrary to their clients' best interests. Indirectly, it can account for considerable unethical conduct that primarily promotes client interests. The fear of losing lucrative clients can lead professionals to act unethically in their behalf. For employed professionals, fear of losing their jobs accounts for a considerable amount of obedience to employers' unethical directives.

The desires for fame or winning a competition, as well as sheer pride, can also lead professionals into unethical conduct. Research scientists have been known to fudge data and professors to steal student ideas to gain a reputation. Lawyers' desires for winning or beating an opponent can lead to unethical conduct. Pride, of course, is involved in both these situations, but it can also make professionals reluctant to admit mistakes and cover them up.

Another major motive for professional misconduct is a desire to benefit clients or employers. The desire to help others, combined with a usually mistaken belief that one knows better than others what will benefit them, is a primary motive behind professional paternalism. Someone once said that if a person in a white lab coat with a strong desire to help comes toward one, one should turn and run as fast as one can. This cynical overstatement does make the point that benevolence does not always lead to correct action.

A final reason for unethical professional conduct to be mentioned here is a simple failure to be aware of, or reflect on, the ethical import of one's conduct. One can easily see an efficient means of achieving a desired end and choose it without thinking. Because third parties are often not immediately before one, one can fail to consider obligations to them. It is a natural human impulse primarily to consider those people with whom one is acquainted—clients and employers. Moreover, if one has never reflected on the ethical implications of various work situations, one might not think of them.

Some proposals and methods to help ensure ethical conduct by professionals are designed to counteract these and other motives for unethical conduct. One approach is for more effective enforcement of ethical codes to increase deterrence. Deterrence changes motivations by providing a fear of discipline for noncompliance. A second approach is increased ethical education to make professionals more aware of their responsibilities. A third approach is to try to change work situations to decrease incentives for unethical and increase those for ethical conduct.

Effective Deterrence

The effectiveness of deterrence depends on the probability of a sanction, how promptly after the conduct it is imposed, and its size. Historically, ethical norms have not been effectively enforced. For the bar, it was recently reported that 90 percent of complaints are not investigated, that less than 3 percent of proper complaints (those within disciplinary jurisdiction) result in public sanctions, and that disbarment results in only 0.8 percent of the cases.[27] Similarly, a detailed study of the medical profession found that physicians did not attend to unethical practice by others, and when they did, official action rarely occurred.[28] From January 1970 through June 1977, the American Institute of Certified Public Accountants disciplined only 121 members.[29] The situation was no better in engineering, where, of the approximately sixty thousand members of the National Society of Professional Engineers, in 1975, it was reported that only about one hundred fifty cases of unethical conduct were heard each year and that twenty of the fifty-two member societies had never processed a single disciplinary case.[30] Despite some evidence of more effective enforcement recently, it is doubtful that it is yet very effective.[31]

There are four main areas of possible improvement of enforcement. The first is the substantive grounds for professional discipline. In most licensed professions, the grounds for discipline by licensing authorities are not as broad as the professions' ethical codes. In itself, that is probably appropriate because not all unethical conduct should be formally regulated. However, too great a gap often exists. For example, even in law, which has the closest correspondence because of the adoption of the ABA *Code* or *Model Rules,* neglecting client affairs and charging excessive fees are not usually disciplinary matters. In many professions, to enforce ethical norms more comprehensively, they would have to be revised to be more explicit because professionals ought not be disciplined without clear norms indicating what is prohibited.

A second requirement for more effective deterrence is the reporting of violations. Presently, most complaints stem from clients. Professionals need to report more violations. They should probably be disciplined for failure to report them. Such discipline would only be enforcing an obligation already recognized by the ethical codes of most professions.[32] Reliance on client complaints and those of professionals concerning economic matters means that sanctions are rarely imposed for violations of obligations to third parties.

A third requirement for effective deterrence is adequate investigation of allegations of misconduct. Many complaints are not investigated because regulatory agencies and societies simply lack the ability to do so. Investigators are especially needed for matters not based on client complaints because they often involve collusion between a professional and a client. Increased funding for more investigation might well increase the probability of being sanctioned for unethical conduct.

A fourth aspect of effective deterrence concerns procedures and delay. Professional discipline is not a criminal proceeding, but revocation of a license to practice a profession does require due process.[33] Nevertheless, what process is due depends on the situation. Generally, an adversary process is appropriate, but it need not include all the features of a full criminal trial.

Three problems arise in disciplinary procedure. First, sanctions are not applied as swiftly as feasible.[34] The many avenues of appeal often take two years or more to complete, and during that time, professionals are usually not suspended from practice. From the public viewpoint, this practice is not justifiable. If a license to practice is a special privilege for the sake of protecting the public, then an initial determination of misconduct and judgment of revocation are sufficient to justify suspension pending the outcome of an appeal. The public good outweighs the professional's interest in continuing practice once a full hearing and presentation of evidence have resulted in a decision against the professional. After all, injunctions are often issued against businesses suspected of engaging in illegal and deceptive practices even before a final determination is made. Because only the economic interest of professionals is at stake, no reason exists to accord them significantly greater rights than businesses.

A related element of delay arises from the fact that court convictions, even criminal convictions for conduct clearly related to professional activity, do not automatically result in suspension of a license to practice. Hearings on fitness to practice are often suspended until the outcome of a court case, and then all issues are reargued in the hearing.[35] Meanwhile, the public is subject to the ministrations of these professionals. At the very least, conviction for some designated crimes should, as it sometimes does, automatically result in loss of a license to practice. No conceivable justification exists for allowing a physician convicted of manslaughter of patients to continue to practice. A study of the twenty disciplinary actions by the American Institute of Certified Public Accountants during the first nine months of 1976 showed that eighteen of them were of people convicted of crimes or who had had their licenses revoked by state boards.[36] One of the remaining two was of a person granted immunity from prosecution for bribing revenue agents. Thus, the sole case in which the Institute needed a hearing was an accountant who solicited business by a letter and used a fictitious name; he was required to take a course in professional ethics!

A second problem of disciplinary procedure is the multiplicity of jurisdictions. Physicians can have their license suspended in one state and still be licensed in another, or they can be denied privileges at one hospital for incompetent or unethical conduct; yet this information might not even be communicated to another hospital at which they practice. National licensing and disciplining would eliminate this problem. During the nineteenth century, when communications and conditions in the states varied greatly, differing state policies were perhaps reasonable. In the last decade of the twentieth century, no justification exists for different professional norms among the states. Professional ethics is not ethically relative, and cultural conditions among the states do not differ sufficiently to support different norms. The existence of national ethical codes testifies to the national character of professional norms. Short of national licensing and disciplining, court and ethics committee decisions in other states should be taken as determinative of the issues so that a professional cannot reargue the same points in another forum.

A third problem concerns the confidentiality of the disciplinary process. Names of professionals charged with misconduct are not often released until all appeals have been exhausted. Such a policy is intended to protect innocent professionals from damage to their reputation and business. Yet the public has two major interests in an open process. One is that of potential clients in information about the ethical character of professionals. That a lawyer has been charged with neglect or misappropriation of client funds is quite relevant to a potential client's decision to employ that lawyer.

Another interest is in public observation of the disciplinary process to ensure that it is fair and just. Sometimes an open hearing is also beneficial to professionals charged with misconduct; this is true, for example, if they are being harassed by other professionals for improperly advertising or holding unpopular views. A Canadian attorney who was president of the Alberta Human Rights and Civil Liberties Association criticized a proposed Edmonton by-law imposing a curfew for juveniles as infringing the civil liberties of parents and children.[37] He also said that if everyone defied the law and pleaded not guilty, its absurdity would become obvious. The law society charged him with attempting to subvert the law. The attorney went to court and asked that the hearing be open to the public and waived his right of privacy. His request was denied on the ground that the right of privacy also extended to the law society. One need not choose between having the process completely open or closed. A reasonable balance of the competing interests would be to withhold names of professionals until the preliminary investigation is completed and a determination made of sufficient evidence to support proceeding to a hearing.[38]

Education

To counteract the lack of awareness and reflection as a factor in unethical conduct, education in professional ethics can be strengthened. Education in professional ethics can take four forms. First, in the so-called pervasive method, ethical considerations are built into all or most aspects of teaching a field. For example, a course on criminal law might consider ethical problems of criminal defense attorneys and prosecutors, and one on genetic diseases might consider the ethics of confidentiality. The pervasive technique suffers two chief defects. Not all faculty are knowledgeable about professional ethics and capable of adequately teaching it. Moreover, the diffuse character of the study prevents sustained consideration of the issues and can lead students to believe ethics is a peripheral concern. Yet the pervasive method is valuable in reinforcing learning from other courses.

The second form is a required course on professional ethics. Although this method enables a more sustained and critical consideration of professional ethics, one course cannot be expected to alter student character. Such courses emphasize conceptual aspects of ethics, but students need to develop dispositions of honesty, candor, loyalty, and so on. As Aristotle noted, such dispositions are learned only by practice.

A third form is clinical education. It allows students more of an opportunity to develop dispositions by having limited practice subject to ethical evaluation. Medical, nursing, and dental education have always had a large clinical component, but overt ethical considerations have been lacking. In the twentieth century, legal education has not included much clinical practice until the last decades. Still, many law students never engage in a clinical program. The other professions, such as engineering and accounting, usually have even less clinical experience.

A fourth form is continuing education. Several benefits might result from continuing education in ethics. Students will have had some experience, so they are more likely to be aware of the problems that arise. It can also serve as a reminder to be sensitive to ethical issues. Frequently, however, continuing education amounts to little more than telling "war stories." Moreover, a half-day or even full-day seminar does not provide time for a detailed analysis of ethical problems. Nonetheless, it can be useful as a supplement to other forms of education.

Work Setting

Education in professional ethics probably does not significantly affect the frequency of professional misconduct. Sociological studies of both the legal and medical professions indicate that the social setting of professional practice is the chief determinant of compliance with professional norms.[39] Two elements of the social setting are crucial—the degree to which a professional is subject to collegial rather than client pressure and the nature of the collegial pressure. One can distinguish professional practice along a continuum from a solo practitioner economically dependent on client opinion to a professional in a large group practice and economically dependent on colleague approval.[40] The more isolated a professional's practice, the less opportunity other professionals have to observe his or her conduct. When professionals consult clients in the privacy of their office protected by professional–client confidentiality, others cannot observe their conduct and subject it to ethical evaluation. A professional who is economically dependent on attracting clients is very susceptible to client pressures for inappropriate conduct, whether a shady legal deal, the prescription of narcotics for nonexistent medical problems, the falsifying of books, or an inexpensive but unsafe design. At the opposite end of the spectrum, salaried professionals practicing as members of a team have little opportunity for misconduct. Their colleagues will know of their conduct.[41]

At this point, the nature of collegial pressures becomes relevant. Colleagues can provide peer support for violations of, or for compliance with, ethical norms.[42] Loyalty to the team can make a professional less apt to criticize the ethics of his or her colleagues and superiors.[43] Involvement of independent laypersons in professional organizations for purposes of ethical review would help ensure that colleague support is for, rather than against, ethical practice.

Although these studies focused on self-employed professionals with individual clients, the same general considerations apply to employed professionals. The primary determinant of ethical conduct will be the extent to which employees believe it is valued by the organization. Employers rarely make direct policy statements that they favor unethical conduct. Indeed, just the opposite is true.

The question is the extent to which incentives in the workplace favor ethical rather than unethical conduct. If raising ethical concerns is discouraged, and those who do so are looked on as troublemakers, then the incentives are in the wrong direction. Moreover, employees should be rewarded, not penalized, for reporting unethical conduct. For example, a nurse who reports improper conduct by another nurse or physician should have this positively noted in the personnel file and taken into account in salary increases and promotions. Instead, at present, such reports are primarily made to avoid possible blame or for spite against a disliked co-worker. Persons or committees could be designated to receive ethical questions and complaints on a confidential basis. In general, people act the way they think they are expected to act and for which they are rewarded by praise or money.

To emphasize the importance of the work setting for ensuring compliance with professional norms does not imply that the other approaches should be neglected. Unless professionals have been educated in professional ethics, they will not recognize ethical issues when they arise or be intellectually equipped to work out reasonable solutions. And should they act unethically, effective discipline will protect others. Thus, the three approaches can work together and perhaps have a synergistic effect.

SUMMARY

This chapter has concerned methods for ensuring compliance with professional norms. The first section considered the points of control—discipline and admission to professional education and practice. Pronounced discrimination occurred in admission to professional education and practice during the first half of this century. Professionals, no less and no more than others in society, discriminated against people on the basis of ethnic origin, race, and sex. Efforts to rectify past discrimination by affirmative action programs were briefly examined; both those for and against such programs are concerned with equality of opportunity but see them differently in terms of who benefits and who loses under such programs. The Supreme Court has held that special (quota) admissions programs are unconstitutional, but that race may be taken into consideration.

Another issue is whether it is justifiable to require applicants for professional licenses to demonstrate good moral character. The argument for doing so is that professional status is not a right but a privilege granted for the benefit of the public. Consequently, applicants should provide some assurance that they will act ethically. The arguments against such a requirement are that it violates a presumption of innocence, predictions are quite unreliable, and the requirement is too ambiguous. Good moral character means possession of those virtues corresponding to the professional responsibilities previously identified. Character traits and conduct do not constitute grounds for denying admission unless they have a close relationship to unethical professional conduct.

The other form of control is discipline of practicing professionals for unethical conduct. Professional societies and licensing agencies can discipline professionals by private and public reprimands, exclusion from membership in professional societies, and suspension or revocation of licenses.

Traditionally, professionals have been self-regulating. To evaluate self-regulation, one should consider its advantages and disadvantages and then compare it with alternatives. In considering the advantages and disadvantages of self-regulation, it is important to distinguish admission to the profession, setting and applying norms, and reporting violations. It is also useful to distinguish economic, ethical, and technical norms. The conclusion was that, except for technical norms, laypersons are probably better suited for being regulators because they do not have conflicts of interest or professional biases.

The alternatives to self-regulation include the use of administrative agencies, malpractice and other lawsuits, and civilian boards. Administrative agencies would differ from the current system by having full-time employees make the decisions. They might not effectively counteract professional bias and are likely to be inefficient. Lawsuits, particularly malpractice actions, arise only after untoward conduct has occurred, do not presently include all unethical conduct, and are more concerned with compensation than prevention. Civilian boards composed predominantly of laypersons could more appropriately distribute tasks in accordance with qualifications. However, they face many practical problems of implementation.

The final section considered professionals' motives for unethical conduct and possible ways of increasing motivation for ethical conduct. Professionals usually act unethically from the same motives as other persons—for personal financial gain and reputation, for the benefit of clients or employers without considering effects on others, and so on. The enforcement of professional ethics has not provided an effective deterrent. More comprehensive substantive rules, better reporting of violations, increased investigation of complaints, and less delay in the process would make deterrence more effective.

Education in professional ethics might increase awareness of ethical problems and reflection on them. It can occur through discussion in all courses, courses on professional ethics, an ethical component of clinical training, and continuing education.

However, the primary factor for or against ethical conduct is the work setting. Collegial pressure and support for ethical conduct are crucial. Employers should also structure the work setting not merely to give lip service to ethics, but to provide incentives for ethical conduct and disincentives for unethical conduct. When the atmosphere and incentives of the work experience support ethical conduct, the motivations for unethical conduct will be fewer or overridden.

NOTES*

1. Auerbach, *Unequal Justice,* chap. 2.

2. Ibid., p. 109.

3. *Regents of the University of California* v. *Bakke,* 438 U.S. 265 (1978).

4. See generally, Frederick A. Elliston, "The Ethics of Ethics Tests for Lawyers," in *Ethics and the Legal Profession,* ed. Davis and Elliston, pp. 50–61; Rhode, "Moral Character."

5. *Schware* v. *Board of Bar Examiners,* 353 U.S. 232, 238–239 (1957).

6. *In re Florida Board of Bar Examiners,* 358 So. 2d 7, 10 (Fla. 1978) (J. Boyd, dissenting).

7. Patterson and Cheatham, *Profession of Law,* pp. 38–39.

8. One could add norms of etiquette, but today most formal norms of etiquette have disappeared.

9. See R. M. MacIver, "The Social Significance of Professional Ethics," in *Cases and Materials on Professional Responsibility,* ed. Pirsig, p. 50.

10. Carlin, *Lawyers' Ethics.* See also Philip Shuchman, "Ethics and Legal Ethics: The Propriety of the Canons as a Group Moral Code," in *1977 National Conference on Teaching Professional Responsibility,* ed. Goldberg, pp. 249–274; Heinz, "Power of Lawyers," pp. 906–907.

---

*See the bibliography at the back of the book for complete references.

11. *Gibson* v. *Berryhill*, 411 U.S. 564 (1973); see also *Allen* v. *California Bd. of Barber Examiners*, 25 Cal. App. 3d 1014, 102 Cal. Rptr. 368 (Cal. Ct. App. 1972) (licenses revoked for too low prices).

12. Thomas D. Morgan, "The Evolving Concept of Professional Responsibility," in *1977 National Conference on Teaching Professional Responsibility*, ed. Goldberg, pp. 275–316.

13. See, for example, National Society of Professional Engineers, "Code of Ethics," Canons 1 and 4.

14. See also Freidson, *Professional Powers*, p. 187.

15. "Malpractice Crisis Largely Due to Few Doctors, Study Finds," *Gainesville Sun*, 14 April 1986, p. 7A. The situation is similar in the legal profession. Most complaints about lawyers come from clients, and lawyers are reluctant to report other lawyers. See F. Raymond Marks and Darlene Cathcart, "Discipline Within the Legal Profession," in *Ethics and the Legal Profession*, ed. Davis and Elliston, p. 72; Cummins, "Reporting Judicial Misconduct."

16. Marks and Cathcart, "Discipline Within the Legal Profession," p. 77.

17. In my twenty-one years at five universities, I know of only one such case. I have heard of a number of others in which it was unquestionably justifiable but not done. For example, to keep an incompetent teacher out of the classroom, one chemistry department put the person in charge of the storeroom.

18. See, for example, Ill. Ann. Stat. ch. 111, sec. 4452 (Smith-Hurd 1978); and 36 Ca. Jur. 3d sec. 120 (1977).

19. All of these are actual examples from personal experience.

20. Professional bias can be overemphasized; see Freidson, *Professional Powers*, p. 195.

21. Morris, "Revocation of Professional Licenses," p. 814.

22. Ibid., p. 789. One can, however, argue generally against the current tort law system; see Bayles, *Principles of Law*, pp. 272–279.

23. "Malpractice Crisis," (see n. 15 above), p. 7A.

24. See also Morris, "Revocation of Professional Licenses," p. 815.

25. At least one-third of the members of local bar grievance committees in Florida are nonlawyers; Integration Rule of the Florida Bar, Art. XI, Rule 11.03(2)(c). New York requires one or two laypersons on each board; Freidson, *Professional Powers*, p. 69.

26. Schneyer, "Moral Philosophy's Standard Misconception of Legal Ethics," pp. 1542–1543.

27. Rhode, "Moral Character," pp. 547–548.

28. Freidson, *Profession of Medicine*, pp. 139, 158.

29. Abraham Briloff, "Codes of Conduct: Their Sound and Their Fury," in *Ethics, Free Enterprise, and Public Policy*, ed. De George and Pichler, pp. 272–273.

30. Dan H. Pletta, "Ethical Standards for the Engineering Profession: Where Is

the Clout?" in *Engineering Professionalism and Ethics,* ed. Schaub and Pavlovic, p. 484.

31. "Record Number of Physicians Lost Their Licenses in 1985," *Gainesville Sun,* 16 November 1986, p. 10A; "Number of Disbarred Lawyers Doubles, Bar Says," *Tallahassee Democrat,* 27 October 1987, p. 1C.

32. ABA, *Code of Professional Responsibility,* DR 1-103(A); ABA, *Model Rules,* Rule 8.3(a); AMA, "Current Opinions," 9.04; ANA, *Code for Nurses,* sec. 3; Engineers' Council, "Suggested Guidelines," 1, d; NASW, "Code of Ethics," Principle V(M)(2).

33. Morris, "Revocation of Professional Licenses," pp. 792, 797.

34. The speed with which action is taken sometimes results from an over-solicitous concern for the rights of the professional. The purpose of licensing is to protect the public, not the licensees; see Morris, *Revocation of Professional Licenses,* p. 10. There is a strong public interest in speedy discipline for misconduct (ibid., p. 16), but the interest of a professional charged with misconduct is often in delay, delay, and more delay.

35. Some courts have made the process even slower by holding that revocation of a license for conviction of a crime cannot occur until all legal appeals of the conviction have been exhausted; see *State* v. *Birdwell,* 592 P.2d 520 (Okla. 1979).

36. Briloff, "Codes of Conduct" (see n. 29 above), p. 274.

37. Jeff Sallot, "Closed Hearing for Rights Lawyer, Court Rules," *The Globe and Mail* (Toronto), 13 February 1980, p. 52.

38. See also Briloff, "Codes of Conduct" (see n. 29 above), p. 278, and the Report of Association of the Bar of the City of New York cited therein.

39. Carlin, *Lawyers' Ethics,* p. 7; Freidson, *Profession of Medicine,* p. 365.

40. Freidson, *Profession of Medicine,* p. 107.

41. See Spangler, *Lawyers for Hire,* pp. 88–89.

42. Carlin, *Lawyers' Ethics,* p. 116.

43. Hazard, *Ethics in the Practice of Law,* p. xv.

STUDY QUESTIONS AND PROBLEMS

1. Reconsider problem 9 in Chapter 6. Should social worker Yellowbird Zurko report the other social workers to the professional society for unethical conduct in being careless with the confidentiality of files? Why or why not? Should she report them to someone at the agency? If so, to whom? If not, why not?

2. Reconsider problem 10 in Chapter 7. Suppose Stacy Trent is a student at the time. The next year she applies for a professional license. Should she be denied admission for lack of good moral character? Why or why not? Does it make any difference for what profession she is an applicant?

3. During the early 1960s, Amy Best spent one summer working with a civil rights organization in a southern state. One evening while Best was encouraging blacks

at a small church to register to vote, she was arrested for disturbing the peace. On conviction, she paid a $75 fine and did not appeal. When appearing before the admissions committee of the state bar after graduating from law school and passing the bar exam, she was asked if she had ever been convicted of a felony or misdemeanor. She frankly told them her story. Should she be denied admission for lack of good moral character? Why or why not? Suppose she had denied the conviction; should she have then been admitted? Why or why not?

4.   Chester Dunbar, a recent law school graduate, is visited in his office by a law student, Eleanor Fredricks. She has just been accused of selling liquor to a minor. She says she knew the person to whom she sold the liquor was too young, but she needed to make some extra money because she was broke. But, Eleanor says, "I told them I thought the person was of age and that he showed me a false driver's license. That is what I will tell everyone but you. If I get convicted, I may not get admitted to the bar." A friend, who was waiting in Chester's outer office to go to lunch, remarks as they eat that he recognized the woman who came into the office. She was Elaine Field, who had led riots on the campus a few years ago. She had been dating a friend of his at the time. What, if anything, may Chester ethically report to the state bar admissions committee? Why? Does he have an obligation to report anything? Why or why not? May or should he report anything to the law school? Why or why not?

5.   A nurse, George Hardy, was working in the emergency room of a small hospital when a patient came in with a sprained shoulder. He phoned the patient's private physician, who arrived a half-hour later. During the examination, both George and the patient noted alcohol on the physician's breath, and when he left the room, the patient remarked that the physician was a little crocked. What should the nurse say? Why? What, if anything, should he subsequently do? Why? If the physician has a high standing at the hospital, George might get fired if he raises a strong complaint. What then is his ethical duty?

6.   A patient arrived at the emergency room, and resident Ivy Jackson examined him. The patient complained of great weight loss over the past ten weeks, loss of appetite, and a lump in his stomach. His private physician could not be reached. The answering service said he was out of town for the weekend and patients with emergencies should report to the emergency room. Ivy's subsequent discussion with the patient revealed that he had seen and complained to his physician last week about the weight loss and other matters. The physician had checked his blood pressure and listened to his heart and pronounced him fine. (The patient had had a heart attack five years earlier.) The patient died on Tuesday morning from cancer of the lymph glands, a greatly enlarged spleen, and peritonitis (infection of the abdominal lining). Jackson considered telling the patient's family that they probably had a good case for negligent malpractice and reporting the physician to the hospital board. However, a senior physician advised her not to get involved because she might be subject to a libel suit. The physician might have diagnosed the case and decided it was best not to tell the patient. What should Ivy do? Why?

7.   Safeguard, Inc.'s engineers prepared plans and specifications for machinery

to be used in manufacturing. Midland Tubing was hired to produce the equipment. Midland's engineers thought Safeguard's design faulty and that the equipment might be dangerous. They reported this to Midland's officials, who so informed Safeguard. After a review, Safeguard replied that their engineers thought the design was satisfactory and to go ahead with production. Midland's officials told their engineers to proceed. What should Midland's engineers do? Why?

8. Pick a profession and investigate how, in your state, its ethical norms are established and who does it. Find out the process for handling complaints of unethical conduct. What sanctions are available? Are they often applied? What recommendations do you have for changes? Why?

9. Kirk Longman is a certified public accountant. After a three-year legal battle, he pleads no contest to a charge of fraud on his personal income tax return and is fined. Should the American Institute of Ceritified Public Accountants automatically revoke his membership? Should he automatically lose his certification? Should the Institute have begun separate proceedings when it learned of Kirk being charged? Why or why not?

10. Does the willingness of professionals to report misconduct by others in their profession differ significantly from that of nonprofessionals to report unethical and even illegal conduct by others? Should it? Why or why not?

11. During this semester, how many times in your other courses has there been a discussion of ethical problems raised by or related to the material studied? Should there have been more? Why or why not?

12. Suppose that without your permission one of your professors remarks in class about your low grade on an exam or paper and states the actual score, thereby violating both your legal and ethical right to confidentiality. In your college, to whom should you report the professor's unethical conduct? Would you report it? Why or why not? At your school, have there been any cases of professors being sanctioned for unethical conduct? If not, why not? Is it plausibly because none of them ever acts unethically?

   Do you know of any students who have cheated on an exam or paper? If so, did you report them? If not, would you report them? Why or why not?

Acknowledgments of Sources of Study Problems

Ideas for study problems have been freely borrowed from other sources. The sources used are indicated below; the page in the source where the problem can be found is indicated in parentheses. The chapter and problem numbers refer to this book. These problems are used with permission.

Alger, Philip L., Christensen, N. A., and Olmstead, Sterling P. *Ethical Problems in Engineering*. Edited by Burrington S. Havens and John A. Miller. New York: Wiley, 1965. Chapter 2, problem 2 (p. 274).

American Psychological Association. *Casebook on Ethical Standards of Psychologists*. Washington, D.C.: American Psychological Association, 1967. Chapter 5, problem 3 (p. 29); and Chapter 7, problem 3 (p. 1).

Baum, Robert J., and Flores, Albert, eds. *Ethical Problems in Engineering*. Troy, N.Y.: Center for the Study of the Human Dimensions of Science and Technology, Rensselaer Polytechnic Institute, 1978. Chapter 4, problem 11 (p. 205); Chapter 7, problems 6, 7 (pp. 210, 178); and Chapter 8, problem 7 (p. 186).

Bok, Sissela. *Lying: Moral Choice in Public and Private Life*. New York: Pantheon, 1978. Chapter 6, problem 11 (p. 221).

Carey, John L. *Professional Ethics of Public Accounting*. New York: American Institute of Accountants, 1946. Chapter 5, problem 7 (p. 64).

Carey, John L., and Doherty, William O. *Ethical Standards of the Accounting Profession*. New York: American Institute of Certified Public Accountants, 1966. Chapter 3, problem 3 (p. 292); Chapter 4, problems 12, 15 (pp. 235, 236).

Christiansen, Harley D. *Ethics in Counseling: Problem Situations*. Tucson: University of Arizona Press, copyright 1972. Chapter 3, problem 7 (p. 205); and Chapter 4, problem 16 (p. 12).

Garrett, Thomas M., Baumhart, Raymond C., Purcell, Theodore V., and Roets, Perry. *Cases in Business Ethics*. Englewood Cliffs, N.J.: Prentice-Hall, 1968. Chapter 5, problem 5 (pp. 203–205).

Heine, William C. *Journalism Ethics: A Case Book*. London, Ont.: University of Western Ontario School of Journalism, 1975. Chapter 5, problem 8 (p. 1).

Mantell, Murray I. *Ethics and Professionalism in Engineering*. New York: Macmillan, 1964. Chapter 4, problem 6 (p. 118); and Chapter 5, problem 4 (p. 113).

Mathews, Robert E. *Problems Illustrative of the Responsibilities of Members of the Legal Profession*, 2d ed. New York: Council on Legal Education for Professional Responsibility, 1968. Chapter 4, problem 10 (p. 116); Chapter 5, problem 6 (p. 124); and Chapter 8, problem 3 (p. 257).

Morgan, Thomas D., and Rotunda, Ronald D. *Problems and Materials on Professional Responsibility*. Mineola, N.Y.: Foundation Press, 1976. Chapter 3, problem 1 (p. 69); Chapter 4, problem 14 (p. 48); Chapter 5, problem 2 (p. 17); Chapter 7, problems 5, 9 (pp. 270, 15); and Chapter 8, problem 4 (p. 141).

Redlich, Norman. *Professional Responsibility: A Problem Approach*. Boston: Little, Brown, 1976. Chapter 4, problem 2 (p. 35); and Chapter 7, problem 8 (p. 65).

Schaub, James H. Chapter 5, problem 13.

Veatch, Robert M. *Case Studies in Medical Ethics*. Cambridge, Mass.: Harvard University Press, 1977. Chapter 4, problem 7 (p. 151); Chapter 5, problem 1 (p. 129); Chapter 7, problem 2 (p. 299); and Chapter 8, problems 5, 6 (pp. 115, 113).

Wilson, Suanna J. "Confidentiality." In *Ethical Issues in Social Work*. Edited by Shankar A. Yelaja. Springfield, Ill.: Charles C. Thomas, 1982. Chapter 6, problem 9 (p. 351).

Select Bibliography

Alger, Philip L., Christensen, N. A., and Olmstead, Sterling P. *Ethical Problems in Engineering*. Edited by Burrington S. Havens and John A. Miller. New York: Wiley, 1965.

American Bar Association. *Code of Professional Responsibility and Code of Judicial Conduct*. Chicago: American Bar Association, 1983.

—————. *Model Rules of Professional Conduct*. Chicago: American Bar Association, 1983.

—————. National Institute Proceedings. "Advisors to Management: Responsibilities and Liabilities of Lawyers and Accountants." *The Business Lawyer* (30 March 1975), special issue: 1–227.

—————. Special Committee on Evaluation of Disciplinary Enforcement. *Problems and Recommendations in Disciplinary Enforcement*. Preliminary draft. January 15, 1970. Chicago: American Bar Association, 1970.

American Institute of Certified Public Accountants. "Rules of Conduct of the Code of Professional Ethics." In *Codes of Professional Responsibility*, pp. 237–240. *See* Gorlin.

American Medical Association. "Current Opinions of the Judicial Council." In *Codes of Professional Responsibility*, pp. 101–125. *See* Gorlin.

—————. *Principles of Medical Ethics*. In *Codes of Professional Responsibility*, p. 101. *See* Gorlin.

American Medical Ass'n v. *FTC*, 638 F.2d 443 (1980).

American Nurses' Association. *Code for Nurses with Interpretive Statements*. Kansas City: American Nurses' Association, 1976.

American Psychiatric Association. "Principles of Medical Ethics with Annotations Especially Applicable to Psychiatry." In *Codes of Professional Responsibility*, pp. 129–135. *See* Gorlin.

American Society of Civil Engineers. *ASCE Guide to Employment Conditions for Civil Engineers*, 2d ed. New York: American Society of Civil Engineers, 1980.

Auerbach, Jerold S. *Unequal Justice: Lawyers and Social Change in Modern America*. New York: Oxford University Press, 1976.

Bates v. *State Bar of Arizona*, 433 U.S. 350 (1977).

Baum, Robert J. "Access to Engineering Services: Rights and Responsibilities of Professionals and the Public." *Business & Professional Ethics Journal* 4, nos. 3 & 4 (1985): 117–135.

———, and Flores, Albert, eds. *Ethical Problems in Engineering,* 2d ed. 2 vols. Troy, N.Y.: Center for the Study of the Human Dimensions of Science and Technology, Rensselaer Polytechnic Institute, 1980.

Baumrin, Bernard, and Freedman, Benjamin, eds. *Moral Responsibility and the Professions.* New York: Haven Publications, 1983.

Bayles, Michael D. *Principles of Law: A Normative Analysis.* Dordrecht, Netherlands: D. Reidel, 1987.

———. *Principles of Legislation: The Uses of Political Authority.* Detroit: Wayne State University Press, 1978.

Beach, John. "Codes of Ethics: Court Enforcement Through Public Policy." *Business & Professional Ethics Journal* 4, no. 1 (1984): 53–64.

Beauchamp, Tom L., and McCullough, Laurence B. *Medical Ethics.* Englewood Cliffs, N.J.: Prentice-Hall, 1984.

Bell, Nora K., ed. *Who Decides? Conflicts of Rights in Health Care.* Clifton, N.J.: Humana Press, 1982.

Benjamin, Martin. "Lay Obligations in Professional Relations." *Journal of Medicine and Philosophy* 10 (1985): 85–103.

———, and Curtis, Joy. *Ethics in Nursing.* New York: Oxford University Press, 1981.

Bloom, Murray Teigh, ed. *Lawyers, Clients, & Ethics.* New York: Council on Legal Education for Professional Responsibility, 1974.

Bok, Sissela. *Lying: Moral Choice in Public and Private Life.* New York: Pantheon Books, 1978.

———. *Secrets.* New York: Pantheon Books, 1983.

Bosk, Charles L. *Forgive and Remember: Managing Medical Failure.* Chicago: University of Chicago Press, 1979.

Bouhoutsos, Jacqueline, et al. "Sexual Intimacy Between Psychotherapists and Patients." *Professional Psychology: Research and Practice* 14 (1983): 185–196.

Bowman, James S., Elliston, Frederick A., and Lockhart, Paula. *Professional Dissent: An Annotated Bibliography and Resource Guide.* New York: Garland, 1984.

Brandt, Richard B. *A Theory of the Good and the Right.* Oxford: Clarendon Press, 1979.

Branson, Roy. "The Secularization of American Medicine." *Hastings Center Studies* 1, no. 2 (1973): 17–28.

Brazil, Percy. "Cost Effective Care Is Better Care." *Hastings Center Report* 16 (February 1986): 7–8.

Brecher, R. "Striking Responsibilities." *Journal of Medical Ethics* 11 (1985): 66–69.

Briloff, Abraham J. *More Debts Than Credits: The Burnt Investor's Guide to Financial Statements.* New York: Harper & Row, 1976.

Buchanan, Allen. "Medical Paternalism." *Philosophy & Public Affairs* 7 (1978): 370–390.

Cahn, Steven M. *Saints and Scamps: Ethics in Academia.* Totowa, N.J.: Rowman & Littlefield, 1986.

Callahan, Daniel. "Recombinant DNA: Science and the Public." *Hastings Center Report* 7 (April 1977): 20–22.

Callahan, Joan C., ed. *Ethical Issues in Professional Life.* New York: Oxford University Press, 1988.

Camenisch, Paul F. *Grounding Professional Ethics in a Pluralistic Society.* New York: Haven Publications, 1983.

Capron, Alexander M. "Containing Health Care Costs: Ethical and Legal Implications of

Changes in the Methods of Paying Physicians." *Case Western Reserve Law Review* 36 (1986): 708–759.

Carlin, Jerome E. *Lawyers' Ethics: A Survey of the New York City Bar*. New York: Russell Sage Foundation, 1966.

Carroll, Mary Ann, Schneider, Henry G., and Wesley, George R. *Ethics in the Practice of Psychology*. Englewood Cliffs, N.J.: Prentice-Hall, 1985.

Case Conference. "Mum's the Word: Confidentiality and Incest." *Journal of Medical Ethics* 11 (1985): 100–104.

Chayes, Abram, and Chayes, Antonia H. "Corporate Counsel and the Elite Law Firm." *Stanford Law Review* 37 (1985): 277–299.

Cheek, James H. "Professional Responsibility and Self-Regulation of the Securities Lawyer." *Washington and Lee Law Review* 32 (1975): 597–636.

Childress, James F., and Siegler, Mark. "Metaphors and Models of Doctor–Patient Relationships: Their Implications for Autonomy." *Theoretical Medicine* 5 (1984): 17–30.

Christie, Ronald J., and Hoffmaster, C. Barry. *Ethical Issues in Family Medicine*. New York: Oxford University Press, 1986.

Cohen, Elliot D. "Pure Legal Advocates and Moral Agents: Two Concepts of a Lawyer in an Adversary System." *Criminal Justice Ethics* 4 (Winter/Spring 1985): 38–59.

Collins, Randall. *The Credential Society: An Historical Sociology of Education and Stratification*. New York: Academic Press, 1979.

Cooper, David E. "Trust." *Journal of Medical Ethics* 11 (1985): 92–93.

Cummins, Robert P. "Reporting Judicial Misconduct." *Loyola University of Chicago Law Journal* 16 (1985): 443–445.

Curran, Barbara H. *The Lawyer Statistical Report*. Chicago: American Bar Foundation, 1985.

D'Amato, Anthony, and Eberle, Edward J. "Three Models of Legal Ethics." *St. Louis University Law Journal* 27 (1983): 761–799.

Davis, John W., Hoffmaster, Barry, and Shorten, Sarah, eds. *Contemporary Issues in Biomedical Ethics*. Clifton, N.J.: Humana Press, 1978.

Davis, Michael. "The Moral Authority of a Professional Code." In *Authority Revisited: Nomos XXIX*. Edited by J. Roland Pennock and John W. Chapman. New York: New York University Press, 1987, pp. 302–337.

———, and Elliston, Frederick, eds. *Ethics and the Legal Profession*. Buffalo: Prometheus Books, 1986.

De George, Richard T. "Ethical Responsibilities of Engineers in Large Organizations: The Pinto Case." *Business & Professional Ethics Journal* 1, no. 1 (1981): 1–14.

———, and Pichler, Joseph A., eds. *Ethics, Free Enterprise, and Public Policy: Original Essays on Moral Issues in Business*. New York: Oxford University Press, 1978.

Dolenc, Danielle A., and Dougherty, Charles J. "DRG's: The Counterrevolution in Financing Health Care." *Hastings Center Report* 15 (June 1985): 19–29.

Drinker, Henry S. *Legal Ethics*. New York: Columbia University Press, 1953.

Dyer, Allen R. "Patients, Not Costs, Come First." *Hastings Center Report* 16 (February 1986): 5–7.

Engelhardt, H. Tristram, Jr. *The Foundations of Bioethics*. New York: Oxford University Press, 1986.

———. "Rights and Responsibilities of Patients and Physicians." In *Medical Treatment of the Dying: Moral Issues*. Edited by Michael D. Bayles and Dallas M. High. Cambridge, Mass.: G. K. Hall and Schenkman, 1978.

Engineers' Council for Professional Development. "Code of Ethics of Engineers." In *Engineering Professionalism and Ethics*, pp. 426–427. *See* Schaub and Pavlovic.

———. "Suggested Guidelines for Use with the Fundamental Canons of Ethics." In *Engineering Professionalism and Ethics*, pp. 427–433. *See* Schaub and Pavlovic.

Feinberg, Joel. *Harm to Self*. Vol. 3 of *The Moral Limits of the Criminal Law*. New York: Oxford University Press, 1986.

Flores, Albert, ed. *Professional Ideals*. Belmont, Cal.: Wadsworth, 1988.

Florida Bar v. *Brumbaugh*, 355 So. 2d 1186 (Fla. 1978).

Franck, Michael. "Referral Fees: Everybody Does It, But Is It OK? No Referral Fee for No Work." *American Bar Association Journal* 71 (February 1985): 40, 42, 44.

Freedman, Benjamin. "A Meta-Ethics for Professional Morality." *Ethics* 89 (1978): 1–19.

Freedman, Monroe H. "Lawyer–Client Confidences Under the A.B.A. Model Rules: Ethical Rules Without Ethical Reason." *Criminal Justice Ethics* 3 (Summer/Fall 1984): 3–8.

———. *Lawyers' Ethics in an Adversary System*. Indianapolis: Bobbs-Merrill, 1975.

———. "Legal Ethics and the Suffering Client." *Catholic University Law Review* 36 (1987): 331–336.

———. "The Problem of Writing, Enforcing, and Teaching Ethical Rules: A Reply to Professor Goldman." *Criminal Justice Ethics* 3 (Summer/Fall 1984): 14–16.

Freidson, Eliot. *Profession of Medicine: A Study of the Sociology of Applied Knowledge*. New York: Harper & Row, 1970.

———. *Professional Powers: A Study of the Institutionalization of Formal Knowledge*. Chicago: University of Chicago Press, 1986.

———, ed. *The Professions and Their Prospects*. Beverly Hills, Cal.: Sage Publications, 1973.

Fried, Charles. *Right and Wrong*. Cambridge, Mass.: Harvard University Press, 1978.

Ganos, Doreen, et al., eds. *Difficult Decisions in Medical Ethics*. New York: Alan R. Liss, 1983.

Gewirth, Alan. "Professional Ethics: The Separatist Thesis." *Ethics* 96 (1986): 282–300.

Glazer, Myron. "Ten Whistleblowers and How They Fared." *Hastings Center Report* 13 (December 1983): 33–41.

Goldberg, Stuart C., ed. *1977 National Conference on Teaching Professional Responsibility: Pre-Conference Materials*. Detroit: University of Detroit School of Law, 1977.

Goldfarb v. *Virginia State Bar*, 421 U.S. 733 (1975).

Goldman, Alan H. "Confidentiality, Rules, and Codes of Ethics." *Criminal Justice Ethics* 3 (Summer/Fall 1984): 8–14.

———. *The Moral Foundations of Professional Ethics*. Totowa, N.J.: Rowman and Littlefield, 1980.

Goldworth, Amnon. "The Moral Limit to Private Profit in Entrepreneurial Science." *Hastings Center Report* 17 (June 1987): 8–10.

Gorlin, Rena A., ed. *Codes of Professional Responsibility*. Washington, D.C.: Bureau of National Affairs, 1986.

Gorovitz, Samuel, et al., eds. *Moral Problems in Medicine*. Englewood Cliffs, N.J.: Prentice-Hall, 1976.

Gross, Leonard E. "Ethical Problems of Law Firm Associates." *William and Mary Law Review* 26 (1985): 259–315.

Grosskopf, I., Buckman, G., and Garty, M. "Ethical Dilemmas of the Doctors' Strike in Israel." *Journal of Medical Ethics* 11 (1985): 70–71.

Halstrom, Frederick N. "Referral Fees Are a Necessary Evil." *American Bar Association Journal* 71 (February 1985): 40, 42, 44.

Hazard, Geoffrey C., Jr. *Ethics in the Practice of Law*. New Haven, Conn.: Yale University Press, 1978.

————, and Rhode, Deborah L., eds. *The Legal Profession: Responsibility and Regulation*. Mineola, N.Y.: Foundation Press, 1985.

Hegland, Kenney. "Beyond Enthusiasm and Commitment." *Arizona Law Review* 13 (1971): 805–817.

Heinz, John P. "The Power of Lawyers." *Georgia Law Review* 17 (1983): 891–911.

Hill, Judith M. "The University and Industrial Research: Selling Out?" *Business & Professional Ethics Journal* 2, no. 4 (1983): 27–35.

In re Primus, 436 U.S. 412 (1978).

In re R.M.J., 455 U.S. 191 (1982).

Jameton, Andrew. *Nursing Practice: The Ethical Issues*. Englewood Cliffs, N.J.: Prentice-Hall, 1984.

Johnson, Deborah G. *Computer Ethics*. Englewood Cliffs, N.J.: Prentice-Hall, 1985.

Kardestuncer, Hayrettin, ed. *Social Consequences of Engineering*. San Francisco: Boyd & Fraser, 1979.

Katz, Jay. *The Silent World of Doctor and Patient*. New York: Free Press, 1984.

Kaufman, Andrew I., ed. *Problems in Professional Responsibility*, 2d ed. Boston: Little, Brown, 1984.

Kelley, Patricia, and Alexander, Paul. "Part-Time Private Practice: Practical and Ethical Considerations." *Social Work* 30 (1985): 254–258.

Kerr, Stephen T. "Referral in Education and Medicine: Differing Patterns of Development in Specialized Professions." *Work and Occupations: An International Sociological Journal* 12 (1985): 416–436.

Kipnis, Kenneth. *Legal Ethics*. Englewood Cliffs, N.J.: Prentice-Hall, 1986.

Klaidman, Stephen, and Beauchamp, Tom L. *The Virtuous Journalist*. New York: Oxford University Press, 1987.

Kleinig, John. *Paternalism*. Totowa, N.J.: Rowman and Allanheld, 1984.

Larson, Magali Sarfletti. *The Rise of Professionalism*. Berkeley: University of California Press, 1977.

Layton, Edwin T., Jr. *The Revolt of the Engineers: Social Responsibility and the American Engineering Profession*. Cleveland: Press of Case Western Reserve University, 1971.

Lebacqz, Karen. *Professional Ethics: Power and Paradox*. Nashville: Abingdon Press, 1985.

Levy, Charles. *Social Work Ethics*. New York: Human Science Press, 1976.

Lieberman, Jethro K. *Crisis at the Bar: Lawyers' Unethical Ethics and What To Do About It*. New York: W. W. Norton, 1978.

Llewellyn, Karl N. "The Bar Specializes—With What Results?" *Annals of the American Academy of Political and Social Science* 167 (May 1933): 177–192.

————. "The Bar's Troubles and Poultices—and Cures?" In *Jurisprudence: Realism in Theory and Practice*. Chicago: University of Chicago Press, 1962, pp. 243–281.

Lomasky, Loren. "Public Money, Private Gain, Profit for All." *Hastings Center Report* 17 (June 1987): 5–7.

Luban, David. "Paternalism and the Legal Profession." *Wisconsin Law Review* (1981): 454–493.

————. "Political Legitimacy and the Right to Legal Services." *Business & Professional Ethics Journal* 4, nos. 3 & 4 (1985): 43–68.

————. "Professional Ethics: A New Code for Lawyers?" *Hastings Center Report* 10 (June 1980): 11–15.

————, ed. *The Good Lawyer: Lawyers' Roles and Lawyers' Ethics*. Totowa, N.J.: Rowman and Allanheld, 1983.

Lynn, Kenneth S., ed. *The Professions in America*. Boston: Beacon Press, 1965.

Macklin, Ruth. "Equal Access to Professional Services: Medicine." *Business & Professional Ethics Journal* 4, nos. 3 & 4 (1985): 1–12.

Martin, Mike W., and Schinzinger, Roland. *Ethics in Engineering*. New York: McGraw-Hill, 1983.

Masters, Roger D. "Is Contract an Adequate Basis for Medical Ethics?" *Hastings Center Report* 5 (December 1975): 24–28.

May, William F. "Code, Covenant, Contract, or Philanthropy?" *Hastings Center Report* 5 (December 1975): 29–38.

McCullough, Laurence B., and Wear, Stephen. "Respect for Autonomy and Medical Paternalism Reconsidered." *Theoretical Medicine* 6 (1985): 295–308.

Meslin, Eric M. "The Moral Costs of the Ontario Physicians' Strike." *Hastings Center Report* 17 (August 1987): 11–14.

Miller, Judith. "Biotechnology and University Ethics." *Westminster Institute Review* 1, no. 3 (1981): 6–8.

Moore, Nancy J. "Limits to Attorney–Client Confidentiality: A 'Philosophically Informed' and Comparative Approach to Legal and Medical Ethics." *Case Western Reserve Law Review* 36 (1986): 177–247.

Moore, Wilbert E. *The Professions: Roles and Rules*. New York: Russell Sage Foundation, 1970.

Morreim, E. Haavi. "The MD and the DRG." *Hastings Center Report* 15 (June 1985): 30–38.

Morris, William O. "Revocation of Professional Licenses." *Mercer Law Review* 37 (1986): 789–815.

————. *Revocation of Professional Licenses by Governmental Agencies*. Charlottesville, Va.: Michie, 1984.

Moss, Frederick C. "The Ethics of Law Practice Marketing." *Notre Dame Law Review* 61 (1986): 601–695.

Muñoz, Ricardo F. "Commentary [on Pope and Winslade]." *Business & Professional Ethics Journal* 4, nos. 3 & 4 (1985): 177–182.

Nader, Ralph, and Green, Mark, eds. *Verdicts on Lawyers*. New York: Thomas Y. Crowell, 1976.

National Association of Social Workers. "Code of Ethics." In *Codes of Professional Responsibility*, pp. 161–167. *See* Gorlin.

National Federation of Societies for Clinical Social Work. "Code of Ethics." In *Codes of Professional Responsibility*, pp. 171–178. *See* Gorlin.

National Society of Professional Engineers. "Code of Ethics for Engineers." In *Codes of Professional Responsibility*, pp. 257–262. *See* Gorlin.

National Society of Professional Engineers v. *United States*, 435 U.S. 679 (1978).

Newman, Joel S. "Representing the Repugnant Client." *Case & Comment* 86 (November/December 1981): 22–27.

Newton, Lisa. "A Framework for Responsible Medicine." *Journal of Medicine and Philosophy* 4 (1979): 57–69.

Nix v. *Whiteside*, 106 S.Ct. 988 (1986).

Note. "Legal Services—Past and Present." *Cornell Law Quarterly* 59 (1974): 960–988.

Note. "Professional Ethics of Criminal Defense Lawyers: Is There a Single Solution to the Issues Raised by a Perjuring Client?" *Memphis State University Law Review* 16 (1986): 531–552.

Note. "Soliciting Sophisticates: A Modest Proposal for Attorney Solicitation." *University of Michigan Journal of Law Reform* 16 (1983): 585–602.

Novak, Dennis H., et al. "Changes in Physicians' Attitudes Toward Telling the Cancer Patient." *Journal of the American Medical Association* 241 (1979): 897–900.

Ohralik v. *Ohio State Bar Association*, 436 U.S. 447 (1978).

Oken, Donald. "What to Tell Cancer Patients: A Study of Medical Attitudes." *Journal of the American Medical Association* 175 (1961): 1120–1128.

Orkin, Mark M. *Legal Ethics: A Study of Professional Conduct.* Toronto: Cartwright & Sons, 1957.

Ozar, David T. "Three Models of Professionalism and Professional Obligation in Dentistry." *Journal of the American Dental Association* 110 (1985): 173–177.

Parsons, Talcott. "Professions." In *International Encyclopedia of the Social Sciences,* 2d ed. Edited by Daniel L. Sills. New York: Macmillan and Free Press, 1968.

Patterson, L. Ray. "An Analysis of Conflicts of Interest Problems." *Mercer Law Review* 37 (1986): 569–597.

————, and Cheatham, Elliott E. *The Profession of Law.* Mineola, N.Y.: Foundation Press, 1971.

Pellegrino, Edmund D., and Thomasma, David C. *A Philosophical Basis of Medical Practice.* New York: Oxford University Press, 1981.

Pierce, Christine, and VanDeVeer, Donald, eds. *AIDS: Ethics and Public Policy.* Belmont, Cal.: Wadsworth, 1988.

Pirsig, Maynard E., ed. *Cases and Materials on Professional Responsibility,* 2d ed. St. Paul, Minn.: West, 1965.

Pope, Kenneth S., and Winslade, William. "Unequal Access to Mental Health Services: The Challenge to Professional Integrity." *Business & Professional Ethics Journal* 4, nos. 3 & 4 (1985): 151–162.

Pound, Roscoe. "What Is a Profession? The Rise of the Legal Profession in Antiquity." *Notre Dame Lawyer* 19 (1944): 203–228.

President's Commission for the Study of Ethical Problems in Medicine and Biomedical and Behavioral Research. *Making Health Care Decisions,* vol. 1, *Report.* Washington, D.C.: U.S. Government Printing Office, 1982.

————. *Securing Access to Health Care,* vol. 1, *Report.* Washington, D.C.: U.S. Government Printing Office, 1983.

Reamer, Frederic G. *Ethical Dilemmas in Social Service.* New York: Columbia University Press, 1982.

————. "Ethical Dilemmas in Social Work Practice." *Social Work* 28, no. 1 (1983): 31–35.

Regan, Tom, ed. *Just Business: New Introductory Essays in Business Ethics.* New York: Random House, 1984.

Regents of the University of California v. *Bakke*, 438 U.S. 265 (1978).

The Report of the Professional Organizations Committee. Toronto: Ministry of the Attorney General, 1980.

Rhode, Deborah L. "Ethical Perspective on Legal Practice." *Stanford Law Review* 37 (1985): 589–652.

——. "Moral Character as a Professional Credential." *Yale Law Journal* 94 (1985): 491–603.

Ringleb, Al H., Bush, Alan J., and Moncrief, William C. "Lawyer Direct Mail Advertisements: Regulatory Environment, Economics, and Consumer Perceptions." *Pacific Law Journal* 17 (1986): 1199–1246.

Robinson, George M., and Moulton, Janice. *Ethical Problems in Higher Education.* Englewood Cliffs, N.J.: Prentice-Hall, 1985.

Robison, Wade L., Pritchard, Michael S., and Ellin, Joseph, eds. *Profits and Professions: Essays in Business and Professional Ethics.* Clifton, N.J.: Humana Press, 1983.

Roscoe Pound–American Trial Lawyers Foundation. Commission on Professional Responsibility. *The American Lawyer's Code of Conduct.* Revised draft, May 1982. In *1987 Selected Standards on Professional Responsibility.* Edited by Thomas D. Morgan and Ronald D. Rotunda. Mineola, N.Y.: Foundation Press, 1987, pp. 205–238.

Rosenthal, Douglas E. *Lawyer and Client: Who's in Charge?* New York: Russell Sage Foundation, 1974.

Schaub, James H., and Pavlovic, Karl, eds. *Engineering Professionalism and Ethics.* New York: Wiley, 1983.

Schneyer, Ted. "Moral Philosophy's Standard Misconception of Legal Ethics." *Wisconsin Law Review* (1984): 1529–1572.

Schware v. *Board of Bar Examiners,* 353 U.S. 232 (1957).

Semad, Stanley A. "Unionization of Law Offices: Some Ethical Concerns." *Ohio State Bar Association Report* 55 (1982): 1314–1318.

Shaffer, Thomas L. "Legal Ethics and the Good Client." *Catholic University Law Review* 36 (1987): 319–330.

——. "The Legal Ethics of Radical Individualism." *Texas Law Review* 65 (1987): 963–992.

Sharswood, George. *An Essay on Professional Ethics,* 6th ed. Philadelphia: George T. Bird, 1844; reprint 1930.

Shelp, Earl E., ed. *The Clinical Encounter: The Moral Fabric of the Patient–Physician Relationship.* Boston: D. Reidel, 1983.

Simon, William H. "The Ideology of Advocacy: Procedural Justice and Professional Ethics." *Wisconsin Law Review* (1978): 29–144.

Smith, Harmon L., and Churchill, Larry R., eds. *Professional Ethics and Primary Care Medicine: Beyond Dilemmas and Decorum.* Durham, N.C.: Duke University Press, 1986.

Snoeyenbos, Milton, Almeder, Robert, and Humber, James. *Business Ethics.* Buffalo: Prometheus Books, 1983.

Spangler, Eve. *Lawyers for Hire: Salaried Professionals at Work.* New Haven, Conn.: Yale University Press, 1986.

Special supplement. "The Public Duties of the Professions." *Hastings Center Report* 17 (February 1987).

Spicker, Stuart F., and Gadow, Sally, eds. *Nursing: Images and Ideals—Opening Dialogue with the Humanities.* New York: Springer, 1980.

Spiegel, Mark. "Lawyers and Professional Autonomy: Reflections on Corporate Lawyering and the Doctrine of Informed Consent." *Western New England Law Review* 9 (1987): 139–152.

Stone, Alan A. "Sexual Misconduct by Psychiatrists: The Ethical and Clinical Dilemma of Confidentiality." *American Journal of Psychiatry* 140 (1983): 195–197.

Strauss, Marcy. "Toward a Revised Model of Attorney–Client Relationship: The Argument for Autonomy." *North Carolina Law Review* 65 (1987): 315–350.

Subin, Harry I. "The Lawyer as Superego: Disclosure of Client Confidences to Prevent Harm." *Iowa Law Review* 70 (1985): 1091–1292.

Swain, Bruce M. *Reporter's Ethics*. Ames: Iowa State University Press, 1978.

Symposium. "Legal Ethics." *Loyola University of Chicago Law Journal* 16 (1985): 429–589.

Tarasoff v. *Regents of the University of California*, 17 Cal. 3rd 425, 551 P.2d 334, 131 Cal. Rptr. 14 (1976).

United States. National Commission for the Protection of Human Subjects of Biomedical and Behavioral Research. *The Belmont Report: Ethical Principles and Guidelines for the Protection of Human Subjects of Research*. Washington, D.C.: U.S. Government Printing Office, 1978. See its other reports and appendixes.

VanDeVeer, Donald. *Paternalistic Intervention: The Moral Bounds on Benevolence*. Princeton, N.J.: Princeton University Press, 1986.

———, and Regan, Tom, eds. *Health Care Ethics: An Introduction*. Philadelphia: Temple University Press, 1987.

Veatch, Robert M. *Case Studies in Medical Ethics*. Cambridge, Mass.: Harvard University Press, 1977.

———. "Medical Ethics: Professional or Universal?" *Harvard Theological Review* 65 (1972): 531–559.

———. "Models for Ethical Medicine in a Revolutionary Age." *Hastings Center Report* 2 (June 1972): 5–7.

———. "Professional Ethics: New Principles for Physicians." *Hastings Center Report* 10 (June 1980): 16–19.

———. "Professional Medical Ethics: The Grounding of Its Principles." *Journal of Medicine and Philosophy* 4 (1979): 1–19.

———. *A Theory of Medical Ethics*. New York: Basic Books, 1981.

Virginia State Board of Pharmacy v. *Virginia Citizens Consumer Council*, 425 U.S. 748 (1976).

Windal, F., and Corley, R. *The Accounting Professional: Ethics, Responsibility and Liability*. Englewood Cliffs, N.J.: Prentice-Hall, 1980.

Yelaja, Shankar A., ed. *Ethical Issues in Social Work*. Springfield, Ill: Charles C. Thomas, 1982.

Young, David. "Licensing and Minorities: A Question of Fairness." *Business & Professional Ethics Journal* 4, nos. 3 & 4 (1985): 185–193.

Zauderer v. *Office of Disciplinary Counsel*, 471 U.S. 626 (1985).

Zuger, Abigail. "AIDS on the Wards: A Residency in Medical Ethics." *Hastings Center Report* 17 (June 1987): 16–20.

Index